Accent On Cooking

CONTENTS

ACCENT ON COOKING

America's Best Homemade Recipes!

CONTENTS

OVER 600 FAMILY–PROVEN RECIPES!

EXCLUSIVELY DISTRIBUTED BY:

P.S.I. & ASSOCIATES, INC.

13322 S.W. 128TH ST.
MIAMI, FL 33186
(305) 255-7959

Address all correspondance to the address above.

© 1992

ISBN# 1-55993-204-X

28826

Appetizers

TO SAVOR

NUTTY WHOLE-GRAIN CRACKERS

1-1/2 cups quick-cooking oats, uncooked
1/2 cup all-purpose flour
1/2 cup whole-wheat flour
1/4 cup wheat germ
1/4 cup ground walnuts or pecans
1 tablespoon sugar
2/3 cup water
1/4 cup vegetable oil
2 teaspoons water, divided
1/4 teaspoon salt, divided

Combine first 6 ingredients in a large bowl; stir well. Add 2/3 cup water and oil, stirring just until dry ingredients are moistened. Divide dough in half. Roll half of dough to a 12x12-inch square on an ungreased baking sheet. Cut into 2-inch squares. Brush dough with 1 teaspoon water; sprinkle evenly with 1/8 teaspoon salt. Repeat procedure with remaining half of dough. Bake at 350 degrees for 25 minutes or until crisp and lightly browned.

Separate crackers; remove from baking sheets and cool on wire racks. Store in an airtight container.

HAYMAKER'S SWITCHEL

Makes 18 (4-ounce) servings

8 cups water
1 cup sugar

1/2 cup cider vinegar
1/2 cup molasses
1/2 teaspoon ground ginger

In saucepan heat together water, sugar, vinegar, molasses, and ginger until sugar is dissolved. Chill before serving.

OLD-FASHIONED SODA CRACKERS

Makes 8 dozen

4-1/2 cups all-purpose flour
1/2 teaspoon baking soda
1/2 teaspoon salt
1/2 cup margarine
1-1/2 cups water
Salt

Heat oven to 350 degrees. In large bowl combine flour, baking soda, and salt. Cut in margarine until crumbly. Add water; stir just until mixed. Turn dough onto lightly floured surface; knead until thoroughly mixed (about 3 minutes). Roll out dough, 1/4 at a time, on well-floured surface to 1/8-inch thickness. Cut into 2-inch squares; place 1 inch apart on ungreased cookie sheets. Prick two or three times with fork; sprinkle with salt. Bake for 20-25 minutes or until lightly browned.

BARBECUE MEATBALLS

2 pounds ground beef
1 envelope dry onion soup mix

2 eggs
1/2 cup bread crumbs

Mix and form into small balls, a little larger than a walnut; sauté over medium heat until done; drain. Place meatballs in a chafing dish or crockpot. Pour sauce over meatballs.

Sauce:
12 ounces chili sauce
10 ounces grape jelly

Mix together; heat thoroughly and pour over meatballs. Simmer in serving dish.

ROCKIN' ROLLER NIBBLES

Makes 6 cups

2 ripe, medium-size bananas, peeled
1 cup cashews
1 cup flaked coconut
1 cup regular oats
1 cup peanuts
1 cup sunflower seeds
2 tablespoons vegetable oil
1 cup raisins, optional

Slice bananas into blender. Whirl until puréed. In a bowl combine bananas, cashews, coconut, oats, peanuts, and sunflower seeds. Spread mixture evenly in 15x9-inch baking pan. Sprinkle oil evenly over mixture. Bake in 350-degree oven for 20 minutes. Remove from oven; stir mixture to separate, then bake 10 minutes longer. Stir again. Bake 10 minutes longer. Cool. Stir in raisins, if desired.

HOT HAMBURGER DIP

1 pound ground beef
½ cup chopped onion
1 (8-ounce) can tomato sauce
¼ cup ketchup
1 (8-ounce) package cream cheese
1 cup grated Parmesan cheese
1 clove garlic, mashed
1 teaspoon oregano
1 tablespoon parsley
1 tablespoon sugar
1 (4-ounce) can mushrooms, chopped
Salt to taste
Pepper to taste

Sauté beef until brown. Add onion and garlic; cook until tender. Add all other ingredients and stir over low heat until cream cheese melts. Pour into Crockpot and keep warm. Serve with corn chips or taco chips.

PEANUT DEVILED-HAM BALL

1 (8-ounce) package cream cheese, softened
1 (4½-ounce) can deviled ham
2 tablespoons grated onion
1 teaspoon horseradish
¼ teaspoon liquid hot pepper seasoning
¼ teaspoon dry mustard
¼ cup chopped, salted peanuts
1 tablespoon dried parsley

Combine first 6 ingredients; beat until smooth and well-blended. Chill. Shape into a ball. Roll in peanuts and parsley to coat outside of cheese ball. Chill for 30 minutes before serving. Serve with party rye bread or assorted crackers.

MUSHROOM TARTS
Makes 60

⅔ cup butter
2½ cups flour
½ teaspoon salt
⅓ cup sour cream
1 egg, slightly beaten

Cut butter into flour and salt. Add sour cream and egg. Cut with pastry blender until well-blended. Using 1 teaspoon dough, press into bottom and side of tart muffin pans. Bake at 400 degrees for 12–15 minutes, or until golden. Remove from tart pan and cool.

Filling:
2 tablespoons chopped green onions
½ pound chopped mushrooms
¼ cup butter
¼ cup flour
½ teaspoon salt
1 cup heavy cream

Sauté mushrooms and onions in butter. Stir in flour and salt. Add cream; stir until thick and smooth. Fill shells; garnish with parsley and serve. Can be frozen. To serve, heat 10 minutes at 400 degrees.

ZUCCHINI APPETIZERS
Makes 4 dozen

3 cups thinly sliced zucchini
1 cup Bisquick
1/2 cup chopped onion
1/2 cup grated Parmesan cheese
2 teaspoons snipped parsley
1/2 teaspoon salt
1/2 teaspoon seasoned salt
1/2 teaspoon oregano
Dash of pepper
1 clove garlic, chopped
1/2 cup oil
4 eggs, slightly beaten

Heat oven to 350 degrees. Grease an oblong 9x13x2-inch pan. Mix all ingredients and spread in pan. Bake until golden brown for about 25 minutes. Cut into pieces, about 2x1-inch.

QUICK PEANUTTY POPCORN BALLS
Makes 8 (2-1/2-inch) balls

1/2 cup light corn syrup
1/4 cup sugar
3/4 cup peanut butter
2 quarts plain popped corn

In a saucepan mix corn syrup and sugar. Cook over medium heat; stir constantly until mixture comes to a boil and sugar is completely dissolved. Remove from heat. Stir in peanut butter until smooth. Immediately pour mixture over popcorn in large bowl. Stir until well-coated. Grease hands and shape into 8 (2-1/2-inch) balls.

CHILI POPCORN

1 tablespoon margarine, melted
1/3 teaspoon chili powder
1/8 teaspoon salt
1/8 teaspoon garlic powder
1/8 teaspoon paprika
6 cups popped corn

Combine margarine, chili powder, salt, garlic powder and paprika; drizzle over warm popcorn. (41 calories per 1-cup serving)

SAUSAGE BALLS
Makes 4 dozen

1 pound hot sausage, at room temperature
10 ounces extra-sharp Cracker Barrel cheese, grated
3 cups Bisquick mix

Mix Bisquick and grated cheese; add sausage. Blend well. Shape into small balls. Freeze on cookie sheet. Store in a plastic bag in the freezer. Place frozen balls on greased cookie sheet. Bake at 300 degrees for 35-45 minutes. Serve hot.

CHEESE DIP
Makes 3-1/2 cups

2 cups sour cream
1-1/2 cups shredded Cheddar
  cheese
1/4 cup sliced pimiento-stuffed
  olives
1/2 teaspoon salt
1/4 teaspoon sage

Blend sour cream with remaining ingredients. Serve chilled. Especially good with saltine crackers!

FRUIT DIP
Make 3 cups

2 cups sour cream
1/4 cup drained crushed pineapple
2/3 cup chopped red apples
1/2 teaspoon curry powder
1/2 teaspoon garlic salt
Apple slices for garnish

Blend sour cream with apple, pineapple, curry powder, and garlic salt. Place in bowl and chill. Garnish with sliced apples around outer edge of bowl.

Good with corn chips or shredded wheat wafers.

MUSHROOM MUNCHIES

1/4 cup vegetable oil
1/4 cup vinegar with lemon
1 tablespoon sugar
1/2 teaspoon onion powder
1/4 teaspoon garlic powder
Pinch of oregano
1 (10-ounce) can whole mushrooms, drained

Mix ingredients together in small bowl. Add mushrooms and marinate for 1 hour. Toothpicks will assist with serving or snacking of the whole mushrooms.

SHRIMP BALL

1 (8-ounce) package cream
  cheese, softened
1 small can shrimp (rinsed,
  drained, shredded)
2 tablespoons grated Romano/
  Parmesan cheese
1 teaspoon parsley flakes
1/2 teaspoon onion salt
1/2 teaspoon garlic salt
2 tablespoons catsup
Chopped walnuts

Mix all ingredients thoroughly (a food processor is helpful). Form into a ball. Roll ball in chopped walnuts. Chill 24 hours before serving. This appetizer freezes well.

NUTTY BLEU CHEESE DIP
Makes 2 cups

1 cup mayonnaise
1 (8-ounce) container sour cream
1/4 cup (1 ounce) bleu cheese,
  crumbled
1 tablespoon finely chopped onion
2 teaspoons instant beef bouillon
1/2 to 3/4 cup walnuts, coarsely
  chopped
Assorted fresh vegetables

In medium bowl, combine mayonnaise, sour cream, bleu cheese, onion, and bouillon; mix well. Stir in nuts; cover and chill. Stir before serving. Garnish as desired. Serve with vegetables. Refrigerate leftovers.

JEZEBEL

1 (18-ounce) jar peach jam
2½ ounces horseradish
1 ounce dry mustard
1 tablespoon ground white pepper
1 (8-ounce) package cream cheese

Mix all ingredients well, except for cream cheese. When ready to serve, pour over a block of cream cheese and serve with crackers.

DOUBLE SHRIMP MOLD

1 can cream of shrimp soup
1 envelope unflavored gelatin
2 (8-ounce) packages cream
  cheese, softened
1 cup mayonnaise
1½ tablespoons green onion,
  chopped
¾ cup celery, finely chopped
2 (6-ounce) cans small
  deveined shrimp
Dash salt and pepper, to taste

Heat undiluted soup to boiling point. Add gelatin to ½ cup cold water. Add to soup; mix well. Add cream cheese; blend well. Cool slightly. Add remaining ingredients; mix well. Spoon into mold or molds. Refrigerate for several hours. Unmold and serve with assorted crackers. May be frozen.

MACARONI PIZZA
Serves 6

2 cups uncooked macaroni
15-1/2-ounce jar spaghetti sauce
1 egg
1/2 teaspoon salt
1/2 cup milk
3 tablespoons Parmesan cheese
1/2 pound ground beef
1/2 cup chopped green pepper
1/2 cup onion, chopped
4-ounce can mushrooms
8-ounce package Mozzarella
  cheese, grated

Cook macaroni according to package directions; drain. Beat together egg, milk, 1 teaspoon Parmesan cheese and salt. Blend into macaroni and spread in greased 9 x 13-inch baking pan. Pour spaghetti sauce over macaroni. Add small bits of raw ground meat. Sprinkle on green pepper, onion, mushrooms and remaining Parmesan cheese. Top with Mozzarella cheese. Bake at 350 degrees for 20 minutes. Let stand 5-10 minutes before cutting.

PARTY MIX

2 cups Cheerios
2 cups Corn Chex
2 cups Rice Chex
2 cups thin pretzels
1-1/2 cups pecans
1 stick margarine
1 teaspoon salt
1 tablespoon Worcestershire sauce
3/4 teaspoon garlic powder

Heat oven to 250 degrees. Melt margarine; stir in salt, worcestershire, and garlic powder. Mix in cereals and nuts; mix well. Heat in 300-degree oven on cookie sheet about 45 minutes, stirring often, until nuts are brown.

CHOCOLATE PEANUT-BUTTER APPLES
Makes 6-8

6-8 medium-size apples
6-8 wooden skewers
1 cup semisweet chocolate mini chips
1 cup peanut-butter-flavored chips
1 tablespoon vegetable oil

Wash apples and dry thoroughly. Insert wooden skewer into each apple. Set aside. Melt mini chips and peanut-butter chips with oil in top of double boiler or in a heavy 1-1/2-quart saucepan over low heat; stir constantly until smooth. Remove from heat; dip apples in mixture (tilting pan as needed). Twirl to remove excess coating; place apples on waxed-paper-covered cookie sheet. Refrigerate until firm.

QUICK CRUSTY HAM BALLS
Makes 16

1 cup cooked ham, chopped
3/4 cup grated Cheddar cheese
2 tablespoons onion, grated

1 egg
1/4 cup dry cracker crumbs
1/2 cup sweet milk
1 cup cornflakes, crushed
Vegetable oil

Combine first 5 ingredients; mix well. Shape into 1-1/2-inch balls. Dip ham balls into milk; coat with cornflakes. Fry in vegetable oil until crusty and golden.

BUBBLING HOT CRAB WITH BEAN SPROUTS

1 (8-ounce) package cream cheese
6 ounces crab
1 tablespoon milk
2 tablespoons minced onion
2 tablespoons mayonnaise
1 teaspoon salt
Dash pepper
1/3 can bean sprouts, drained
2 tablespoons chopped chives
1/2 cup grated Parmesan cheese
1/3 cup sliced almonds

Mix all together, except cheese and almonds. Bake at 350 degrees for 20-25 minutes. Top with cheese and almonds. Serve with crackers.

CHEESY HASH BROWNS

1 (2-pound) package frozen hash browns, thawed
1 stick butter, melted
2 cups sour cream
2 cups Cheddar cheese, grated
1 can cream of chicken soup
1 cup chopped onions
1 teaspoon salt
1/2 teaspoon pepper
2 cups crushed corn flakes
1/2 stick margarine

Mix and combine all ingredients. Pour into a 13x9-inch dish. Top with 2 cups crushed corn flakes, mixed with 1/2 stick melted margarine. Bake in 350 degree oven 30-40 minutes.

VEGETABLE DIP

1 cup mayonnaise
1/2 teaspoon lemon juice
1/4 teaspoon salt
1/4 teaspoon paprika
1 teaspoon chopped onions
1 teaspoon salad herbs
1 teaspoon garlic salt
1 teaspoon dried chives
1/8 teaspoon curry powder
1/2 teaspoon Worcestershire sauce
1/2 cup sour cream

Mix ingredients together and serve with raw celery, carrots, cauliflower, and broccoli.

RADISH SPREAD

1 (8-ounce) package cream cheese, softened
1/2 cup butter, softened
1/2 teaspoon celery salt
1/8 teaspoon paprika
1/2 teaspoon Worcestershire sauce
1 cup finely chopped radishes
1/4 cup finely chopped green onions

Combine cheese and butter, and mix until thoroughly creamed. Add remaining ingredients and mix. Serve on party rye bread or crackers.

CREAMED ONIONS WITH NUTMEG
Serves 6

24 small white onions
3 tablespoons butter
3 tablespoons flour
1-1/2 cups milk
Salt and pepper to taste
1/4 teaspoon nutmeg
1/4 teaspoon garlic powder
Paprika

Peel onions and steam for about 20 minutes or until tender. Heat butter in saucepan; add flour; stir in milk. Stir constantly until mixture is smooth and thick. Add salt, pepper, nutmeg, and garlic powder. Blend well. Drain onions and pour cream sauce over them. Sprinkle with paprika. Keep in warm oven until ready to serve.

SALMON LOG

1 (1-pound) can salmon
1 (8-ounce) package cream cheese, softened
1 tablespoon lemon juice
2 tablespoons grated onion
1 teaspoon prepared horseradish
1/4 teaspoon salt
1 teaspoon liquid smoke seasoning
1/2 cup chopped walnuts
3 tablespoons snipped parsley

Drain and flake salmon, removing skin and bones. Combine salmon with the next 6 ingredients; mix well. Chill several hours. Combine walnuts and parsley. Shape salmon mixture into 8x2-inch log, or use a fish mold. Roll in nut mixture. Chill well. Serve with crisp crackers.

CRAB PUFFS

1 cup water
1 stick margarine
1 cup flour
4 eggs

Bring water to boil and add margarine, return to boil. Add flour all at once. Remove from heat and beat in 1 egg at a time. Then add all the following ingredients:

3 scallions, chopped
1 teaspoon dry mustard
1 (6½-ounce) can crabmeat
1 teaspoon Worcestershire sauce
½ cup sharp cheddar cheese, grated

Drop on cookie sheet by spoonfuls. Bake at 400 degrees for 15 minutes. Turn oven down to 350 degrees and bake 10 additional minutes.

These can also be frozen.

SAVORY CHEESE BITES
Makes 7 dozen

1 cup water
1/8 teaspoon salt
4 eggs
1/2 cup butter
1 cup flour
1 cup shredded Swiss cheese

Combine water, butter, and salt in a pan; bring to a boil. Stir until butter melts. Add flour; stir vigorously until mixture leaves sides of pan to form a smooth ball. Remove from heat. Add eggs, one at a time; stir until well-blended. Return to heat and beat mixture until smooth. Remove from heat; stir in cheese. Drop batter by heaping teaspoonfuls onto a greased baking sheet. Bake 400 degrees for 20 minutes, or until puffed and golden brown.

SAUSAGE TEMPTERS IN APPLESAUCE
Makes 4 dozen

1 pound pork sausage
2 cups applesauce
1 ounce cinnamon red candies
2 drops red food coloring

Form sausage in ¾-inch balls. Brown and cook meatballs in a skillet. Turn them so they brown evenly. Place a toothpick in each ball. Heat applesauce, candies and food coloring until candies dissolve. Place sausage balls in sauce, toothpick side up. Serve hot.

Note: A chafing dish would be ideal in which to keep sausages hot while serving.

BRAUNSCHWEIGER BALL

1 (8-ounce) package cream cheese, softened
1 pound braunschweiger, at room temperature
1/4 cup mayonnaise
1/4 teaspoon garlic salt
2 tablespoons dill pickle juice
1/2-3/4 cup chopped dill pickle
1/4 cup (or more) chopped onion
3 drops Tabasco sauce
1 tablespoon Worcestershire sauce
1/2 cup salted peanuts, chopped

Combine half the cream cheese with the remaining ingredients, except peanuts; mix well. Spread in a mold. Chill for several hours. Unmold. Frost with remaining cream cheese. Garnish with chopped peanuts. Snack with assorted crackers or slices of party loaf bread.

DILL WEED DIP

2/3 cup real mayonnaise
2/3 cup sour cream
1 tablespoon dried onion
1 tablespoon dried parsley
2 teaspoons dill weed
1 teaspoon Lawry's seasoning salt
Dash pepper
2 drops Tabasco sauce
1/2 teaspoon Worcestershire sauce
1/2 teaspoon Accent

Mix together and let set at least 2 hours before serving. Fresh vegetables and bread cubes are great to serve with the dip.

CREAMY CHEESE SPREAD

1/2 cup sour cream
6 ounces processed American cheese, cut in cubes
1 (3 ounce) package cream cheese, cut in cubes
2 tablespoons chopped onion
2 teaspoons Worcestershire sauce
2 teaspoons chopped dried chives
2 teaspoons parsley flakes
1/4 teaspoon dried minced garlic
1/4 teaspoon cracked black pepper

Put all ingredients in food processor or blender and process until smooth. Chill and serve with pretzels, crackers, chips, and/or raw vegetables.

SAUSAGE-CHEESE BALLS

Makes 75 appetizers

1-1/2 cups biscuit mix.
1 pound grated Cheddar cheese
1 pound lean ground pork sausage or "hot" ground sausage

Preheat oven to 350 degrees. Combine ingredients until dough sticks together. Roll into 1-1/2 inch balls. Bake about 25 minutes. Drain on paper towels. Serve warm on toothpicks.

Note: Spray baking sheet with no stick coating before putting sausage balls on sheet.

HAM 'N CHEESE SNACKS

1-1/2 cups finely chopped, cooked ham
1 (8 ounce) carton plain yogurt
1/4 cup shredded Swiss cheese
1/4 cup finely chopped crackers
2 tablespoons butter or margarine
2 teaspoons caraway seed
6 eggs

Combine first six ingredients. Beat eggs until thick lemon-color.. Fold eggs into yogurt mixture; blend well. Pour evenly into 8-inch square pan. Bake in preheated 375 degree oven for 15-17 minutes, until nicely browned. Cut into squares and serve hot.

FRIED CHEESE

4 slices Swiss cheese, cut 3/4 inch thick
Salt to taste
1/2 cup flour
1 egg, beaten
2/3 cup bread crumbs
1 cup shortening

Sprinkle cheese with salt. Dip slices first in flour, then in beaten egg, fry quickly in hot shortening until golden brown.

SODA CRACKERS

4 cups flour
3 tablespoons lard or shortening
1/2 teaspoon baking soda
1/8 cake yeast
1 teaspoon sugar
Pinch of salt
1/2 teaspoon malt extract
Water sufficient to make stiff dough

Roll out 1/4 inch thick on lightly floured board. Cut into desired shapes. Brush lightly with milk. Bake on ungreased baking sheet at 425 degrees for 15 to 18 minutes, or until lightly browned.

CROUTONS

Makes 2 cups

4 slices firm bread (stack slices and trim off crusts)
Cut bread into 1/2 inch cubes
1-1/2 ounces unsalted butter
1 teaspoon vegetable oil

Melt butter with oil in a heavy pan. Add bread cubes. Although white bread is most traditional for croutons, any good-quality bread will do. Experiment with whole wheat, rye, pumpernickel. Sauté bread cubes, about 2 minutes, turning to brown cubes evenly. Remove croutons with slotted spoon; drain on paper towels. Serve or keep warm in low oven until ready to serve.

CHICKEN HORS D'OEUVRES

Makes 38

1 (3 ounce) package cream cheese, softened
1 (5 ounce) can chicken spread
1/3 cup chopped apples
1/4 cup chopped walnuts
5 tablespoons chopped parsley
1/2 teaspoon Worcestershire sauce
Dash of cayenne pepper
Toasted wheat germ

Stir cream cheese in bowl until smooth; blend in remaining ingredients except wheat germ. Chill. Shape into thirty-eight (38) balls; roll in wheat germ. Place on serving platter.

PRETZELS

2 eggs, separated
1/4 cup butter, softened
2 cups flour
Salt & pepper
Milk
Coarse salt

Beat egg whites until stiff, but not dry. Beat egg yolks until lemony. Work (with hands or a spoon) the butter and egg yolks into the flour. Fold in beaten egg whites. Season with salt and pepper. Roll out; slice and shape as desired. Brush pretzels with milk and sprinkle with coarse salt. Bake on cookie sheets in preheated 350 degree oven for about 10 minutes, turning once.

CHEESE DIP
Makes 3-1/2 cups

2 cups sour cream
1-1/2 cups shredded Cheddar cheese
1/4 cup sliced pimiento-stuffed olives
1/2 teaspoon salt
1/4 teaspoon sage

Blend sour cream with remaining ingredients. Serve chilled. Especially good with saltine crackers!

DIPPETY DOO DIP

1 squeeze tube of hickory smoked cheese
1 cup sour cream
1 can bean with bacon soup (undiluted)
2 or 3 minced green onions (use all)

Combine all ingredients and warm over double boiler or in Microwave. Mix well. Serve with tortilla chips.
You can't eat just one!

BLUE CHEESE DIP

3 ounces blue cheese, crumbled
1/2 cup sour cream
1/2 cup mayonnaise
Dash of paprika
Dash of garlic powder
Assorted vegetables, cut in strips

Mix together all ingredients except vegetables and chill 2 hours to blend flavors. Serve with vegetables.

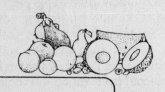

FRUIT DIP
Make 3 cups

2 cups sour cream
1/4 cup drained crushed pineapple
2/3 cup chopped red apples
1/2 teaspoon curry powder
1/2 teaspoon garlic salt
Apple slices for garnish

Blend sour cream with apple, pineapple, curry powder, and garlic salt. Place in bowl and chill. Garnish with sliced apples around outer edge of bowl.

Good with corn chips or shredded wheat wafers.

SNACKIN DIPS FOR CHIPS
Serves 4

1 can (6 1/2 ounce) chunk tuna
1 envelope instant onion soup mix
1 cup dairy sour cream
1 tablespoon prepared horseradish
Parsley for garnish
Potato chips - celery sticks - cherry tomatoes

Drain tuna. Combine tuna with soup mix, sour cream, and horseradish. Garnish with parsley. Arrange potato chips, celery sticks, and tomatoes on platter.

RAW VEGETABLE DIP
Yield - 2-1/2 cups

2 cups applesauce
1/2 pint dairy sour cream
2 tablespoons minced onion
1 teaspoon Worcestershire sauce
1/2 teaspoon salt

Slowly cook applesauce abut 5 minutes to evaporate some of the liquid; chill. Combine the applesauce, sour cream, onion, Worcestershire sauce and salt. Mix well. Use as a dip for fresh, raw vegetables of your choice.

FRESH MUSHROOM DIP

1-8 ounce package cream cheese, softened
2 tablespoons snipped ripe olives
2 tablespoons snipped parsley
3/4 teaspoon seasoned salt
4 drops bottled hot pepper sauce
1/2 cup sour cream
1/2 pound fresh mushrooms, finely chopped

Combine cream cheese and seasonings; fold in sour cream and chill. Stir in mushrooms just before serving.

LOW CAL CLAM DIP
Makes 2 cups

1-8 ounce can minced clams
1-1/2 cups cottage cheese
1/2 teaspoon seasoned salt
2 teaspoons lemon juice
1 teaspoon Worcestershire sauce
1 tablespoon minced green onions
Assorted crisp vegetable dippers

In blender container, combine clams with liquid, cottage cheese, seasoned salt, lemon juice, and Worcestershire sauce. Cover and whirl around until smooth. Stir in green onions. Cover and chill at least two hours to blend flavors. Serve with cauliflower, broccoli, and strips of carrots, zucchini, and cucumbers.

CHEESE BALL

8 ounce cream cheese
6 ounce blue cheese, crumbled
6 ounce jar Old English cheese
2 tablespoons mayonnaise
Dash of garlic salt
2 tablespoons finely chopped onion
6 ounce chopped walnuts

Mix all three (3) cheeses together with an electric mixer. Add mayonnaise, garlic salt, onion, and walnuts to cheese mixture. Shape into a ball and wrap with plastic wrap. Refrigerate twenty-four (24) hours before serving. When ready to serve, sprinkle paprika.

CHEESE-COCONUT BALLS
Makes about 30

2 packages (3 ounces each) Roquefort cheese
1 package (4 ounces) shredded cheddar cheese
1 package (8 ounces) cream cheese, softened
1 package (3 1/2 ounces) flaked coconut

Mash cheeses and combine them thoroughly with electric mixer. Chill for at least one hour. Shape into 1-inch balls and roll in coconut. Serve with fresh apple slices.

PINEAPPLE CHICKEN WINGS
Serves 4

12 chicken wings
3 tablespoons butter
1 small onion, sliced
8 1/2-ounce can pineapple chunks, drained, juice reserved
Orange juice
1/4 cup soy sauce
2 tablespoons brown sugar
1 tablespoon vinegar
1 teaspoon ground ginger
1/2 teaspoon salt
1/2 teaspoon ground mace
1/2 teaspoon hot pepper sauce
1/4 teaspoon dry mustard
1 1/2 tablespoons cornstarch

Fold chicken wing tips under to form triangles. Melt butter in large skillet; add wings and onion. Cook until wings are brown on both sides, about 10 minutes. Measure reserved pineapple syrup and add enough orange juice to make 1 1/4 cups liquid. Blend in soy sauce, sugar, vinegar, ginger, salt, mace, hot pepper sauce and mustard. Pour over chicken.

Cover and simmer 30 minutes, or until chicken is tender, basting top pieces once or twice. Remove chicken to hot plate. Add a small amount of water to cornstarch, blending to dissolve. Add slowly to the hot liquid in pan, stirring, and bring to boil to thicken. Return chicken to skillet, along with pineapple chunks.

Serve chicken wings and sauce with steamed rice.

BROILED CHICKEN LIVER ROLL-UPS

2 cans water chestnuts
1 pound chicken livers
1/2 pound bacon (cut each slice into thirds)
1 bottle soy sauce
1/2 cup brown sugar

Drain water chestnuts and slice each into 3 pieces. Wrap each water chestnut with a small piece of chicken liver and bacon piece. Secure with a toothpick and marinate in soy sauce for at least 4 hours.

Just before serving, remove roll-ups from soy sauce and roll each in brown sugar. Place on broiler rack and broil for about 10 minutes, or until crisp. Serve at once.

TASTY CHICKEN BASKETS
Makes 40-50 baskets

Baskets (directions follow)
Filling:
2 cups chopped cooked chicken meat
5 slices bacon, fried and crumbled
3 tablespoons diced, pared apple
1/2 teaspoon salt
1/8 teaspoon pepper
1/4 cup mayonnaise
1/4 cup finely chopped pecans
4-ounce can mushrooms, chopped

Combine and mix all filling ingredients. Cover and refrigerate for 2 hours. Makes 2 1/2 cups filling, enough for 40-50 baskets.

To make Baskets:
Cut 90-100 rounds from regular sliced bread using a 1 1/2-inch round cookie cutter. Spread half the rounds with softened butter.

Cut a small hole from the centers of remaining bread rounds, "doughnut" fashion. Place each "doughnut" atop a buttered round, and fill center with chicken filling, mounding high. Garnish with sprigs of parsley.

ROLLED SANDWICHES
Makes 25-30 sandwiches

1 loaf of bread, sliced into lengthwise slices
Filling:
1/4 pound (1 stick) butter, softened
4 ounces cream cheese
1/4 teaspoon paprika
1/4 teaspoon salt
1 tablespoon mayonnaise
3/4 cup minced nuts, raisins, dates and/or figs

Slice crusts from long pieces of bread. Combine *Filling* ingredients well. Spread on bread slices. Roll up from narrow ends. (Before rolling, strips of sweet pickles or olives may be placed over filling for colorful variations.) Press end of roll firmly and wrap each roll tightly in plastic wrap. Store in refrigerator overnight.

Before serving, slice each roll into 1/4-inch slices. Arrange on serving plate.

Note: Instead of the nuts-and-dried-fruit filling, you can use one of the following: 1 1/2 cups tuna salad, crab, shrimp, salmon, finely chopped raw vegetables, grated cheddar cheese, chicken, turkey or ham filling.

SHRIMP PUFFERS
Makes 60 appetizers

8 tablespoons softened butter or margarine
2 eggs, separated
3 cups shredded sharp cheddar cheese
15 slices white bread (thin-sliced)
60 cooked shrimp, shelled and deveined

Blend butter, cheese and egg yolk until smooth. Beat egg whites until stiff; fold into cheese mixture.

Trim crusts from thinly sliced bread; cut each piece in quarters diagonally. Top each slice with a shrimp and 1 teaspoon of the cheese mixture. Bake in a preheated 350-degree oven on lightly greased cookie sheets for about 15 minutes, or until puffy and golden.

RYE CRACKERS

2 cups rye flour
2 cups wheat flour
Salt to taste
1/4 teaspoon baking soda
1/2 cup vegetable oil
1 cup (or more) water
1 tablespoon caraway seeds

Mix together. Roll out thinly on floured surface. Cut into desired shapes. Bake on cookie sheets at 275 degrees for about 30 minutes.

DILL CRACKERS

2/3 cup Wesson oil
1 envelope ranch-style dry salad dressing
1 teaspoon dill
1/2 teaspoon lemon pepper
1/4 teaspoon garlic salt
10 ounce package oyster crackers

Mix all together, except crackers. Coat crackers with mixture, tossing until well coated, about 5 or 6 minutes.

NUT BALLS

1 stick butter
1 cup pecans
1 teaspoon vanilla
2 tablespoons sugar
1 cup flour

Mix all ingredients and roll into tiny balls and bake at 250 degrees for one hour. Cool slightly and roll in confectioners' sugar. Roll in sugar again about half-hour later.

TUNA SPREAD

1 can tuna (water packed), drained

1 (8-ounce) package cream cheese, softened
1 small onion, finely chopped
Salt and pepper to taste

Blend all ingredients until smooth. Serve with crackers. This can be rolled into a log and used for all types of festive entertaining.

NUTS, BOLTS AND SCREWS

1 pound pecans
1 large box Cherrios
1 medium box stick pretzels
1 tablespoon Worcestershire sauce
1 box Wheat Chex
2 tablespoons salt
1 tablespoon garlic salt
1 pound oleo or butter
8 8

Melt butter in large roaster. Pour in all cereals, nuts and pretzels and seasonings. set oven at 200 degrees. Stir every 15 minutes for 1 hour.

WHEAT GERM CRUNCHIES
Makes 3-1/2 dozen

1/2 cup all-purpose flour
1/2 teaspoon soda
2 teaspoons baking powder
1/4 teaspoon salt
1 cup brown sugar, firmly packed
1/2 cup shortening
1 egg, beaten
1/2 teaspoon vanilla
1/2 cup coconut
1/2 cup uncooked oatmeal
1 cup wheat germ
1-1/2 cups corn or wheat flakes

Sift flour, soda, baking powder and salt. Cream shortening and sugar. Add egg and vanilla. Add dry ingredients and wheat germ. Mix well. Stir in coconut, oatmeal and cornflakes just enough to mix. Drop by teaspoons on greased cookie sheet or roll into walnut-sized balls with fingers and place on greased cookie

sheet. Bake 15 minutes at 350 degrees.

TAFFY APPLES

1 large can crushed pineapple (save drained juice)
2-1/2 cups miniature marshmallows
1 egg
1 tablespoon flour
12 ounces Cool Whip
3/4 cup cocktail or Spanish peanuts
1-1/2 tablespoons vinegar
1/2 cup sugar
4-6 apples, unpeeled and chopped

Combine drained pineapple and marshmallows; refrigerate overnight. Beat pineapple juice, egg, flour, vinegar and sugar; heat until thick, stirring constantly. Cool and refrigerate overnight, separate from pineapple.

Next day: Mix sauce and Cool Whip; add peanuts, marshmallow mixture and apples; stir. Refrigerate at least 2 hours before serving.

CELERY PINWHEELS

1 medium stalk celery
1 (3-ounce) package cream cheese
2 tablespoons crumbled Roquefort cheese
Mayonnaise
Worcestershire sauce

Clean celery and separate branches. Blend together the softened cream cheese with the Roquefort cheese. Add mayonnaise to make the mixture of spreading consistency and season with a dash of Worcestershire sauce. Fill the branches of celery with cheese mixture. Press branches back into the original form of the stalk. Roll in waxed paper and chill overnight in refrigerator. Just before serving, slice celery crosswise forming pinwheels. Arrange pinwheels on crisp lettuce for serving.

HAM BALLS
Makes approximately 48 appetizers

4 cups ground lean ham
1/2 cup finely chopped onion
1/4 teaspoon pepper
2 eggs
1 cup plain bread crumbs

Combine and mix all ingredients. Shape into 1-inch balls. Place in a shallow pan and bake at 400 degrees for 25 minutes.

Sour Cream Gravy:
2 tablespoons shortening
2 tablespoons flour
1/4 teaspoon dill seed
1/4 teaspoon marjoram
1/2 cup water
1 1/2 cups sour cream

Melt shortening; add flour and seasonings. Cook until it bubbles. Add water and sour cream, stirring constantly. Cook until thick. Makes 2 cups sauce.

Serve *Ham Balls* with *Sour Cream Gravy;* provide toothpicks for dipping.

DEVILED TURKEY BONBONS

1 cup cooked, finely chopped turkey
1 cup finely chopped nuts
1 tablespoon chopped onion
2 tablespoons chopped pimiento
1/4 teaspoon salt
Hot pepper sauce to taste
1/4 cup cream of mushroom soup.

Combine turkey and 1/2 cup nuts. Add remaining ingredients except remaining nuts; mix well. Shape into small balls and roll in remaining chopped nuts. Chill until serving time.

SIMPLE HORS D'OEUVRES

It's true that these tempting tidbits have a French name, may be very elaborate, and are usually met in hotels, but that's no reason for not serving them simply, in the home, for a little variety.

Try a bit of pink, moist salmon on a piece of rye toast . . . some ripe olives . . . celery, stuffed with cream cheese flavored with mayonnaise, salt and paprika, or filled with a mixture of equal parts cream cheese and Roquefort cheese which has been seasoned with Worcestershire sauce . . . slices of salami. . . . All these are as truly and delightfully "hors d'oeuvres" as the most elaborate arrangement of caviar and egg.

CHEESE SURPRISE APPETIZERS

2 cups grated sharp cheddar cheese
1/2 cup softened butter
1 cup flour
1 small jar green, pimiento-stuffed olives

Mix cheese, butter and flour to form dough. Shape into small balls about 1 inch in diameter. Flatten ball with hands; place one olive in center, wrap dough around it, sealing edges completely. Freeze until just before ready to serve. (These *must* be frozen.)

When ready to serve, place frozen appetizers on baking sheet and immediately place in 375-degree oven. Bake about 10 minutes, or until golden. Cheese will puff up and melt.

ASPARAGUS ROLLS
Makes 20 appetizers

20 slices bread
1 package frozen asparagus
1 5-ounce jar processed pimiento cheese spread

Trim crusts from bread slices; spread each with cheese. Cook asparagus until just tender. Chill. Lay one piece asparagus diagonally across slice of bread. Turn opposite corners over asparagus, overlapping. Press firmly to seal. Wrap several sandwiches together in waxed paper. Place in covered container and chill for several hours.

MEATBALL APPETIZERS
Makes about 8 dozen tiny meatballs and 2 cups sauce

1 1/2 pounds ground beef
2 eggs
1/4 cup milk
1 cup plain bread crumbs
1/4 cup chopped onion
1 1/2 teaspoons chopped parsley
1 1/2 teaspoons salt
1/8 teaspoon pepper
3 tablespoons oil
10-ounce bottle chili sauce
1/2 cup grape jelly
1 tablespoon instant coffee

Combine meat, eggs, milk, crumbs, onion, parsley, salt and pepper and mix well. Shape into tiny meatballs and brown well on all sides in skillet in hot oil. Remove meatballs from pan. Drain excess drippings, leaving just 2-3 tablespoons. Add chili sauce, jelly and instant coffee to pan drippings and simmer, stirring occasionally, until jelly melts (about 4 minutes). Add meatballs and simmer 10 more minutes. Serve on toothpicks.

Meatballs can be browned, refrigerated, then cooked with sauce just before serving.

ANTIPASTO

2 cans tuna fish, undrained
1 can anchovies, undrained
1 small jar stuffed olives, drained
1 small bottle cocktail onions, drained
1 medium can mushrooms, cut up and drained
1 jar sweet pickled cauliflower, drained and cut in small pieces
1 small jar tiny sweet pickles, drained and cut in small pieces
1 No. 2 can green beans, drained
1 cup carrots, cooked crisp, cut in small rings
1 bottle chili sauce
1 bottle catsup

Mix all ingredients. Add a little salad oil if not moist enough. Marinate in refrigerator for at least one day. Eat with crackers. Makes a delicious hors d'oeuvre.

CANAPE PUFFS
Makes about 25 puffs

1/2 cup water
1/4 cup (1/2 stick) butter
1/2 cup flour
2 eggs

Heat water and butter to boiling; reduce heat and stir in flour all at once. Stir about 1 minute until mixture forms ball around spoon. Remove from heat and beat in eggs, one at a time, until mixture is smooth.

Place by rounded teaspoonsful onto ungreased cookie sheets. Bake in a preheated 400-degree oven for about 25 minutes or until golden. Remove and cool on racks.

Slice off tops; remove any doughy insides. Fill with any sandwich filling; chill until serving time.

EGG & HAM HORS D'OEUVRES
Makes 20 appetizers

5 hard-cooked eggs
1 teaspoon minced chives
Salt and paprika
1-2 drops hot pepper sauce
Mayonnaise
1/2 pound boiled ham

Separate yolks and whites of eggs. Force yolks through a sieve; add chives, seasonings and mayonnaise to moisten. Beat to a smooth paste. Chop egg whites and ham together and mix with yolks. Form into 1-inch balls and garnish with additional mayonnaise.

BLUE CHEESE MUSHROOMS

1 pound mushrooms (1-1 1/2 inches in diameter)
1/4 cup green onion slices
2 tablespoons butter or margarine
1 cup (4 ounces) crumbled blue cheese
1 small package (3 ounces) cream cheese, softened

Remove stems from mushrooms; chop stems. Saute stems and green onion in margarine until soft. Combine with cheeses, mixing well. Stuff mixture into mushroom caps. Place on a broiler pan rack and broil for 2-3 minutes or until golden brown. Serve hot.

SWEET AND SOUR MEATBALLS

1 pound lean ground beef
1 envelope dry onion-soup mix
1 egg

Combine beef, soup mix and egg and form into tiny meatballs. Brown in skillet; discard all but 1 tablespoon fat.

Sauce:
8-ounce can tomato sauce
16-ounce can whole-berry cranberry sauce

Combine ingredients for sauce with reserved tablespoon of fat from meat in saucepan. Heat; add meatballs. Cover and simmer for about an hour. Serve with toothpicks.

PEPPERONI BALLS

1 package hot roll mix
1/4 pound mozzarella cheese, cut in cubes
1/4-1/2 lb.pepperoni, thinly sliced

Prepare roll mix according to package directions, but *omitting egg* and using *1 cup water*. Dough does *not* need to rise. Place one cheese cube on one pepperoni slice. Pinch off a piece of dough and shape carefully around cheese and pepperoni, forming a ball. Repeat until all ingredients are used.

Fry in deep hot oil for about 5 minutes, or until golden brown, turning once. Drain on paper towels and serve warm.

BLUE CHEESE BITES
Makes 40 appetizers

1 package (10-count) refrigerated biscuits
1/4 cup margarine
3 tablespoons crumbled blue cheese or grated Parmesan cheese

Cut each biscuit into four pieces. Arrange pieces on two greased 8x1 1/2-inch round baking pans. Melt margarine; add cheese and stir to blend. Drizzle cheese mixture over biscuits. Bake in 400-degree oven for 12-15 minutes.

CHICKEN WINGS

1 pound chicken wings
1/4 pound (1 stick) butter
1/4 teaspoon garlic powder
2 tablespoons parsley
1 cup fine, dry bread crumbs
1/2 cup Parmesan cheese
1 teaspoon salt
1/4 teaspoon pepper

Cut off tips from chicken wings and discard; split remaining portion of wing at joint to form two pieces. Melt butter, mixing in garlic powder. Combine bread crumbs, Parmesan cheese and seasonings. Dip chicken wing portions in seasoned butter, then roll in crumbs. Bake on a greased baking sheet (use one with edges) in a preheated 325-degree oven for about 50 minutes.

These can be frozen and baked later.

DEVILED EGGS

4 hard-cooked eggs
1/3 cup grated Parmesan cheese
1 teaspoon prepared mustard
Pepper
Skim milk
Paprika

Halve the eggs lengthwise; remove yolks and mash. Add the cheese, mustard, few grains pepper, and enough milk to moisten well. Beat until fluffy and refill the egg whites. May want to garnish with paprika for added color. (65 calories per egg half)

Brunch
FARE

THANKSGIVING MORN PUMPKIN COFFEE CAKE
Serves 12

½ cup butter
¾ cup sugar
1¼ teaspoons vanilla extract
3 eggs
2 cups all-purpose flour
1 teaspoon baking powder
1 teaspoon baking soda
½ cup sour cream
1¾ cups solid-pack pumpkin
1 egg, lightly beaten
⅓ cup sugar
1½ teaspoons pumpkin pie spice
  Streusel (recipe follows)

Cream butter, ¾ cup sugar and vanilla; add eggs; beat well. Combine dry ingredients; add to butter mixture alternatly with sour cream. Combine pumpkin, beaten egg, ⅓ cup sugar and pie spice. Spoon half of batter into 13 x 9 x 2-inch baking pan; sprinkle half of streusel mixture over batter; spread remaining pumpkin mixture over streusel; sprinkle remaining streusel over top. Bake at 325 degrees for 50–60 minutes, or until tested done in middle.

Streusel:

1 cup brown sugar
⅓ cup butter
2 teaspoons cinnamon
1 cup chopped nuts

Mix all together.

REUBEN BRUNCH CASSEROLE

10 slices rye bread, cubed
1-1/2 pounds cooked corned beef
2-1/2 cups shredded cheese
  (American, Swiss, or Cheddar, or
  combination)
6 eggs, lightly beaten
3 cups milk
1/4 teaspoon pepper

Grease 13x9-inch baking dish. Arrange bread cubes on bottom. Coarsely shred corned beef. Layer beef over bread. Sprinkle with cheese. Beat eggs, milk, and pepper until well blended. Pour over corned beef mixture. Cover with foil. Refrigerate several hours or overnight. When ready to bake, preheat oven to 350 degrees; bake covered for 45 minutes, then uncover and bake for 10 additional minutes or until bubbly and puffed.

POACHED EGGS ON CHICKEN MUFFINS
Serves 6

1 (4-3/4 ounce) can chicken spread
1/2 teaspoon ground thyme
3 English muffins, split and toasted
6 eggs, poached
Chopped chives, optional

Mix chicken with thyme; spread on English muffins. Top each muffin half with an egg and sprinkle with chives.

COTTAGE CHEESE WAFFLES

½ cup sifted flour
½ teaspoon salt
4 eggs
½ cup milk
⅓ cup vegetable oil
1 teaspoon vanilla
1 cup cottage cheese

Sift flour and salt together. Set aside. Beat eggs, milk, vegetable oil and vanilla together. Add cottage cheese and beat until smooth. Combine with flour. Cook as usual.

BAKED PINEAPPLE TOAST
(Serves 6)

1/4 cup butter or margarine, melted
1/2 cup firmly packed brown sugar
1 (8-ounce) can crushed pineapple,
  drained
6 white bread slices
2 eggs
1-1/2 cups milk
1/2 teaspoon salt

Combine butter, sugar, and pineapple. Spread on bottom of 13x9-inch baking dish. Top with bread. Beat eggs, milk, and salt together; pour over bread. Bake, uncovered, at 325 degrees for 25 minutes or until golden brown. Cool slightly; invert on heated serving platter.

HAM PANCAKE PIE
Serves 6

2 medium sweet potatoes, peeled and thinly sliced
3 cups diced, cooked ham
3 medium apples, peeled, cored and sliced
½ teaspoon salt
¼ teaspoon pepper
3 tablespoons brown sugar
¼ teaspoon curry powder
⅓ cup apple juice *or* water
1 cup pancake mix
1 cup milk
½ teaspoon dry mustard
2 tablespoons butter, melted

In a 2-quart greased casserole dish, layer half the potatoes, half the ham and half the apples. Combine salt, pepper, brown sugar and curry powder; sprinkle half the mixture over layers in dish. Repeat this process with remaining potatoes, ham, apples and brown sugar mixture. Pour apple juice or water over all. Cover dish and bake at 375 degrees until potatoes are tender, about 40 minutes. Beat together pancake mix, milk, mustard and butter. Remove casserole from oven when potatoes are done; pour pancake batter over top. Bake 20 minutes more, uncovered, or until pancake is puffed and golden.

WINTER BERRY FRENCH TOAST
Serves 4

½ cup (canned *or* fresh) whole-berry cranberry sauce
1 (10-ounce) package frozen, sliced strawberries in syrup, thawed
2 teaspoons orange peel, finely grated
4 eggs
1¼ cups milk
1 tablespoon sugar

¼ teaspoon nutmeg
8 (1-inch-thick) slices day-old French bread (about 8 ounces)
3 tablespoons butter *or* margarine
Confectioners' sugar

In 1-quart saucepan melt cranberry sauce over low heat, stirring constantly. Mix in strawberries and orange peel. Heat just to boiling; set aside. In shallow bowl beat eggs, milk, sugar and nutmeg to blend thoroughly. Soak bread slices in egg mixture to saturate. Melt some of the butter in large skillet over medium heat. Fry bread slices until browned, about 5 minutes on each side, adding butter to skillet as needed. Transfer to heated platter; dust with confectioners' sugar. Served with warm sauce.

CINNAMON RAISIN BATTER BREAD

1 package active dry yeast
1-1/2 cups warm water (105-115 degrees)
2 tablespoons honey
2 tablespoons butter
1 teaspoon salt
3 cups flour, divided
1 tablespoon cinnamon
1 cup raisins

In a large bowl, dissolve yeast in warm water. Stir in honey. Add butter, salt, and 2 cups of the flour. Beat with electric mixer on low speed until blended. Beat 1 minute on high speed. Stir in remaining flour with a wooden spoon. Cover and let rise in a warm place until doubled in size. Punch down by stirring with a heavy spoon. Add cinnamon and raisins. Spoon batter into a loaf pan. Let rise again until batter reaches the top of the pan (not over!). Bake in preheated 350-degree oven for about 40 minutes or until loaf sounds hollow when lightly tapped. Cool on wire rack.

This batter bread is a wonderful treat for breakfast or in the "munchkin's" lunch sack as a peanut-butter-and-jelly sandwich.

REUBEN BRUNCH CASSEROLE

10 slices rye bread, cubed
1-1/2 pounds cooked corned beef
2-1/2 cups shredded cheese (American, Swiss, or Cheddar, or combination)
6 eggs, lightly beaten
3 cups milk
1/4 teaspoon pepper

Grease 13x9-inch baking dish. Arrange bread cubes on bottom. Coarsely shred corned beef. Layer beef over bread. Sprinkle with cheese. Beat eggs, milk, and pepper until well blended. Pour over corned beef mixture. Cover with foil. Refrigerate several hours or overnight. When ready to bake, preheat oven to 350 degrees; bake covered for 45 minutes, then uncover and bake for 10 additional minutes or until bubbly and puffed.

BAKED DOUGHNUTS

⅓ cup sugar
2 teaspoons nutmeg
2 teaspoons salt
⅓ cup shortening
2 eggs
2 cakes yeast
¼ cup lukewarm water
3¾ cups flour

In saucepan add sugar, nutmeg salt and shortening to milk. Stir until shortening is melted over low heat. Cool to lukewarm; add well-beaten eggs and yeast dissolved in ¼ cup lukewarm water. Add flour and beat briskly. Let rise until double in bulk, or about an hour. Roll to ½-inch thickness and cut with floured cutter; place on greased pan and brush with melted butter. A cookie sheet is good for this. Let rise about ½ hour, or until about double. Bake at 450 degrees for about 10 minutes. Brush with butter when done, then dust with confectioners' sugar. These are also great with a brown-sugar frosting.

PIMIENTO-CHEESE SOUFFLE

6 tablespoons butter
6 tablespoons flour
⅛ teaspoon dry mustard
   Dash cayenne pepper
1½ cups milk
6 large eggs, separated
1½ cups shredded Swiss cheese
1 (4-ounce) jar pimientos,
   drained and chopped

Heat oven to 350 degrees. Lightly grease a quart soufflé dish. Melt butter in a medium saucepan. Stir in flour, mustard and cayenne. Gradually stir in milk over medium heat until mixture thickens and begins to boil, about 5 minutes. Stir in cheese and pimientos. When cheese is melted, set aside. Beat yolks in a large bowl until light and lemon colored. Stir cheese mixture into beaten yolks. Beat egg whites in a large bowl until soft peaks form. Gently fold beaten whites into cheese-yolk mixture. Pour mixture into soufflé dish. Bake until golden, puffy and a knife inserted comes out clean, approximately 45 minutes.

BREAKFAST BAKED FRENCH TOAST
Serves 4

3 eggs
1 tablespoon all-purpose flour
¼ cup sugar
½ teaspoon cinnamon
¼ teaspoon allspice
¼ teaspoon salt
½ teaspoon baking powder
½ teaspoon vanilla extract
1 cup milk
8 (1-inch) slices French bread
2 tablespoons butter *or* margarine, melted

Beat eggs; add flour, sugar, cinnamon, allspice, salt, baking powder and vanilla; mix until smooth. Beat in milk; pour into baking dish. Dip bread into mixture; turn over; cover; refrigerate overnight. Before baking turn slices over; melt butter; drizzle over top. Bake at 400 degrees for 10 minutes; turn bread; bake an additional 5 minutes until golden brown. To serve, sprinkle with confectioners' sugar, maple syrup, honey, sour cream, jelly or preserves of your choice. Can be sprinkled with cinnamon-sugar or topped with fruit.

POACHED EGGS ON CHICKEN MUFFINS
Serves 6

1 (4-3/4 ounce) can chicken spread
1/2 teaspoon ground thyme
3 English muffins, split and toasted
6 eggs, poached
Chopped chives, optional

Mix chicken with thyme; spread on English muffins. Top each muffin half with an egg and sprinkle with chives.

BAKED WESTERN OMELET
Serves 4

4 large eggs
1/4 cup water
4 ounces cooked ham, cut into thin strips
1 cup sliced mushrooms
1/2 cup chopped tomato
1/4 cup sliced scallions
1/4 cup chopped green bell pepper
1/8 teaspoon freshly ground pepper

Preheat oven to 375 degrees. Lightly spray a 10-inch glass pie pan with non-stick cooking spray. In medium bowl, with wire whisk, beat eggs with 1/4 cup water until well-blended. Stir in remaining ingredients. With rubber spatula, scrape into prepared pie pan. Bake 20-30 minutes until omelet is set, slightly puffed, and browned. Cut into four servings and serve at once. (141 calories per serving)

QUICK & EASY PUFFY OMELET

2 tablespoons bread crumbs
3 eggs
⅛ teaspoon pepper
4 tablespoons milk
½ teaspoon salt
3 tablespoons butter

Soak bread crumbs in milk. Separate eggs. Beat yolks until thick and lemon colored. Add crumbs and milk, salt and pepper. Beat egg whites until stiff. Gradually, fold the egg yolk mixture into the whites. Melt butter in the omelet pan or frying pan and allow it to run around the sides of the pan. Pour mixture into the pan and cook slowly for 10 minutes, or until lightly brown underneath. Put pan in a moderate 350-degree oven for 5–10 minutes until it is dry on top. Fold and turn onto a hot platter. Serve at once.

HAM GRIDDLE CAKES
Makes 11

1 cup milk
1 cup quick-cooking oats, uncooked
2 tablespoons vegetable oil
2 eggs, beaten
½ cup all-purpose flour
2 tablespoons sugar
2 teaspoons baking powder
1 cup diced, cooked ham
   Maple syrup

Combine milk and oats in a large bowl; let stand 5 minutes. Add oil and eggs, stirring well. Combine flour, sugar and baking powder; add to oat mixture, stirring just until moistened. Stir in ham.

For each pancake, pour about ¼ cup batter onto a hot, lightly greased griddle. Turn pancakes when tops are covered with bubbles and edges look cooked. Serve with maple syrup.

BACON PUFFED PANCAKES

Makes about 15

2 eggs
3/4 cup sweet milk
2-1/3 cups baking mix (I use Bisquick)
2 tablespoons sugar
1/4 cup oil
8 slices bacon, fried and crumbled

Beat eggs with mixer on high speed for about 5 minutes or until thick and lemon colored. Add remaining ingredients. Pour about 1/4 cup batter onto hot, ungreased griddle or use skillet. Cook as usual, turning once.

Kids love these because they are so light and have the bacon right inside. Awfully good on a cold day or any day!

OATMEAL PANCAKES

2 cups milk
1-1/2 cups quick rolled oats (uncooked)
1 cup sifted flour
2-1/2 teaspoons baking powder
1 teaspoon salt
2 tablespoons sugar
2 eggs, beaten
1/3 cup melted butter or margarine

Pour milk over oats and let stand 5 minutes. Sift together flour, baking powder, salt, and sugar. Add beaten eggs to rolled oats mixture. Add butter. Add sifted dry ingredients; mix quickly and lightly. If not used right away, store in refrigerator and mix again just before using. Keeps for several days in refrigerator.

POTATO PANCAKES

Serves 6

4 large potatoes
1 small onion
1/2 cup milk
1 teaspoon salt
1 egg, beaten
2 tablespoons flour
Fat for frying

Peel and grate potatoes; mix with onion and milk. Mix with salt, egg, and flour. Drop by tablespoonsful into hot fat in skillet. Brown on both sides and serve immediately.

POTATO PANCAKES WITH CHEDDAR

Serves 4

1 egg
1/3 cup milk
1/2 teaspoon salt
3 tablespoons flour
1 small onion, grated or chopped fine
1/2 cup grated Cheddar cheese
4 medium potatoes
Shortening or salad oil for frying
Applesauce

In bowl, beat egg; beat in milk, salt and flour. Add grated or chopped onion and grated cheese. Wash and peel potatoes. Grate directly into egg mixture, working rapidly as grated potatoes tend to darken.

In heavy skillet, heat shortening or salad oil, using enough to coat surface generously. Add potato mixture by tablespoons; cook until brown and crisp on both sides. Serve hot with applesauce.

SOUFFLE PANCAKES

Serves 6

6 egg yolks
1/3 cup pancake mix
1/3 cup sour cream
1/2 teaspoon salt
6 egg whites

Beat egg yolks until thick and lemon colored; fold in pancake mix, sour cream and salt, until well blended. Beat egg whites until stiff but not dry. Carefully fold into yolk mixture. Drop by tablespoonsful onto hot, well greased griddle. Cook until golden brown on both sides.

Serve hot with butter, maple syrup, honey or favorite fruit sauce.

MAPLE PANCAKE SYRUP

Makes 2-1/2 cups

2 cups sugar
2 cups water
1 teaspoon maple flavoring

Combine sugar, water, and maple flavoring in small saucepan. Bring to boil; cook for 5 minutes. Bottle and refrigerate.

CORN FRITTERS

1 to 2 cups corn
1 egg, well beaten
1 teaspoon sugar
1/2 teaspoon salt
1 tablespoon butter, melted
2 teaspoons baking powder
1 cup flour
2/3 cup milk

Mix thoroughly. Drop spoonfuls of batter into fat in hot frying pan. Brown both sides.

BUFFET RYE SLICES

1 cup Swiss cheese, grated
1/4 cup bacon, cooked and crumbled
1/4 cup mayonnaise
1 teaspoon Worcestershire sauce
1/4 cup green onions, chopped
1/2 cup chopped ripe olives

Mix all ingredients and spread on party rye slices. Bake in 375 degree oven for 8-10 minutes; serve warm.

SWEET POTATO DOUGHNUT SOFTIES
Makes 30

3 eggs
¾ cup sugar
3 tablespoons butter *or* margarine, melted
¾ cup mashed sweet potato
3 cups all-purpose flour
1½ tablespoons baking powder
2 teaspoons allspice
1 teaspoon cloves
¼ teaspoon salt
Spiced Sugar (recipe follows)

Beat eggs; add sugar and beat until light; stir in butter and sweet potato. (Do not use a mixer—it toughens the doughnuts.) Combine flour, baking powder, allspice, cloves and salt; stir into the wet ingredients. Cover; chill overnight. Roll out dough ¼ inch thick; cut with a 2½-inch doughnut cutter. Fry until golden brown; turn once. Drain on paper towels; roll in spiced sugar. Serve warm and fresh.

Spiced Sugar:
1½ teaspoons cinnamon
¼ teaspoon nutmeg
¾ cup sugar

CHEDDAR EGG BAKE

6 eggs, slightly beaten
1 cup shredded cheddar cheese (4 ounces)
½ cup milk
2 tablespoons margarine, softened
1 teaspoon prepared mustard
½ teaspoon salt
¼ teaspoon pepper

Heat oven to 325 degrees. Mix all ingredients. Pour into an ungreased 8 x 8 x 2-inch pan. Bake 25–30 minutes, or until eggs are set. A simple and delicious way to make eggs!

BAKED PINEAPPLE TOAST
(Serves 6)

1/4 cup butter or margarine, melted
1/2 cup firmly packed brown sugar
1 (8-ounce) can crushed pineapple, drained
6 white bread slices
2 eggs
1-1/2 cups milk
1/2 teaspoon salt

Combine butter, sugar, and pineapple. Spread on bottom of 13x9-inch baking dish. Top with bread. Beat eggs, milk, and salt together; pour over bread. Bake, uncovered, at 325 degrees for 25 minutes or until golden brown. Cool slightly; invert on heated serving platter.

PUMPKIN FRITTERS
Makes 36

2 cups coarsely shredded pumpkin
1 teaspoon butter
1 large egg
1½ cups milk
3 tablespoons light brown sugar
¼ teaspoon salt
1 teaspoon cinnamon
½ teaspoon nutmeg
1 teaspoon vanilla extract
2 cups unsifted all-purpose flour
3 teaspoons baking powder
Vegetable oil for frying
Confectioners' sugar

In skillet, sauté shredded pumpkin in butter until no longer raw-looking. Drain. Wash and dry skillet. Add oil to make 2 inches; heat to 350 degrees. In bowl, combine egg, milk, brown sugar, salt, cinnamon, nutmeg, vanilla and pumpkin. Add flour and baking powder to pumpkin mixture; stir until well-combined. Drop fritter batter by heaping teaspoonfuls into hot fat. Fry on all sides for 2–3 minutes. Remove with slotted spoon. Drain on paper toweling. Serve hot, sprinkled with confectioners' sugar.

BREAKFAST HONEY MUFFINS
Makes 9

1 cup sifted all-purpose flour
2 teaspoons baking powder
½ teaspoon salt
½ cup unsifted whole-wheat flour
½ cup milk
1 egg, well-beaten
½ cup honey
½ cup coarsely chopped, cooked prunes
1 teaspoon grated orange peel
¼ cup salad oil *or* melted shortening

Preheat oven to 400 degrees, and lightly grease 9 (2½-inch) muffin pan cups. In large bowl, sift the all-purpose flour with the baking powder and salt. Stir in whole-wheat flour. Combine milk and rest of ingredients in medium bowl. Add, all at once, to flour mixture, stirring only until mixture is moistened. Spoon into cups; bake 20–25 minutes, or until nicely browned. Serve warm.

HAM AND MUSHROOM TOAST
Serves 6

3 cups sliced mushrooms
6 tablespoons butter or margarine
2 tablespoons flour
3/4 cup bouillon
1 pint (16 ounces) sour cream
Salt
Pepper
6 slices ham
6 slices hot, buttered toast

Sauté mushrooms in butter (6 tablespoons) for 5 minutes. Add flour, then stir in 3/4 cup bouillon and the sour cream. Cook, stirring, until smooth; season with salt and pepper, and if you wish with chives, tarragon, or dill. Put sliced ham on the hot, buttered toast. Top with mushrooms, and serve at once.

LUNCHEON TUNA IN TOAST CUPS

2 ribs celery, thinly sliced
1 medium onion, chopped
1 small green pepper, chopped
1 tablespoon vegetable oil
1 package white sauce mix
1 cup American cheese, cut into small cubes
1 (7-ounce) can tuna, drained and flaked
3 tablespoons pimiento, chopped
Toast cups (recipe follows)

In a skillet, cook celery, onion, and green pepper, in vegetable oil until tender. Prepare white sauce as instructed on package. Into the white sauce, stir the celery, onion, green pepper, cheese, tuna, and pimiento; heat until cheese melts and is hot and bubbly. Serve in warm toast cups.

Toast Cups:

Trim crusts from fresh wheat or white bread; spread lightly with soft butter. Press buttered side down into muffin cups. Bake 10-12 minutes in a 350 degree oven or until lightly toasted.

ELEGANT QUICHE LORRAINE

3 eggs, slightly beaten
1 cup light cream
5 slices bacon, crisply cooked and crumbled
3 tablespoons Dijon type mustard
1/4 cup finely minced onion
1 cup grated Swiss cheese
1/4 teaspoon salt
1/8 teaspoon pepper
1 unbaked 9-inch pie shell

Combine all ingredients, except pie shell. Pour into pie shell and bake in a pre-heated 375 degree oven for 35-40 minutes, or until knife inserted in filling comes out clean.

BACON ROLL-UPS
Makes 6 dozen

1/2 cup margarine
3 cups herb-seasoned stuffing mix
2 eggs, beaten
1/4 pound ground beef
1/4 pound hot sausage, crumbled
1 pound sliced bacon, cut slice into thirds

Melt margarine in 1 cup water in saucepan. Remove from heat. Combine with stuffing. Mix in large bowl, mixing well; chill. Add remaining ingredients except bacon, mixing well.

Shape into pecan-shaped balls. Wrap with bacon; secure with toothpicks. In baking dish, bake at 375 degrees for 35 minutes or until bacon is crisp.

CHEESE, HAM 'N OLIVE SWIRLS
Makes 45

1-one pound loaf frozen ready-dough
6 thin slices cooked ham (4 x 7 inches)
4 ounces softened cream cheese
6 tablespoons chopped olives (black or green)

Let frozen dough thaw until pliable. (To thaw dough in the microwave, wrap in plastic wrap and cook on lowest setting for six minutes, rotating occasionally.) On a lightly floured board, roll thawed dough out to a 14-inch square. Cut in half. Cover each half with three slices of meat. Spread each half with two ounces softened cream cheese and sprinkle with 3 tablespoons chopped olives.

Beginning with 14-inch sides, roll each half in jelly-roll fashion. Pinch long edge to seal. Cut rolls into 1/2 inch slices. Place slices on greased baking sheets. Let rise for 30 minutes. Bake in 350 degree oven for 15 minutes or until golden brown. Remove from pan immediately.

ZUCCHINI QUICHE
Serves 8

2 cups zucchini, sliced thin
1 cup onion, sliced
3 tablespoons oil
1 clove garlic, minced
1-1/2 teaspoons salt
4 eggs, beaten
1 cup milk
1 cup heavy cream
1/2 cup mozzarella cheese, grated
10-inch pie crust

Saute zucchini, onion, and garlic in oil. Season with salt. Cover pie crust with this mixture. Combine remaining ingredients and pour into pie shell. Bake in preheated 375 degree oven 30-35 minutes until custard is set. Serve hot.

COCONUT CRUNCH CEREAL
Yields 8 cups

3 cups rolled oats
1-1/2 cups shredded coconut
1/3 cup wheat germ
1 cup toasted, unsalted sunflower kernels
1/3 cup sesame seeds
1/4 cup soy flour
2 teaspoons cinnamon
1/4 cup honey
1/4 cup vegetable oil
1/2 cup water
1 cup almonds, chopped

Mix first seven ingredients. Heat honey and water; pour slowly over cereal. Pour oil over cereal and mix until crumbly. Pour mixture into a heavy, shallow baking pan that has been oiled. Bake in a 325 degree oven for 1-1/2 hours; stirring every 15 minutes. Add chopped almonds and bake for 30 additional minutes. Cereal should be crisp. Turn off the oven; cool. Store cereal mixture in a tightly covered container. Serve plain with fresh fruit or milk.

19

BREAKFAST EGG DISH

Serves 6

8 slices bread
1/2 cup melted butter
1 cup grated Cheddar cheese
Bacon or ham bits
Chopped green pepper
Sliced mushrooms, optional
2 cups milk
1/4 teaspoon salt
1/8 teaspoon pepper

Cut crust off the slices of bread and cube bread. Put in a 9x13 inch buttered pan. Pour the melted butter over the bread cubes; sprinkle on bacon bits, green pepper, and mushrooms.

Separate the eggs. Beat the yolks with the milk, salt, and pepper; pour over ingredients in the pan. Beat egg whites until stiff. Seal above mixture with egg whites. Cover and keep in the refrigerator overnight.

Bake at 325 degrees for 40-45 minutes.

EGG 'N' CHIPS

Serves 6

6 hard-boiled eggs, chopped
2 tablespoons chopped green pepper
1/2 teaspoon salt
2/3 cup mayonnaise or salad dressing
1-1/2 cups diced celery
3/4 cup coarsely chopped walnuts
1 teaspoon minced onion
1/4 teaspoon pepper
1 cup grated Cheddar cheese
1 cup crushed potato chips

Combine eggs, celery, walnuts, green pepper, onion, salt, pepper and salad dressing or mayonnaise. Toss lightly, but thoroughly, so ingredients are evenly moistened. Use additional salad dressing if needed. Place in a greased 1-1/2 - quart baking dish. Sprinkle with cheese and top with crushed chips. Bake at 375 degrees for about 25 minutes or until thoroughly heated and cheese has melted.

FOOLPROOF SCRAMBLED EGGS

Serves 3-4

6 eggs
1/3 cup light cream
3/4 teaspoon salt
1/8 teaspoon pepper
1/2 teaspoon Worcestershire sauce

Beat eggs; beat in cream and seasonings. Cook in upper part of double boiler, over hot water, until just set, stirring often. Serve at once with toast.

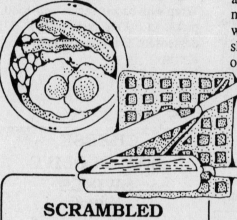

SCRAMBLED BAGEL ROYALE

Serves 2

2 bagels
1-1/2 tablespoons butter
  or margarine
4 eggs
2 tablespoons milk
3 tablespoons chopped onion
1/4 cup lox pieces or smoked salmon
2 ounces cream cheese
2 slices tomato garnish

Slice bagels in half horizontally. Lightly spread with one tablespoon of butter or margarine; toast lightly. Over medium high heat, saute chopped onion in remaining half tablespoon of butter or margarine until translucent. Beat eggs with milk; add to onions. Stir eggs. When eggs are almost set, add lox pieces and cream cheese that has been cut into small chunks; scramble in pan until cheese begins to melt.

Spoon mixture over bagels. Garnish with tomato slices.

TOLEDO HAM AND EGGS

Serves 6

1 cup chopped, cooked ham
1 tablespoon olive oil
2 cups cooked peas
2 canned pimentos, chopped
1/4 cup chopped green olives
Salt and pepper, if desired
6 eggs.
2 tablespoons olive oil

Saute ham in olive oil for 2-3 minutes. Combine with peas, pimento, and olives. Heat well; add salt and pepper if desired. Put in the middle of a hot platter and surround with the eggs, which have been slowly cooked in the 2 tablespoons of olive oil.

TUNA STUFFED EGGS

Makes 24 halves

12 eggs
6 slices bacon
1 - 3-1/4 to 3-1/2 - ounce can tuna, drained and finely flaked
3/4 cup mayonnaise
1 tablespoon lemon juice
1/2 teaspoon hot pepper sauce
1/2 teaspoon salt

In 4-quart saucepan, place eggs and enough water to come one inch above tops of eggs over high heat; heat to boiling. Remove saucepan from heat; cover tightly and let eggs stand in hot water 15 minutes; drain.

Meanwhile, in 10-inch skillet, cook bacon until browned, remove to paper towel to drain. Crumble bacon, set aside.

Peel and slice eggs lengthwise in half. Remove yolks and place in medium bowl. With fork, finely mash yolks. Stir in tuna, mayonnaise, lemon juice, hot pepper sauce and salt until smooth. Pile egg yolk mixture into egg whites center. Sprinkle with bacon. Cover and refrigerate.

OMELET SUPREME
Serves 3

3 slices bacon, cut into small pieces
2 small potatoes, peeled and sliced
8 fresh spinach leaves, stems removed, sliced into 1/4 inch slices
6 eggs, lightly beaten with fork
1/2 cup yogurt
Salt and pepper to taste

In skillet, heat bacon; add potatoes; fry until bacon is crisp, and potatoes lightly browned. Add spinach; remove mixture to bowl. In shallow bowl, mix eggs, yogurt, salt, and pepper; pour into skillet. Distribute potato mixture evenly over eggs; cook over low heat without stirring. As eggs set on bottom, lift edges; let uncooked mixture run underneath. When omelet is set, fold with fork. Serve immediately.

BROCCOLI OVEN OMELET
Serves 6

9 eggs
1 (10 ounce) package frozen chopped broccoli, thawed and drained
1/3 cup finely chopped onion
1/4 cup grated Parmesan cheese
2 tablespoons milk
1/2 teaspoon salt
1/2 teaspoon dried basil
1/4 teaspoon garlic powder
1 medium tomato, cut into 6 slices
1/4 cup grated Parmesan cheese

Beat eggs with whisk in bowl until light and fluffy. Stir in broccoli, onion, 1/4 cup Parmesan cheese, milk, salt, basil, and garlic powder. Pour into ungreased 11x7x2 inch baking dish. Arrange tomato slices on top. Sprinkle with 1/4 cup Parmesan cheese. Bake uncovered in 325 degree oven until set, 25-30 minutes.

Great for holiday brunch, also as vegetable side dish.

GARDEN MEDLEY
Serves 6

1/4 cup butter or margarine
2 cups cauliflower
1/4 cup chopped onion
2 cups sliced zucchini
1/2 cup halved cherry tomatoes
1/4 teaspoon salt
1/4 teaspoon thyme leaves, crushed
2 tablespoons grated Parmesan cheese, if desired

In large skillet, melt butter. Add cauliflower and onion; sauté 2-3 minutes. Add zucchini; cover and cook over medium heat, stirring occasionally, 3-5 minutes, or until vegetables are crisp-tender. Stir in tomatoes, salt, and thyme; cook 1-2 minutes until thoroughly heated. Spoon into serving dish; sprinkle with Parmesan cheese. (100 calories per serving)

OLD FASHIONED BREAD OMELET

Combine and soak for 10 minutes:
2 cups bread cubes
1 cup milk

Preheat oven to 325 degrees.
Combine in bowl:

5 eggs, beaten
1/2 cup grated cheese
1 cup alfalfa sprouts, chopped
1 small onion, finely chopped
1 tablespoon parsley flakes
1 teaspoon garlic powder
Salt and pepper to taste
Bread and milk mixture

Heat in skillet:
1/4-1/2 cup bacon pieces until done

Pour in egg mixture and cook over medium heat without stirring, about 5 minutes. When browned underneath, place pan in oven for 10 minutes to finish cooking the top. Turn out onto hot platter. Omelet can be folded in half.

QUICHE LORRAINE

1 (9-inch) pie crust
1 tablespoon soft butter
12 bacon slices
4 eggs
2 cups whipping cream
3/4 teaspoon salt
1/8 teaspoon nutmeg
1/4 pound natural Swiss cheese, shredded (1 cup)

Spread crust with soft butter; beat eggs, cream, salt, and nutmeg with wire whisk; stir in cheese and pour egg mixture into crust. Fry bacon until crisp and brown. Drain on paper towels and crumble; sprinkle in pie crust. Bake 15 minutes at 400 degrees; turn oven to 325 degrees and bake 35 minutes. Quiche is done when knife inserted in center comes out clean. Let stand 10 minutes before serving.

QUICK AND EASY BUCKWHEAT PANCAKES

1/2 cup bread crumbs
2-1/2 cups scalded milk
2 cups buckwheat flour
1/2 teaspoon salt
1/2 yeast cake
2 tablespoons molasses
1/4 teaspoon baking soda

Add bread crumbs and salt to scalded milk. Cool. When lukewarm add yeast and stir until yeast is dissolved. Add buckwheat flour and stir until smooth. Put in warm place overnight. In the morning add molasses and soda mixed with a little lukewarm water. Beat smooth. Bake on hot griddle.

These pancakes are delicious and more healthful than the regular kind. Your family will love them!

MAPLE BUTTER TWISTS

2 Coffee Cakes, Serves 16

3-1/4 - 3-1/2 cups flour
3 tablespoons sugar
1-1/2 teaspoons salt
1 package yeast
3/4 cup milk
1/4 cup butter
2 eggs

Filling:
1/2 cup brown sugar
1/3 cup white sugar
2 tablespoons flour
1/2 teaspoon cinnamon
1/4 cup softened butter
1/4 cup maple syrup
1/2 teaspoon maple extract
1/2 cup chopped nuts

Glaze:
1/2 powered sugar
2-3 teaspoons milk
1/4 teaspoon maple extract

Grease 2 - 8 inch round cake pans. In large bowl, combine 1-1/2 cups flour with the next 3 ingredients. In a small saucepan, heat milk and margarine until very warm. Add with the eggs to the flour mixture. Beat with electric mixer on low speed until moistened, then beat 3 minutes on medium speed. Stir in remaining flour. Place in greased bowl, cover and let rise 1-1/2 hours.

Combine all filling ingredients, except nuts, in small bowl. Beat with electric mixer on medium speed, 2 minutes. Stir in nuts.

Divide dough in half. Roll each half to a 14 x 8 inch rectangle. Spread each with half of filling. Roll up from long side as for jellyroll; seal edges. Cut each roll in half lengthwise. Twist the two halves together and seal ends. Place each twisted roll in a prepared pan circle; flatten with fingertips. Cover; let rise 1 hour.

Heat oven to 350 degrees. Bake 25-30 minutes. Remove from pans immediately. Combine glaze ingredients until smooth and drizzle over coffee cake while still warm.

BAKED CHEESE GRITS

Serves 6

2-2/3 cups water
2/3 cup hominy grits, quick-cooking
2 tablespoons butter or margarine
1-1/2 cups pasteurized process American cheese, shredded
2 eggs, beaten
1/8 teaspoon pepper

Preheat oven to 350 degrees. Grease a 2-quart baking dish. Bring water to a full rolling boil. Add grits; return to boiling point. Cook, stirring constantly, until very thick, about 6 minutes. Remove from heat. Add butter or margarine and mix cheese, eggs, and pepper. Stir into grits. Pour into baking dish and bake 40 minutes or until lightly browned.

CORNMEAL PANCAKES

1/2 cup cornmeal
1/2 cup flour
2 teaspoons baking powder
1/2 teaspoon salt
2 tablespoons sugar
1 egg
1 cup milk
2 tablespoons margarine, melted

Mix first 5 ingredients; stir in egg, milk, and margarine. Blend until smooth. If batter is too thick, thin with additional milk. Cook on a hot, lightly-oiled griddle.

APPLE PECAN CREPES

Serves 8

16 crepes
1 (1-pound, 5-ounce) can apple pie filling
1/2 teaspoon cinnamon
1/2 cup broken pecan pieces
Custard sauce

Combine apple filling, cinnamon, and pecan pieces. Spoon 2-1/2 tablespoons filling down center of each crepe and overlap edges. Place in chafing dish or oven-proof serving dish. Heat through. Serve with custard sauce.

EGGNOG FRENCH TOAST

Loaf of Italian or French bread, cut in 12 3/4-inch slices (day-old bread is best)
1-1/2 cups dairy eggnog
1/4 cup butter
Cinnamon
Confectioners' sugar
Syrup

Place bread in single layer in shallow dish. Pour eggnog over bread. Let stand, turning bread once, until eggnog is absorbed, about 5 minutes.

In large skillet cook slices in butter until golden on both sides. Sprinkle with cinnamon and confectioners' sugar. Serve hot with syrup.

NORWEGIAN COFFEE CAKE

4 cups flour
6 teaspoons baking powder
1 cup sugar
1/2 teaspoon salt
2 eggs
1 cup milk
1 cup butter or margarine

Sift together dry ingredients. Blend in shortening as for pie crust. Beat eggs and milk; add to dry ingredients. Do not mix too much. Grease two 9-inch cake pans and put half of mixture in each pan by putting spoonfuls around the edge. Bake at 400 degrees for about 20 minutes. Frost and add nuts to the top. Great with breakfast!

TALLAHASSEE HASH PUPPIES

2 cups cornmeal
2 teaspoons baking powder
1 teaspoon salt
1-1/2 cups sweet milk
1/2 cup water
1 large onion, chopped fine

Sift dry ingredients together. Add milk, water; stir in chopped onion. Add more meal or milk, if necessary, to form a soft dough. Mold with hands. Fry in deep, hot fat until brown.

BAGEL CHIPS

4 bagels
3 tablespoons butter or margarine
3 tablespoons vegetable oil
2 cloves crushed garlic
1/8 teaspoon salt
1/8 teaspoon paprika

Slice each bagel horizontally in 6 pieces. In small pan, saute garlic in 1 tablespoon butter or margarine until lightly browned. Add remaining ingredients; stir until margarine is melted. Spread bagels out on cookie sheet. Brush both sides of bagel slices with mixture. Bake at 375 for 5 minutes on each side. Baking time may vary according to oven and how thin bagels are sliced. After bagels are cooled, place in airtight container.
NOTE: Variation-sprinkle with Parmesan cheese the last 2 minutes of baking.

STRAWBERRIES 'N' CREAM BAGEL

2 bagels
1 teaspoon butter or margarine
4 ounces cream cheese
1/2 cup strawberries, mashed
1/2 teaspoon of vanilla
2 tablespoons powdered sugar

1/2 cup sliced strawberries for garnish

Slice bagels in half horizontally. Lightly spread with one teaspoon of butter or margarine; toast lightly. Mix together cream cheese, mashed strawberries, vanilla and powdered sugar. Spread mixture over bagels. Garnish top of each bagel with sliced strawberries.

BREAKFAST BARS
Makes 18 bars

1/4 cup butter or margarine
3 cups miniature marshmallows
1/2 cup peanut butter
1/2 cup nonfat milk
1/4 cup orange - flavored instant breakfast drink
1 cup raisins
3 cups Cheerios cereal

Butter a 9 x 9 x 2 inch pan. Melt butter and marshmallows over low heat, stirring constantly. Stir in milk, breakfast drink, and peanut butter. Fold in raisins and cereal, stirring until coated. With buttered hands, pat evenly in pan. Cool. These are delicious with coffee for breakfast or anytime.

BRUNCH IN A SHELL

1 slice ham, cut 1/4 inch thick
1 unbaked 9 inch pie shell
1/2 can, (10-1/2 ounces) cream of mushroom soup
2/3 cup dairy sour cream
3 eggs
1 to 2 tablespoons chopped chives
1/4 teaspoon salt
Dash pepper

Cut ham slice so it will cover bottom of pie shell evenly. Combine remaining ingredients with rotary beater and pour into ham-lined pie shell. Cover crust edge with 1-1/2 inch aluminum foil. Bake in preheated 425 degree oven for 40-45 minutes, removing protective foil from crust 15 minutes before end of baking time. Pie puffs up near end of baking and sinks back after removal from oven.

BANANA BONANZAS

1 cup sifted flour
3 tablespoons sugar
2-1/2 teaspoons baking powder
1/2 teaspoon salt
1 cup whole bran
1 beaten egg
1/4 cup milk
2 tablespoons oil
1 cup mashed bananas
1/2 cup walnuts (optional)

Sift together flour, sugar, baking powder, and salt. Stir in bran. Combine egg, banana, milk, and oil. Add liquid ingredients all at once, stirring just until flour mixture is moistened. Fill well-greased muffin pans 2/3 full. Bake at 400 degrees for 25 minutes.

OLD-FASHIONED "EGGSPARAGUS"
Serves 4

1 pound fresh asparagus (or use canned)
Boiling salted water
4 eggs, separated
2 tablespoons milk or cream
1 tablespoon butter, melted
Salt and pepper to taste

Trim asparagus; cook in boiling salted water until stalks are tender, about 20 minutes. Drain and arrange in lightly-greased 9 x 13-inch shallow baking dish. Beat egg whites to stiff froth. Fold in beaten egg yolks, milk or cream, butter, salt and pepper to taste. Pour egg-mixture evenly over asparagus. Bake at 325 degrees for about 10 minutes, or until eggs are set.

23

CHOCOLATE-ALMOND ZUCCHINI BREAD
Makes 2 loaves

3 eggs
2 cups sugar
1 cup vegetable oil
2 squares (2 ounces) unsweetened chocolate
1 teaspoon vanilla
2 cups finely grated zucchini
3 cups flour
1 teaspoon salt
1 teaspoon cinnamon
1/4 teaspoon baking powder
1 teaspoon baking soda
1 cup coarsely chopped almonds

Preheat oven to 350 degrees. In small bowl, beat eggs until lemon colored; beat in sugar and oil. Melt chocolate over hot water. In large bowl, add egg mixture, vanilla, and zucchini to chocolate.

Sift together flour, salt, cinnamon, baking powder, and baking soda. Stir into zucchini mixture. Mix in nuts. Pour batter into 2 well-greased 9x5x3 inch loaf pans. Bake 1 hour and 20 minutes or until done. Cool in pans 15-20 minutes. Turn out onto rack. Cool thoroughly before serving.

JIFFY RAISIN LOAF
Makes 1 loaf

3/4 cup golden seedless raisins
Hot water
2 cups prepared biscuit mix
3/4 cup sugar
1 teaspoon cinnamon
1/3 cup chopped nuts
1 egg
3/4 cup milk

Rinse raisins in hot water. Drain. Combine with biscuit mix, sugar, cinnamon, and nuts. Beat egg slightly. Add to milk. Stir into dry ingredients. Pour batter into greased 8-1/2x4-1/4x2-1/2 inch loaf pan. Bake at 350 degrees for 50-60 minutes. Cool on wire rack.

GRANOLA

4 cups uncooked oatmeal
1-1/2 cups wheat germ (raw or toasted)
1 cup grated coconut
1/4 cup powdered milk
1/2 tablespoon cinnamon
1 tablespoon brown sugar
1/3 cup vegetable oil
1/2 cup honey
1 tablespoon vanilla
1/2 cup sesame seeds (optional)
1/2 cup raw nuts, seeds, or raisins, etc. (optional)

In a large bowl, mix dry ingredients. In a saucepan, combine oil, honey, and vanilla; warm. Add these to the dry ingredients; stir until all the particles are coated. Hand mixing works well here. Spread this mixture out in a long, low pan or rimmed baking sheets that have been well greased; bake at either 250 degrees for 1 hour or 300 degrees for 30 minutes. Turn mixture with spatula from time to time. When finished toasting, add dried fruits, such as raisins. Cool and store in an airtight container.

LUSCIOUS BANANA-APRICOT BREAD
Makes 2 loaves

2 cups white flour
1-1/2 cups whole wheat flour
2 teaspoons baking powder
1 teaspoon baking soda
1 teaspoon salt
4 eggs
1 cup sugar
2/3 cup shortening
1/2 cup sour milk
6-7 bananas, mashed
1/4 cup wheat germ
1 cup chopped dried apricots
3 teaspoons black walnut flavoring (or 3 cups chopped nuts)

Mix first 5 ingredients by sifting into bowl. Blend in eggs, sugar, shortening, and sour milk, beating well into dry ingredients. Add bananas, flavoring or nuts, apricots, and wheat germ. Stir well. Bake in greased and floured loaf pans at 350 degrees for 50 minutes.

HAM 'N EGG CREPES
(Serves 4-6)

1 (10-1/2 ounce) can condensed cream of chicken soup
1 cup dairy sour cream
1 cup finely chopped cooked ham
6 hard cooked eggs, chopped
1 tablespoon chives, chopped
1/4 teaspoon dry mustard
1/4 cup milk
1/4 cup grated Parmesan cheese
1 recipe for basic crepes

Mix 1/2 can of soup, sour cream, ham, eggs, chives, and mustard; set aside. Combine remaining soup, milk, and half the cheese; set aside. Put about 1/4 cup ham-egg filling on each crepe and roll up. Arrange filled crepes in greased 13x9x2-inch baking dish. Pour sauce over top and sprinkle with remaining cheese. Bake in preheated 350 degree oven for 30 minutes, or until hot and bubbly.

MEAT BALL PANCAKES

3 egg yolks, lightly beaten
1/2 pound ground beef, browned
1/4 teaspoon baking powder
1/2 teaspoon salt
Dash of pepper
1 tablespoon grated onion
1 teaspoon lemon juice
1 tablespoon parsley
3 egg whites, stiffly beaten

Mix all ingredients, *excluding* egg whites. Blend well. Fold in egg whites. Drop by spoonfuls onto greased hot griddle. When puffed and browned, turn and brown other side. Serve at once, with a mushroom sauce or a creamed vegetable.

SURPRISE MUFFINS
Makes 20 small muffins

2 cups sifted flour
1 teaspoon salt
4 teaspoons baking powder
1 tablespoon sugar
4 tablespoons butter
3/4 cup milk
1/4 cup shredded dates
1/4 cup chopped walnuts
20 marshmallows

Sift together flour, salt, baking powder, and sugar into mixing bowl. Cut in butter. Add milk gradually to make a soft dough. Place a teaspoon of the dough in small greased muffin pans. Place over this a marshmallow, some shredded dates, and chopped nuts. Bake in a very hot oven, 450 degrees for 15 minutes, until delicately browned. Serve hot.

BASIC CAMPERS' MIX
Makes 7-1/2 cups)

4-1/2 cups sifted flour
3 tablespoons baking powder
2 teaspoons salt
1 cup shortening, soft
1-1/2 cups quick or old fashioned oats, uncooked

Sift together flour, baking powder, and salt into large bowl. Cut in shorting until mixture resembles coarse crumbs. Stir in oats. Store in airtight container in cool dry place until ready to use.

BAKED EGGS COUNTRY STYLE

1 (10-3/4-ounce) can cream of tomato soup
6 eggs
Salt and pepper to taste
1/8 teaspoon cayenne
1/8 teaspoon nutmeg
1/4 cup Swiss cheese, grated
1/4 cup Parmesan cheese, grated

1/4 cup parsley, chopped
1 teaspoon onion, grated

In a buttered shallow baking dish, pour can of undiluted cream of tomato soup; carefully drop in 6 eggs; sprinkle with salt, pepper, cayenne, nutmeg, and cheeses. Sprinkle parsley mixed with grated onion over all. Bake at 325 degrees for 26 minutes or until eggs are set. Serve immediately over slices of crisp hot toast, or over split toasted English muffins.

BACON AND EGG POCKETS
Serves 2

2 pita bread rounds (whole wheat is better for you)
4 slices bacon
4 eggs
1 tablespoon milk
Salt and pepper to taste
Sliced Cheddar cheese (optional)

Cut pita in half crosswise. Warm in oven as it preheats to about 300 degrees. Meanwhile, in medium skillet, fry bacon until crisp; drain on paper towel. Pour off all grease except what clings to skillet. Whisk eggs with milk, salt and pepper. Pour into skillet; cook, stirring, over medium heat until softly scrambled; crumble in bacon. Stuff pita pockets with cheese, if using, then eggs with bacon.

OATMEAL FLAPJACKS
Makes 12-18

3 cups Basic Campers' Mix
3 tablespoons sugar
2 cups milk
2 eggs

Combine Basic Campers' Mix and sugar. Add milk and eggs; stir until just blended. Pour batter onto hot, lightly greased griddle. Turn pancakes when tops are covered with bubbles and edges look cooked. Turn only once. Serve with butter and syrup.

HASH BROWN OMELET

1/2 pound bacon
Frozen hash brown potatoes, enough to fill bottom of large skillet
6 eggs
1/4 cup milk
1/2 teaspoon salt
1/2 teaspoon pepper
1/4 cup onion, chopped
1 cup grated American cheese
1/4 cup green pepper, mushroom, celery (optional)

Cook bacon until crisp; remove bacon from pan. Cook potatoes in bacon drippings over low heat until thawed. Combine eggs, milk, salt, and pepper; pour over potatoes. Sprinkle bacon, onions, and other vegetables on top of egg mixture. Cover and cook on low heat for 20 minutes or until set. Top with cheese and cover pan until cheese melts. Slice into pie-shaped pieces and serve.

Sausage or shaved ham with mushrooms may be used instead of bacon.

CHOCOLATE WAFFLES

2 cups flour
3 teaspoons baking powder
1/2 teaspoon salt
3 tablespoons cocoa
1/4 cup sugar
2 eggs, separated
1/4 cup melted margarine
1-1/4 cups milk
1 teaspoon vanilla

Sift first 5 ingredients together into a large mixing bowl. Stir in the well-beaten egg yolks, margarine, milk, and vanilla. Beat egg whites until stiff peaks form and fold into flour mixture. Fill the hot waffle iron with batter and close; bake until browned.

If you are a "chocoholic" you'll love these! All my family loves this special breakfast treat.

BLUEBERRY SAUCE

2 cups fresh or frozen blueberries
1/3 cup sugar
1 tablespoon lemon juice
1/4 teaspoon salt
1/2 teaspoon vanilla

Crush blueberries; add sugar, lemon juice, and salt. Mix well. Bring to a boil and boil 1 minute. Add vanilla. Serve over pancakes or blintzes.

CHOCOLATE WAFFLES

1/2 cup melted butter
1 cup sugar
2 squares melted chocolate
3 eggs, well beaten
1 teaspoon salt
1-1/2 cups flour
1 cup milk
1/4 teaspoon vanilla

Cream butter (or margarine) and sugar; add chocolate and eggs. Mix well. Sift in salt and flour; mixing well. Add milk and vanilla. Pour 1/4 cup batter onto greased waffle iron and cook each waffle about 3 minutes.

OATMEAL-RAISIN MUFFINS

1-1/4 cups flour
1 cup rolled oats
1/2 cup raisins
1/4 cup packed dark brown sugar
3 teaspoons baking powder
1/2 teaspoon salt
3/4 teaspoon cinnamon
1 cup milk
1/4 cup oil
1 egg

In large bowl, combine flour, oats, raisins, sugar, baking powder, cinnamon and salt; set aside.

In small bowl, beat remaining ingredients until well blended. Pour into flour mixture and stir just until moistened (batter will be lumpy). Divide among 12 greased or paper-lined 2-1/2-inch muffin cups. Bake in 400 degree oven for 20-25 minutes, or until toothpick inserted in center of muffin comes out clean. Remove from pan and cool on rack. Wrap in plastic wrap or sandwich bags. Will keep 2 to 3 months when frozen.

SAUSAGE MUFFINS
Makes 1 dozen

1/2 pound bulk pork sausage
Butter or margarine, melted
2 cups all-purpose flour
1 tablespoon baking powder
1/4 teaspoon salt
2 tablespoons sugar
1 egg, slightly beaten
1 cup milk
1/2 cup shredded cheese

Cook sausage over medium heat until browned, stirring to crumble; drain well; reserve drippings. Add butter to drippings to measure 1/4 cup. Set sausage and drippings aside.

Combine flour, baking powder, salt, and sugar in a medium bowl. Mix egg, milk, and 1/4 cup reserved drippings; stir well. Add liquid mixture to dry ingredients, stirring just until moistened. Stir in cheese and sausage. Spoon batter into paper-lined muffin pans, filling 3/4 full. Bake at 375 degrees for 18 minutes. Remove from muffin pan immediately.

OVEN OMELET WITH HAM AND CHEESE
Serves 2

1 cup ham in bite-size pieces
1 tablespoon butter or margarine
4 large eggs
1/2 cup whipping cream
1-1/2 tablespoons flour
1/4 teaspoon salt
Pinch pepper
1/3 cup grated sharp Cheddar cheese

Preheat oven to 450 degrees. Spray 10-inch non-stick skillet with pan release; wrap skillet handle with foil to ovenproof it. (If cheese is in a chunk, grate and set aside to soften.)

Heat butter in skillet until bubbly. Add ham; sauté on medium-low heat until beginning to brown. Meanwhile, in a medium bowl, whisk eggs to blend well. Whisk in cream, flour, salt and pepper. If you have fresh chives, snip some into the egg mixture. Pour over ham. Bake until puffy and golden, about 15 minutes. Sprinkle with cheese. Slip out of skillet onto serving plate.

BRIGHAM YOUNG'S BUTTERMILK DOUGHNUTS

2-1/2 cups sifted flour
1 teaspoon baking soda
3/4 teaspoon salt
3/4 teaspoon grated nutmeg
1/2 teaspoon baking powder
1 cup buttermilk
1/2 cup sugar
1 egg, beaten
1 teaspoon vanilla
2 tablespoons melted butter or shortening
Oil for frying
Confectioners' sugar

Sift together first 5 ingredients. Blend together buttermilk, sugar, egg, and vanilla. Beat buttermilk mixture into dry ingredients and stir in butter or shortening. Chill dough 30 minutes. Roll dough out onto a lightly-floured board to 3/8 to 1/2 inch thickness. Cut with 2-1/2 inch doughnut cutter. Fry in 3 inches of hot oil (375 degrees) until golden on both sides (about 2 minutes total). Drain on paper towels. Dust with confectioners' sugar, if desired. Fry doughnut holes in same manner.

This recipe is adapted from Mrs. Young's Cookbook.

MONSTER TOAST

1 loaf sliced bread
1 (6 ounce) can frozen concentrated
  orange juice, thawed, undiluted
Cinnamon

With cookie cutters, cut monster shapes out of bread slices or make a paper pattern and cut out monsters with kitchen scissors.

Dip each cut-out into concentrated orange juice, place on a cookie sheet.

Bake in a 250 degree oven until lightly toasted, about 20 minutes. Sprinkle with cinnamon, if desired.

JURY DUTY WAFFLES
Serves 3

6 eggs
1 cup cottage cheese
1/2 cup flour
1/4 cup milk
1/4 cup oil
Sprinkle of salt
1 teaspoon vanilla

Blend all ingredients together at once, in blender. Only until combined. Do not over-mix. Bake in hot waffle iron. Makes enough for 3 moderate appetites, or 2 big ones. Freeze leftovers and reheat in toaster.

OLD-FASHIONED WAFFLES

1 cup milk
2 eggs, separated
1/4 cup melted margarine or butter
2 teaspoons baking powder
1-1/2 cups flour
Pinch of salt

Beat flour and milk; add margarine; beat. Add well beaten egg yolks; beat again. Add baking powder and pinch of salt; beat very hard for few minutes. Fold in well beaten egg whites. Have waffle iron very hot.

Pile small amount of batter in center of waffle iron. It will spread when cover comes down. Don't use much batter as it will ooze out the sides of the waffle iron.

This recipe has been in our family for decades.

ORANGE GRIDDLE CAKES

1 cup flour
2-1/2 teaspoons baking powder
3/4 teaspoon salt
1 tablespoon sugar
1 egg, well beaten
1-1/4 cups milk
3 tablespoons butter or margarine,
  melted
1-1/2 cups corn flakes
Grated rind of 1 orange
Sauce:
1/2 cup honey
1/2 cup orange juice

Sift dry ingredients together. Combine egg and milk; add gradually to dry ingredients, mixing only until smooth. Add butter or margarine, corn flakes and rind. Bake on hot griddle. Serve immediately with sauce made by combining honey and orange juice.

MELTAWAY PAN-CAKES
Makes 10 pancakes

3 eggs, separated
1/2 cup sour cream
1/4 cup sifted flour
1/4 teaspoon salt
1 tablespoon sugar

Beat egg yolks well; combine with sour cream. Sift dry ingredients together; stir into egg yolk mixture. Beat egg whites until stiff; fold in. Drop by large spoonfuls onto hot griddle until tops are bubbly; turn and brown on other side.

APPLESAUCE PANCAKES
Makes 16 pancakes

2 cups flour
3 tablespoons sugar
1 teaspoon soda
3/4 teaspoon salt
2 cups buttermilk
2 eggs, slightly beaten
2 tablespoons melted butter
2/3 cup finely chopped apples
Spiced Apple Syrup (recipe below)

Sift flour with sugar, soda and salt. Combine buttermilk, eggs and melted butter; add to dry ingredients. Stir just enough to mix. Fold in chopped apples. Bake on hot, lightly greased griddle or electric skillet until golden brown on both side. Serve with syrup.

Spiced Apple Syrup:
Makes 2 cups
2 apples
1 cup apple cider
3/4 cup brown sugar
1 tablespoon butter or margarine
1/4 teaspoon cinnamon

Peel, core and thinly slice apples. In saucepan, combine apple cider, brown sugar, butter or margarine and cinnamon. Heat to boiling. Add apples; simmer about 10 minutes, or until apples are tender.

This makes a wonderful breakfast with link sausage or crisp bacon.

DUTCH POTATO PANCAKES
Serves 4 - 6

4 cups mashed potatoes
2 tablespoons flour
2 eggs, lightly beaten
1 tablespoon baking powder
Pinch of salt
1 cup milk

Mix all together and beat into batter. Place on hot, greased grill; fry on both sides until golden brown.

Fantastic FRUITS

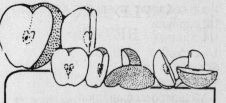

BASIC GOLDEN APPLE PIE

- 6 to 7 medium (about 2½ pounds) Golden Delicious apples
- ¼ cup sugar
- 2 tablespoons flour
- ½ teaspoon ground cinnamon
- ¼ teaspoon ground ginger
- ¼ teaspoon salt
- ⅛ teaspoon ground mace **or** cardamom
- 1 teaspoon vanilla
  Pastry for 2-crust (9-inch) pie
- 2 tablespoons butter **or** margarine

Pare apples, if desired. Core and thinly slice apples to equal 7 cups. Combine dry ingredients. Stir in apples and vanilla; place in pastry-lined 9-inch pie plate. Dot with butter; adjust top crust. Seal and flute edges; cut vents and brush with cream or milk. Bake at 425 degrees for 50–60 minutes, or until apples are tender. If necessary, cover edges with foil partway through baking time to prevent over-browning.

SPICY APPLESAUCE

- 5 pounds cooking apples
- 2 cups water
- 1½ cups sugar
- ¼ teaspoon salt

- ½ teaspoon cinnamon
- ¼ teaspoon cloves
- ¼ teaspoon nutmeg
- 1 teaspoon vanilla

Core, peel and slice apples. Put them in a heavy kettle with water, sugar and spices. Cover and simmer until the apples are tender. Put them through a food mill. If the sauce is too liquid, boil it down further, stirring constantly, until thick. Add vanilla for additional flavoring.

SPICY BAKED APPLES
Serves 4

- 4 medium (about 2 pounds) Rome Beauty apples, cored
- ¼ cup raisins
- ¼ cup chopped walnuts
- 1 tablespoon butter **or** margarine
- 1 tablespoon packed brown sugar
- ¼ cup lemon juice
- ¼ cup water
- ½ teaspoon ground cinnamon
- ¼ teaspoon ground nutmeg
  Half-and-half **or** ice cream (optional)

Pare skin ⅓ way down from top of apples. Place in an 8-inch round baking dish. Combine raisins, walnuts, butter and brown sugar; stuff centers of apples. Combine lemon juice, water and spices; pour over and around apples. Bake, uncovered, at 350 degrees for about 1 hour, or until apples are tender.

Baste every 15 minutes. Serve with half-and-half or ice cream.

Microwave Method: Prepare dish as above; use microwave-safe dish. Micro-cook at HIGH (100 percent), uncovered, 10–12 minutes; turn dish one-quarter turn and baste every 2 minutes. Recipe developed for 600–700-watt microwave ovens.

APPLE MERINGUE SWIRL
Serves 8

- 3 tablespoons butter **or** margarine
- ½ cup brown sugar, divided
- 3 teaspoons cinnamon, divided
- 2 (10-ounce) cans apple slices
- 3 egg whites
- ½ cup sugar
  Dash salt

In the bottom of a shallow 1½-quart baking dish melt butter; sprinkle with half the brown sugar and cinnamon. Arrange apple slices evenly in dish; sprinkle with remaining brown sugar and cinnamon. Beat egg whites until stiff; beat in sugar and salt. Swirl meringue on top of apple slices; bake at 325 degrees for 35–40 minutes, or until meringue is golden.

COUNTRY BAKED APPLES
Serves 5

5 large baking apples, peeled and cored
1/2 cup brown sugar
1 teaspoon cinnamon
1 teaspoon nutmeg
1 cup apple jelly
1-1/4 tablespoons butter or margarine
1/2 cup apple juice

Place apples in an 8-inch square baking dish. Combine next four ingredients; spoon about 1 tablespoon of mixture into apple cavity; dot each apple with butter. Bring apple juice to a boil; pour juice into baking dish. Cover; bake at 350 degrees for 40 minutes.

APPLE BROWN BETTY
Serves 6

1/2 cup sugar
2/3 teaspoon cinnamon
1/3 teaspoon salt
3 cups dry stale bread crumbs, fine texture
6 pared, diced apples
5 tablespoons melted butter or margarine

In a cup combine sugar, cinnamon, and salt thoroughly. Cover with layer of apples. Sprinkle with sugar mixtur. Repeat layers, and top with crumbs. Drizzle melted butter over crumbs. Bake at 375 degrees for 40 minutes. Uncover pan for last 10 minutes.

SCALLOPED APPLES
Serves 6

6 apples, peeled and sliced
1/4 teaspoon cinnamon
1/4 teaspoon salt
1 tablespoon lemon juice
1/4 cup water
3/4 cup brown sugar

1/4 cup flour
1/3 cup margarine

Peel and slice apples. Place apples in a buttered baking dish; cover with cinnamon, salt, lemon juice and water. Mix sugar, flour and margarine until crumbly; sprinkle over apples. Bake at 400 degrees for 30 minutes.

FARM-STYLE FRIED APPLES

1/2 pound bacon
3 large onions, sliced
4 large tart apples
2 tablespoons brown sugar

Fry bacon until crisp; set aside. Peel and slice onions. Core apples (leave skin on); cut cross-wise in 1/4-inch circles. Drain all but 1 tablespoon bacon drippings from pan. Cook onions in reserved bacon drippings 3 minutes; cover with apple slices in an even layer. Sprinkle brown sugar over all; cover. Cook until apples are tender. Serve with crisp bacon slices.

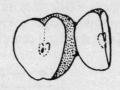

VIRGINIA FRIED APPLES
Serves 4

2 pounds cooking apples
3 tablespoons butter *or* margarine
2 tablespoons brown sugar

Wash and core apples. Cut into 1/4-inch-thick slices. Heat butter in skillet. Sprinkle with sugar. Add apples; cook about 20 minutes, until brown on both sides. Add more butter, if needed, to prevent sticking.

BAKED APPLESAUCE
Serves 6

6 large cooking apples, peeled and cored
2 tablespoons artificially sweetened orange marmalade
1/2 cup orange juice

Preheat oven to 350 degrees. In 3-quart casserole, place apples; dot with marmalade; then pour orange juice over apples. Cover and bake 1 hour or until apples are soft. Stir until apples are chunky.

To cook on range: Prepare ingredients as above but place in 5-quart Dutch oven. Over high heat, cook to boiling. Reduce heat to low; cover; simmer 25 minutes until apples are tender. Stir until apples are chunky. (Exchanges per 1/2-cup serving: 1 fruit)

PLUM KUCHEN
Serves 6

1/2 cup margarine
1/2 cup sugar
2 eggs
3/4 teaspoon almond extract
1/2 teaspoon vanilla
1 cup flour
1 teaspoon baking powder
20 plum halves

Topping:
1/2 cup sugar
1 teaspoon cinnamon
1/4 teaspoon nutmeg

In bowl, cream margarine and 1/2 cup sugar until light and fluffy. Beat in eggs, 1 at a time; add flavorings; beat well. In other bowl, sift flour and baking powder together; blend into first mixture. Pour batter into a 9-inch round pan. Arrange plum halves in batter, cut side down. Mix together topping ingredients; sprinkle over plums. Bake at 400 degrees for 30 minutes. Serve warm or cold with whipped cream.

APRICOT FOOL
Serves 4

1 (8-3/4-ounce) can apricot halves, drained
1-1/2 teaspoons lemon juice
1/4 teaspoon almond extract
1 cup heavy or whipping cream
2 tablespoons confectioners' sugar
2 tablespoons sliced, toasted almonds

In blender at medium speed, blend apricots, lemon juice, and extract until smooth. In small bowl, with mixer at medium speed, beat cream and sugar until stiff. Fold in apricot mixture just enough to marble. Spoon into 4 dessert dishes. Sprinkle with almonds.

SPICY APRICOTS

1 (30-ounce) can whole apricots
¼ cup honey
2 tablespoons vinegar
1 cinnamon stick
3 whole cloves

Drain apricots and reserve ½ cup syrup. Combine honey, vinegar and spices with reserved syrup in saucepan. Bring to a boil and pour over apricots in bowl. Chill several hours.
Great served with pork dishes!

APRICOT WHIP

1 (3-ounce) package orange-flavored gelatin
½ cup hot water
1 (8¼-ounce) can apricots
1½ teaspoons lemon juice

Drain apricots, reserving juice. Dissolve gelatin in hot water. Add ½ cup apricot juice and lemon juice. Chill until slightly thickened. Whip with rotary beater until fluffy and thick. Chop the drained apricots and

fold into mixture. Pour into 4 individual molds. Chill until firm and unmold on serving dishes. Top with 1 tablespoon whipped topping, if desired.

BANANA TURNOVERS

4 cups flour
2 teaspoons salt
1⅓ cups shortening
⅓ cup cold water
4 bananas
8 tablespoons raisins
8 teaspoons sunflower seeds

Mix flour and salt together. Cut in shortening until mixture resembles coarse meal. Sprinkle with water and mix lightly with fork. Divide into 8 balls. Roll each ball out into an 8-inch square on floured board. Cut bananas into slices and put half on 1 half of the square. Add 1 tablespoon raisins and 1 teaspoon sunflower seeds. Fold dough over to make triangle. Seal edges. Bake at 400 degrees for 15–20 minutes on an ungreased cookie sheet. Remove from sheet and cool slightly.

BANANA BONANZA

1 dozen bananas
1 medium container Cool Whip
1 cup chopped nuts
½ cup lemon juice
3 eggs
½ cup sugar

In top of double boiler, combine eggs and sugar well, then add lemon juice until thickened. Let cool; add to Cool Whip. Pour over diced bananas and nuts. Serve at once.

PEARS IN CHOCOLATE SAUCE
Serves 6

1 (29-ounce) can pear halves
8 ounces semisweet chocolate
2 tablespoons hot water
1 tablespoon butter
1 egg yolk
½ cup heavy cream
1 egg white
¾ cup chopped walnuts

Drain pear halves; arrange in 6 serving dishes.
Put chocolate in top of double boiler. Stir in water. Melt chocolate over boiling water; remove from heat. Stir in butter until melted. Add egg yolk and cream. Beat egg white until stiff peaks form; fold into warm chocolate sauce. Spoon chocolate sauce over pears. Sprinkle with chopped walnuts.

SAUCY POACHED PEARS

3 large pears, pared
12 whole cloves
1/2 cup sugar
1/3 cup orange juice
2 tablespoons lemon juice
1/3 cup white grape juice
1 whole stick cinnamon
1 large orange, peeled and thinly sliced
6 maraschino cherries

Cut pears in half lengthwise; insert 2 cloves in broad end of each pear half. Heat sugar, orange juice, lemon juice, white grape juice, and cinnamon stick to boiling, stirring constantly until sugar is dissolved; place pears in fruit syrup. Simmer uncovered, 10-15 minutes, turning occasionally, until pears are tender. Remove cinnamon stick. Place pears on serving dish; add orange slices and cherries. Pour fruit sauce over pears.

ORANGE & BANANA AMBROSIA

2 medium-size oranges
2 ripe bananas
2 tablespoons sugar
1/2 cup shredded coconut

Peel oranges and cut crosswise into thin slices, removing seeds and fibrous portions. Peel and slice bananas. Arrange a layer of orange slices on a serving dish. Add a layer of banana slices, and sprinkle with sugar. Make additional alternate layers of orange and bananas until the fruit is used up.

Top with coconut and chill for 1 hour.

BAKED BANANAS
Serves 4

4 large bananas
Butter
1/2 cup pineapple juice
1/4 cup brown sugar
1/4 teaspoon cinnamon
1/4 teaspoon allspice
1/2 cup sherry
3 tablespoons rum

Preheat oven to 450 degrees. Peel bananas and place in buttered baking dish after splitting them lengthwise. Place pineapple juice, brown sugar, spices, and sherry in saucepan. Heat and pour over bananas. Dot with butter and bake for about 15 minutes, basting often. Remove from oven; sprinkle with rum and serve at once.

MAPLED PEACHES
Serves 5

3½ cups or 1 (1-pound, 13-ounce) can peach slices, undrained
½ teaspoon maple flavoring
¼ teaspoon cinnamon
⅛ teaspoon ground nutmeg

In an 8 x 8-inch baking dish, combine all ingredients; mix well. Bake, covered, at 350 degrees for 15 minutes, or until hot and bubbly. Drain and serve, or chill and serve.

PEACHES IN CUSTARD SAUCE
Serves 6

1 (1-pound) can sliced cling peaches
1-2/3 cups evaporated milk
1 (3-1/2-ounce) package instant vanilla pudding mix
1/2 cup water
1/8 teaspoon nutmeg

Drain peaches well. Cut peaches in chunks. Place evaporated milk and water in mixing bowl. Add nutmeg and pudding mix. Beat slowly with rotary beater until smooth. Stir in peaches. Chill thoroughly before serving.

CHICKEN BREASTS WITH CHERRIES

3 chicken breasts, split
1 tablespoon cornstarch
1 pound pitted cherries
½ teaspoon ground cinnamon
¼ teaspoon allspice
½ cup flour
¼ teaspoon vegetable oil
2 tablespoons lemon juice

Dissolve cornstarch in lemon juice. Add cherries. Substitute cloves for cinnamon, if desired; add salt and pepper, as desired. Combine spices with flour in paper bag; add chicken to coat. Brown chicken in large skillet and then simmer for about 20 minutes. Cover with foil and place on warm serving plate. Remove all but 1 tablespoon drippings from skillet and add cherry mixture. Bring to boil until sauce is thickened. Pour over warm chicken.

CHERRY SALAD WITH APPLE JUICE DRESSING

2 cups pitted cherries
½ honeydew melon, sliced
1 grapefruit, peeled with membranes removed
1 orange, peeled with membranes removed

Dressing:
Makes 1 cup
½ cup apple juice
½ cup orange juice
2 tablespoons brown sugar
½ teaspoon nutmeg
1 cinnamon stick or 1 teaspoon ground cinnamon

To make dressing, combine all ingredients and bring to a boil in saucepan. Reduce heat and simmer for about 5 minutes, or until liquid is reduced by one-half. Cool.

CHERRIES SABAYON
Serves 4

2 cups fresh sweet cherries
2 egg yolks
⅓ cup dry white wine
¼ cup sugar
¾ teaspoon grated orange rind

Place ½ cup cherries in each of 4 individual serving dishes; set aside. Combine egg yolks, wine, sugar and orange rind in top of double boiler; stir well. Place over boiling water; cook 8–10 minutes, or until thickened, beating constantly with a wire whisk. Spoon one-fourth of warm mixture over each serving of cherries. Serve immediately.

SWEET-AND-SOUR HAM (OR TURKEY OR CHICKEN)

2 cups halved, pitted cherries
1½ cups julienne ham
1 cup diagonally sliced celery
1 cup diagonally sliced green onions
¼ cup sliced water chestnuts

Combine ingredients and serve with bottled Italian dressing ... or your own. Try adding ½ cup French-style green beans.

HAM WITH CHERRIES

2 (¾-inch) slices ham
¾ cup cherries
½ cup water
2 tablespoons sugar
1 tablespoon flour
2 tablespoons water
1 tablespoon candied ginger (optional)

Pit and cook cherries with ½ cup water until juices run. Pile cherries on ham slices; adding sugar, flour and water combination which has been cooked until thickened. Add ginger and bake at 350 degrees for 1 hour. Sauce freezes well.

MARASCHINO CHERRIES

4-1/2 pounds pitted cherries
2 quarts water
1 tablespoon pickling salt
1 teaspoon alum
4-1/2 pounds sugar
Juice of 1 lemon
1 ounce red food coloring
1 ounce almond extract

Soak cherries overnight in water, salt and alum. Next day: Drain and rinse cherries in cold water. Combine sugar, lemon juice and food coloring; add cherries and bring to boil. Remove from heat and let stand 24 hours.

Next day: Bring to boil again and let stand 24 hours.

Next day: Bring to boil, add almond extract. Can while boiling hot.

CHERRY FRITTERS
Serves 4

1 cup flour
1/2 teaspoon salt
1 teaspoon baking powder
1 tablespoon melted butter
1 egg
1/3 cup milk
1/4 cup drained cherries
2 tablespoons sugar

Mix dry ingredients. Beat egg; add melted butter. Combine with milk and add to dry ingredients. Fold in cherries. Drop by small teaspoon into 1-1/2 or 2 inches of hot fat. Fry 2 or more minutes until brown. Drain and dust with confectioners' sugar. Fresh peaches, apricots, apples, or pineapple may be used instead of cherries.

SCALLOPED PINEAPPLE
Serves 8–10

4 cups bread chunks (French-style bread is best)
1 (20-ounce) can pineapple chunks, drained
3 eggs
2 cups sugar
1 cup butter, melted

Place bread chunks in the bottom of a well-greased 9 x 12 x 2-inch baking dish. Spread drained pineapple chunks over bread. Beat eggs slightly. Mix in sugar and melted butter. Pour over chunks of bread and pineapple. Bake at 375 degrees for about 40 minutes.

PINEAPPLE, FRUIT AND CREAM

2 (20-ounce) cans chunk pineapple, drained
2 (11-ounce) cans mandarin oranges, drained
3 cups seedless grapes
2 cups small marshmallows
2 cups coconut
1 cup nuts (walnuts or pecans)
1½ cups sour cream

In large bowl combine all ingredients together well; chill for 4–6 hours before serving.

BAKED PINEAPPLE
Serves 6

½ cup butter or margarine
1 cup sugar
4 eggs
1 (1-pound, 4-ounce) can crushed pineapple, drained
5 slices white bread, cubed

Cream together butter and sugar. Beat in eggs, 1 at a time. Stir in pineapple. Fold in bread cubes; turn into greased 1½-quart casserole. Bake, uncovered, at 350 degrees for 1 hour. Good either hot or chilled.

PEACH AND COTTAGE CHEESE SALAD
Single serving

2/3 cup cottage cheese
1/8 teaspoon cinnamon
Artificial sweetener to equal 2 teaspoons sugar
1/2 cup cooked, enriched rice
1 medium peach, sliced
1/4 cup skim milk

Combine cottage cheese, cinnamon, and sweetener; mix well. Add rice and peach. Toss lightly until well-mixed. Chill. Just before serving, pour skim milk over mixture.

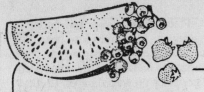

FRESH FRUIT FANTASY
Serves 12

- 2 cups watermelon cubes
- 2 cups cantaloupe
- 2 cups green grapes
- 2 cups strawberries, hulled
- 2 cups fresh blueberries
  Mandarin Dressing (recipe follows)

Combine all fruits in large bowl; toss gently; cover and chill if desired. Serve with Mandarin Dressing.

Mandarin Dressing:
- 1 cup mayonnaise
- 1 cup marshmallow creme
- 1 teaspoon grated orange rind
- 1 teaspoon grated fresh gingerroot

Combine all ingredients in bowl; stir gently. Makes 2 cups dressing.

FRUIT TACOS WITH CREAM CHEESE
Serves 10

- 16 ounces cream cheese, softened
- 2 tablespoons grated orange rind
- 2–3 tablespoons sugar
- 3 tablespoons orange juice
- 2 oranges, peeled and cubed
- 1 cup strawberries, halved
- 1 kiwi, peeled, halved and sliced
- 1 banana, peeled, halved and sliced
- 1 (20-ounce) can pineapple chunks, drained
- 1 cup shredded coconut
- 1 box taco shells

In medium bowl, blend cream cheese, orange rind, sugar and orange juice; chill. Combine cut-up fruit, pineapple and coconut; chill. Heat taco shells according to package directions. Spread cream cheese mixture on shells; top with fruit mixture. Serve immediately.

BRANDIED FRUIT

- 1/3 cup pineapple chunks
- 1/3 cup apricot chunks
- 1 cup sugar
- 1/3 cup sliced peaches
- 7 maraschino cherries

To start culture, mix all of the ingredients together and allow to stand for 2 weeks. Add 1 cup sugar and 1 cup fruit—this sugar-and-fruit mixture may be added every two weeks. Fruit is ready to eat in 2 weeks. Any assortment of canned fruits may be used. Stir mixture occasionally to mix sugar in well. Good over ice cream or angel food cake with whipped cream.

BAKED FRUIT COCKTAIL

- 1 cup sugar
- 1 cup flour
- 1 teaspoon baking soda
- 1 teaspoon salt
- 1 egg
- 1 (1-pound) can fruit cocktail
- 1 teaspoon vanilla
- 1/2 cup brown sugar
- 1/2 cup chopped nuts

In a 6-cup baking dish combine sugar, flour, soda and salt; add egg, fruit cocktail with liquid, and vanilla. Mix well. Combine brown sugar and nuts; sprinkle over the top. Bake in a 325-degree oven for 45 minutes. Serve with whipped cream or ice cream.

HOT SPICED FRUIT
Serves 8–10

- 1 (16-ounce) can mandarin oranges
- 1 (29-ounce) can sliced peaches
- 1 (29-ounce) can sliced pears
- 1 (16-ounce) can pineapple chunks
- 1 (16-ounce) can stewed prunes
- 1 cup syrup from fruit
- 1/4 to 1/2 cup brown sugar
- 2 tablespoons butter
- 1/2 teaspoon nutmeg
- 1 teaspoon cinnamon
- 1/4 teaspoon ground cloves

Drain and layer fruits in casserole. Bring to a boil 1 cup syrup from fruit, brown sugar and butter. Add nutmeg, cinnamon and ground cloves. Pour over fruit and refrigerate overnight. Bake at 350 degrees for 30 minutes.

BLUEBERRY SCONES
Makes 12

- 3 cups buttermilk baking mix
- 4 tablespoons sugar
- 1-1/2 teaspoons grated lemon peel
- 1 cup fresh or frozen blueberries
- 3 eggs
- 1/4 cup milk

Preheat oven to 400 degrees. In a medium bowl, combine baking mix, 2 tablespoons sugar, lemon peel, and blueberries. With fork, blend in 2 eggs beaten with the milk. On lightly floured baking sheet, press dough into 11x1/2-inch circle. Brush with remaining egg, beaten, then sprinkle with remaining sugar. Cut into 12 wedges. Separate wedges about 1/4 inch apart. Bake 12 minutes or until golden. Serve hot with butter and preserves.

PEACH CLAFOUTI
Serves 6

5 tablespoons sugar, divided
3 cups sliced, peeled fresh peaches
1 cup milk
1 cup half-and-half cream
3 eggs
1/4 cup flour
Pinch of salt
1 teaspoon vanilla
Confectioners' sugar or vanilla ice cream

Sprinkle a well-buttered 1-1/2-quart shallow, oval baking dish with 2 tablespoons sugar. Distribute peaches over the sugar. In a blender, combine milk, cream, eggs, flour, and salt for 2 minutes. Add vanilla and remaining sugar. Blend mixture for a few seconds; then pour over fruit. Bake in preheated 375-degree oven for 45-50 minutes or until puffed and golden.

Sprinkle the Clafouti with confectioners' sugar or top with vanilla ice cream. Serve immediately.

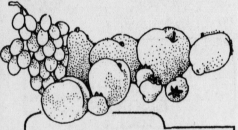

PEACH EASE
Serves 8

1 (29-ounce) can sliced peaches
3 tablespoons quick-cooking tapioca
1/2 teaspoon cinnamon
4 tablespoons butter or margarine, melted
1/2 cup flour
1/2 cup sugar
1/3 cup milk
2 teaspoons baking powder
1 teaspoon vanilla

Preheat oven to 400 degrees. Place peaches with juice in a 7x11-inch baking pan. Stir in tapioca and cinnamon. In mixing bowl, combine remaining ingredients. Spoon batter over peaches. Bake 25-30 minutes or until cake tests done.

For an extra crunch, sprinkle 1/4 cup chopped pecans over batter before baking.

FRUIT ICE

1/2 cup orange juice or 1/3 cup pineapple juice
1 tablespoon lemon juice
1/2 cup water
1 egg white

Combine fruit juices and water; freeze. Stir mixture often while freezing. When almost hard, fold in one stiffly beaten egg white. Place in an individual mold and allow to set by returning to freezer.

FRUIT PANCAKE PUFF
Serves 4

1/2 cup butter
1 cup all-purpose flour
1 cup milk
4 eggs
1/4 teaspoon salt
2 (10-ounce) packages frozen mixed fruit, thawed and drained
2 tablespoons firmly packed brown sugar
Pinch of freshly grated nutmeg

Preheat oven to 425 degrees. Melt 1/4 cup butter in heavy 10-inch skillet in oven, 3 to 5 minutes. Mix flour, milk, eggs, and salt in blender until smooth. Pour batter into hot skillet. Bake until pancake is puffed and golden brown, 20 to 25 minutes.

Meanwhile, combine remaining 1/4 cup butter, fruit, brown sugar and nutmeg in medium saucepan. Stir over low heat until butter is melted and sauce is warm, about 5 minutes. Place pancake on serving platter. Cut into 4 wedges. Top with fruit, using slotted spoon, and serve, passing sauce separately.

CHOCOLATE-COVERED STRAWBERRIES

1/2 cup semi-sweet chocolate chips
1 tablespoon corn syrup
5 tablespoons butter or margarine
36 strawberries

Place chips, syrup, and butter in saucepan. Melt over low heat. Stir until smooth. Remove from heat; place in pan of water. Dip berries into chocolate; place on waxed paper. Chill.

FRITTURA DIFICHI RUSPOLI—(HOT FRIED FIGS)

8 firm black figs or extra large fresh prunes, peeled
1/2 cup dark rum
1/3 cup all-purpose flour
1/4 cup chopped walnuts
1/2 teaspoon vanilla extract
1/2 cup water (Mix vanilla and water together)
Vegetable oil for frying
Confectioners' sugar

Soak figs in the rum for 1 hour; turn often to completely even out flavor. In a bowl slowly stir the flour into the water and vanilla mixture. Beat until smooth and creamy. Add walnuts and mix well. Put about 3/4 inch of oil into skillet and set on medium high heat. When oil is hot; dip each fig or prune into the prepared batter and drop into the hot oil. Fry until golden brown on each side (about 3 minutes). Sprinkle confectioners' sugar over top and serve hot.

BLUSHING PEACHES
Serves 6

6 canned peach halves
1 cup (sugar-free) strawberry-flavored carbonated beverage
1/2 cup low-calorie raspberry preserves
1 tablespoon cornstarch
6 tablespoons low-calorie whipped topping

Place 1 peach half each (cut side up) in 6 dessert dishes. Heat remaining ingredients, except topping, to boiling, stirring constantly. Boil and stir 1 minute; cool. Top each peach with 1 tablespoon whipped topping. Pour sauce on peach halves. Refrigerate for 2 hours.

MOCK MARASCHINO CHERRIES

2 pounds Royal Ann Cherries, not too ripe
2 tablespoons salt
1 teaspoon powdered alum
1 quart water
2-1/2 cups sugar
1-1/2 cups water
1 tablespoon red food coloring (optional)
1-1/2 tablespoons fresh lemon juice
1-1/2 tablespoons almond extract

Pit cherries; place them in a glass or ceramic mixing bowl. Dissolve salt and alum in the quart of water; pour over cherries and let them soak overnight. Drain; rinse in cold water until salt taste is completely gone. Drain all water. In a glass or enamel pot, bring sugar, 1-1/2 cups water, and food coloring to a boil. Turn off heat, gently stir in cherries, coating all. Let stand for 24 hours, covered only by a single layer of cheesecloth. Return pot of cherries to boiling; turn off heat; stir in lemon juice and almond extract. Pack hot cherries into clean jars or plastic containers. Store up to 4 months in your refrigerator or freeze in small containers for future use.

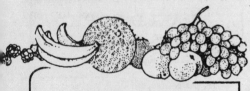

EASY FRUIT COBBLER

2/3 stick butter
1 cup sugar
1/4 cup milk
1-1/2 teaspoons baking powder
4 cups fresh peaches or berries of your choice

Melt butter in 8-inch square baking pan. Mix sugar, flour, and baking powder. Add milk. Mix and pour into baking pan with butter. No need to stir. Add fruit evenly over top, and sprinkle with more sugar. Bake at 375 degrees for 25 minutes. (This recipe can be doubled.)

ANYTIME FRUIT COBBLER
Serves 8

1/2 cup butter or margarine
1 cup milk
1 cup self-rising flour
1 cup sugar
4 cups sliced and sweetened fruit or berries

Melt butter or margarine in an 8x12-inch baking dish. Mix in milk, flour, and sugar. Pile fruit on top, but do not stir. Bake at 375 degrees for about 40 minutes or until lightly browned on top. Serve with whipped cream or ice cream.

I have successfully used the following fruits for this recipe: blackberries, blueberries, raspberries, strawberries, peaches, nectarines, and plums.

EASY NO-COOK BLUEBERRY JAM
Makes 5-6 jars

1 quart fresh blueberries
4 cups sugar
2 tablespoons lemon juice
1/2 bottle liquid pectin

Have ready five or six small jelly glasses, about 8-ounce; sterilized, or freezer containers. Remove stems from berries; discard wilted ones; rinse well. Mash with large spoon or potato masher. Mix berries and sugar thoroughly. Mix lemon juice with pectin; add to berries and stir well for 4-5 minutes. Pour into glasses or freezer containers; cover. Let jam stand at room temperature overnight. Store in refrigerator for use up to three weeks, or freeze to use within a year.
Note: A pretty touch for serving can be added by pouring jam into decorated mugs, cream pitchers, juice glasses, etc., instead of jelly glasses for refrigerator storage.

Enjoy blueberries . . . the elite of the berry kingdom!

MELON AMBROSIA
Serves 6

1 cup watermelon balls
1 cup cantaloupe balls
1 cup honeydew balls
1/2 cup lemon or lime juice
Artificial sweetener to equal 2 tablespoons sugar
1/4 cup shredded coconut

Place melon balls in a serving bowl. Sprinkle with juice and artificial sweetener. Top with coconut. Toss well and refrigerate for at least 1 hour. Garnish with mint, if desired.

About 50 calories per serving.

PEACH COBBLER

6 large or 12 small peaches
6 tablespoons sugar
1 teaspoon lemon juice, fresh
1/2 teaspoon cinnamon
1/4 teaspoon salt
2 cups all-purpose biscuit mix
1/2 cup cold water

Peel peaches; remove pits and cut peaches into slices. Place slices in an 8x8-inch greased baking dish. Sprinkle with sugar, lemon juice, cinnamon, and salt.

Combine biscuit mix and water; form into a ball; place on floured board and knead five times. Roll out into an 8-inch square.

Place pastry over peaches. Press dough gently to sides of dish. Bake in 400-degree oven for 30-40 minutes, until topping is browned. Cool slightly. Serve with Hard Sauce.

Hard Sauce:

1/2 cup soft butter or margarine
1-1/2 cups sifted confectioners' sugar
2 tablespoons brandy *or*
1 teaspoon vanilla

Cream butter or margarine. Gradually beat in sugar and brandy *or* vanilla. Blend until smooth.

Meat
DISHES

CORNED BEEF AND CABBAGE

2 medium onions, sliced
1 (2 1/2-to 3-pound) corned beef brisket
1 cup apple juice
1/4 cup packed brown sugar
2 teaspoons orange peel, finely shredded
2 teaspoons prepared mustard
6 whole cloves
6 cabbage wedges

Place onions in crockpot. Trim away any fat that might be present on the corned beef brisket. If needed, cut brisket to fit into Crockpot; place on top of onions. In a bowl combine apple juice, sugar, orange peel, mustard, and cloves; pour over brisket. Place cabbage on top of brisket. Cover; cook on *low* setting for 10-12 hours or on *high* setting for 5-6 hours.

SOUPY PORK CHOPS

6 pork chops, ½ inch thick, fat removed
1 can tomato soup
1 package dry onion soup mix
1 medium onion, sliced
1 green pepper, sliced
1 cup mushrooms, sliced

Arrange chops in an oblong casserole. Mix remaining ingredients and pour over chops. Cover with waxed paper. Microwave at 70 percent for 30 minutes.

PORK CHOP 'N' POTATO BAKE

1 can cream of celery soup
½ cup milk
½ cup sour cream
1 package hash brown potatoes
1 cup shredded cheddar cheese
1 can French onion rings
6 medium pork chops
Seasoned salt
¼ teaspoon salt
¼ teaspoon pepper

Brown chops and sprinkle with seasoned salt. Mix soup, milk, sour cream, potatoes, salt, pepper, ½ cup of the cheese and ½ can of the onion rings. Spoon into a greased casserole or 9 x 13-inch pan, and arrange chops over top. Cover and bake at 350 degrees for 40 minutes. Top with remaining cheese and onion rings. Bake, uncovered, 5 minutes more.

CHERRY PORK CHOPS
Serves 6

6 pork chops, cut 3/4-inch thick
1/4 teaspoon salt
1/4 teaspoon pepper
1/2 can cherry pie filling (1 cup)
2 teaspoons lemon juice

1/2 teaspoon instant chicken bouillon granules
1/8 teaspoon ground mace

Trim excess fat from pork chops. Brown pork chops in hot skillet with butter or oil. Sprinkle each chop with salt and pepper. Combine cherry pie filling, lemon juice, chicken bouillon granules, and ground mace in cooker. Stir well. Place pork chops in Crockpot. Cover. Cook on *low* for 4-5 hours. Place chops on platter. Pour cherry sauce over meat.

BAKED PORK CHOPS & APPLES
Serves 4

4 pork chops
¼ teaspoon nutmeg
1 tablespoon shortening
1¼ cups apple juice
2 cups sliced raw potato
1 tablespoon cornstarch
1 cup sliced onion
1 teaspoon salt
2 apples, cored and cut into wedges

In skillet, brown chops on both sides in shortening. Remove chops from skillet; arrange in 2-quart casserole. Add potato and onion to pan drippings; heat thoroughly, stirring carefully. Sprinkle with salt and nutmeg; stir in apple wedges. Spoon mixture over chops. Add 1 cup apple juice to skillet; heat until simmering;

OVEN FRIED PORK CHOPS
Serves 4

- 3 tablespoons margarine *or* butter
- 1 egg, beaten
- 2 tablespoons milk
- 1 cup corn bread stuffing mix
- 4 pork loin chops (about 1½ pounds), cut ½ inch thick

Set oven to 425 degrees. Place margarine or butter in a 13 x 9 x 2-inch baking pan. Place pan in the oven about 3 minutes, or until margarine melts. Stir together egg and milk. Dip pork chops in egg mixture. Coat with stuffing mix. Place chops on top of melted margarine in pan. Bake 20 minutes. Turn. Bake 10–15 minutes more, or until pork is no longer pink.

These are delicious and so tender!

TROPICAL PORK CHOPS
Serves 4

- 4 thin pork chops
- 1 small can crushed pineapple
- 1 cup orange juice

Preheat oven to 325 degrees. Place chops in shallow baking dish. Top with pineapple and orange juice. Bake for 1 hour, uncovered.

SPARERIBS "ALOHA"

- 3 pounds spareribs
- ½ cup finely chopped onion
- ¼ cup green pepper, chopped
- 1 (16-ounce) can tomato sauce
- ½ teaspoon dry mustard
- 1 tablespoon Worcestershire sauce
- 1 (2½-cup) can crushed pineapple
- ¼ cup brown sugar

Cut every third rib about halfway through the strip. Sprinkle with salt and pepper. Place in shallow pan. Bake 1¼ hours at 350 degrees. Pour off fat. Mix remaining ingredients and let stand to blend flavor. Pour over ribs. Bake 45–50 minutes, basting frequently to glaze ribs.

SWEET SOUR PORK STEAKS
Serves 4

- 1 tablespoon cooking oil
- 2 pork steaks
- ¾ cup chicken broth
- ¼ cup finely chopped celery
- 1 tablespoon brown sugar
- 1 tablespoon vinegar
- 1 teaspoon prepared mustard
- ¼ teaspoon salt
  Dash of pepper
- 2 tablespoons crushed gingersnaps (2 cookies)
  Hot cooked noodles

Heat skillet over high heat. Add oil to skillet. Cook steaks in oil about 8 minutes, or until meat is no longer pink, turning once. Remove steaks and keep warm. Drain fat from skillet. In same skillet, stir together chicken broth, celery, brown sugar, vinegar, mustard, salt and pepper. Stir in gingersnaps. Cook and stir until mixture is thick and bubbly. Serve meat and sauce over hot cooked noodles.

SAUSAGE 'N' CHEESE TURNOVERS
Makes 10 sandwiches

- 1 (10-ounce) can refrigerated big flaky biscuits
- ½ pound Italian bulk sausage *or* ground beef, browned and drained
- ¼ teaspoon Italian seasoning
- 1 (4-ounce) can mushroom pieces and stems, drained
- 4 ounces (1 cup) shredded mozzarella or provolone cheese
- 1 egg, slightly beaten
- 1–2 tablespoons grated Parmesan cheese

Heat oven to 350 degrees. Grease a cookie sheet. Separate dough into 10 biscuits; press or roll each to a 5-inch circle. In a medium bowl, combine browned sausage, seasoning, mushrooms and mozzarella cheese. Spoon about 3 tablespoons meat mixture onto center of each flattened biscuit. Fold dough in half over filling; press edges with fork to seal. Brush tops with beaten egg; sprinkle with Parmesan cheese. Place on prepared cookie sheet. Bake for 10–15 minutes, or until deep golden brown.

Tip: To reheat, wrap loosely in foil. Heat at 375 degrees for 10–15 minutes.

BAKED BEEF CUBES CACCIATORE
Serves 4

- 3½ pounds lean beef, cut into 1-inch cubes
  Flour for dredging
  Vegetable oil
- 1 large onion, chopped
- 1 clove garlic, minced
- ¼ teaspoon salt
- ½ teaspoon oregano
- ½ teaspoon red pepper, crushed
- 1 (10½-ounce) can crushed tomatoes
- 1 (1-pound, 12-ounce) can crushed tomatoes
- 1 large green pepper, cut into strips
- 12 ounces thin noodles, cooked, drained

Dredge beef with flour; brown in skillet with vegetable oil. Remove from heat; place beef in a large ovenproof casserole; add next 8 ingredients; cover. Bake at 300 degrees for 2½ hours. Remove from oven; stir in cooked noodles.

BAKED PORK TENDERLOINS

Serves 6–8

2 tablespoons oil
2 tablespoons butter or margarine
2 (1-pound) whole-pork tenderloins
½–1 cup sliced celery
½–1 cup sliced carrots
1 medium onion, sliced
½ cup sliced mushrooms
2 tablespoons dry white wine
2 tablespoons flour
1 cup chicken or beef stock
Salt and pepper to taste
Chopped parsley for garnish

In heavy skillet, heat oil and melt butter. When hot, add meat; brown on all sides. Remove from pan. Add celery, carrots, onions and mushrooms; sauté until slightly limp. Add wine. Cook 5 minutes on medium-low heat. Sprinkle on flour. Cook 2–3 minutes. Add stock; cook to thicken. Season with salt and pepper. Place meat in baking dish; pour vegetable mixture over top. Cover and bake at 325 degrees for 1½ hours, or until tender. Sprinkle with parsley. Thicken sauce to gravy consistency. Slice tenderloin and pour sauce over meat.

SASSY SAUSAGES

Serves 5–6

1 cup water
⅓ cup red cinnamon candies
Red food coloring
3 red tart apples, cored and cut into ½-inch rings
1 pound pork sausage links
3 tablespoons water

In skillet, heat 1 cup water, the cinnamon candies and a few drops red food coloring until candies are melted. Place apple rings in syrup; cook slowly, turning occasionally, about 20 minutes, or until tender. Place links in another skillet; add 3 tablespoons water. Cover tightly; cook slowly for 8 minutes. Uncover; cook, turning sausages until well-browned. To serve, insert hot sausage link in center of each apple slice.

SMOKED SAUSAGE CASSEROLE

2 pounds smoked sausage, cut into 4-inch lengths
1 teaspoon butter or margarine
1 medium onion, cut into wedges
2 (16-ounce) cans sauerkraut
1 cup apple juice
2 medium apples, cut into wedges
4 medium potatoes, cut in half
Salt and pepper

Brown sausage in butter in a 1½-quart Dutch oven or large casserole. Arrange onion, sauerkraut, apples and potatoes around sausage. Top with apple juice; salt and pepper to taste. Cover tightly and simmer over low heat for 30–40 minutes, or until potatoes test done with a fork. Stir once during cooking time.

HERB-STUFFED HAM SLICES

Serves 6

4 tablespoons butter or margarine
1 onion, finely chopped
10 mushrooms, finely chopped
1¼ teaspoons prepared mustard
2 tablespoons parsley, finely chopped
2 tablespoons chives, finely chopped
¼ teaspoon ground sage
¾ cup herb bread crumbs
½ to 1 cup chicken stock
Salt and pepper to taste
6 large slices cold boiled or baked ham, ¼–½ inch thick

Heat half the butter in a skillet; add onion and mushrooms; sauté 5 minutes; remove to bowl.

Add rest of ingredients with enough chicken stock to moisten the mixture and hold it together. Spread the prepared mixture on ham slices; fold slices in half; arrange on shallow, buttered baking dish. Melt remaining butter; pour over ham slices. Cover; bake at 375 degrees for 20 minutes.

HAM LOAF

2 pounds ground beef
2 pounds ground ham
4 slices bread, cut up
¼ pound soda crackers, crushed
1 small onion
2 cans tomato soup
4 eggs
1 teaspoon salt
½ teaspoon pepper
4 tablespoons mustard
2 tablespoons Worcestershire sauce

Mix well and add just enough milk to give a soft consistency. Bake in preheated oven at 350 degrees for 2 hours.

HAM CASSEROLE

½ pound egg noodles, cooked
2 cups ham, cubed
1 to 1½ cups cheddar cheese, shredded
1 can cream of mushroom soup
¾ cup milk
1 teaspoon dry mustard
1 box frozen peas

Pierce box of peas in several places. Microwave for 5 minutes; set aside. Combine ham, cheese, soup, milk and mustard in a 3-quart glass casserole. Add noodles and peas; stir to blend. Microwave on HIGH for 6–8 minutes, stirring one time.

MUSTARD-GLAZED HAM LOAF
Serves 8–10

- 1½ pounds ground ham
- 1 pound boneless pork shoulder, trimmed and ground
- 3 eggs, slightly beaten
- ½ cup finely crushed saltine crackers (14 crackers) **or**
- ½ cup finely crushed bread crumbs (3 or 4 slices)
- ½ cup tomato juice
- 2 tablespoons chopped onion
- 1 tablespoon prepared horseradish
- ½ teaspoon salt
- ⅛ teaspoon pepper
- 1–2 recipes Mustard Sauce (recipe follows)

Mix ingredients. Shape into a 9 x 5-inch loaf in shallow baking dish. Bake in a 350-degree oven for 1¼ hours.

Meanwhile prepare Ham Loaf Mustard Sauce. Drain fat from pan. Pour Mustard Sauce over loaf. Bake 30 minutes more, basting with sauce occasionally.

Mustard Sauce:
- ½ cup brown sugar, firmly packed
- 2 tablespoons vinegar
- ½ teaspoon dry mustard

HAM ROLL-UPS WITH CHEESE SAUCE

- 2 cups flour
- 3 tablespoons baking powder
- ½ teaspoon salt
- 4 tablespoons shortening
- 1 cup milk
- 2 cups cooked ham, cubed
- 4 tablespoons butter, melted
- 2 tablespoons cream
- 2 teaspoons mustard

Sift flour, baking powder and salt together in mixing bowl. Add shortening and milk; mix well. Roll dough out on floured table in a long rectangle. Mix ham with butter, cream and mustard; spread thick layer of ham mixture over dough; roll up like a jelly roll. Cut in slices about 1½ inches thick. Place on a cookie sheet; pat each roll sharply to flatten. Bake in oven at 450 degrees for 20–25 minutes; serve with hot Cheese Sauce (recipe follows).

Cheese Sauce:
- ½ stick butter
- 3 tablespoons flour
- 3 cups milk
- ½ teaspoon salt
- 1 pound processed American cheese

Make a cream sauce with the butter, flour and milk. Cook until thickened. Add salt and cheese. Stir until cheese is melted. Serve over hot Ham Roll-Ups.

REAL BAKED HAM

- 5 pounds ham
- Cider to cover
- ½ cup brown sugar
- 1 teaspoon mustard
- 20 whole cloves

Cover the ham with cold water and bring slowly to the boil. Throw out the water and replace with the cider to cover ham. Bring this to a boil; lower heat, keeping the liquid barely simmering for 20 minutes to the pound of ham; remove from heat and allow to stand in the liquid for 30 minutes. Take out ham; skin it and score fat with a sharp knife in a diamond pattern. Stud with whole cloves. Mix the sugar and mustard; rub well into ham. Bake in a preheated oven for an additional 10 minutes to the pound in a 400-degree oven. Carve; serve with sweet potatoes or a salad.

BEEF RING WITH BARBECUE SAUCE

- 1½ pounds ground chuck
- ¾ cup quick-cooking oats
- 1 cup evaporated milk
- 3 tablespoons onion, finely chopped
- 2 tablespoons Worcestershire sauce
- 3 tablespoons vinegar
- 2 tablespoons sugar
- 1 cup ketchup
- ½ cup water
- 6 tablespoons onion, finely chopped

Mix together ground chuck, oats, evaporated milk and 3 tablespoons onion. Pack into an 8-inch ring mold and bake 10 minutes. Remove to a larger pan.

Combine remaining ingredients to form the sauce. Pour sauce over beef ring. Bake at 350 degrees for approximately 1½ hours. Baste frequently with sauce during baking time.

This has been a family favorite for years and is absolutely delicious!!

COUNTRY ROAST AND VEGETABLES
Serves 6-8

- 1 roast, thawed
- Several potatoes, canned sliced or whole
- Several carrots
- Green beans, corn (optional)
- 1 onion, sliced
- 1 cup water
- 1/4 teaspoon salt
- 1/4 teaspoon pepper
- 3 tablespoons butter or margarine
- 1/4 cup flour (optional)

Place roast in Crockpot. Add peeled potatoes, carrots, beans, corn, sliced onion, and butter. Add water and flour for gravy. Sprinkle with salt and pepper. Cook on *low* for 6-12 hours, *high* for less than 6 hours.

SUKIYAKI
Serves 8

- 2 pounds lean ground beef
- 2 tablespoons sugar
- ⅓ cup soy sauce
- ¼ cup A-1 steak sauce
- 1 teaspoon salt
- 1 (6-ounce) can sliced mushrooms
- 2 medium onions, thinly sliced
- 1 green pepper, sliced in thin strips
- 6 scallions, cut in 1-inch pieces
- 1 cup thinly sliced celery
- 1 (8-ounce) can water chestnuts, thinly sliced
- 1 (8-ounce) can bamboo shoots
- 1 tablespoon cornstarch
  Cooked rice

In large skillet, brown beef until crumbly. In small bowl, mix sugar, soy sauce, A-1 steak sauce and salt. Set aside. Drain mushrooms, reserving liquid. When meat is cooked, mix in vegetables. Add sauce. Simmer for 3 minutes, or until vegetables are just crisp-tender. Combine cornstarch and reserved mushroom liquid. Stir into sukiyaki. Cook just until thickened. Serve over rice.

TENDER MEATBALLS IN MUSHROOM GRAVY
Serves 4-6

- 1 pound hamburger
- 4 slices soft white bread
- 1 teaspoon salt
- 1/4 teaspoon pepper
- 1 tablespoon minced onion
- 1 can mushroom soup
- 1/3 cup water

Pull apart bread into small, dime-size pieces. Combine hamburger, bread, salt, pepper, and minced onion in large mixing bowl. Using a spoon, scoop out rounds of meat, or shape into several round, 2-inch balls by hand.

Brown meatballs in a hot skillet using a small amount of butter or oil. Turn them occasionally so all sides are browned. Place meat in cooker. Add soup and water. Cook on *low* for 6 to 12 hours, *high* for up to 6 hours.

BEEF IN OYSTER SAUCE
Serves 6-8

- 1½ to 2 pounds round steak
  Meat marinade
- 1 (10½-ounce) can condensed oyster stew (1¼ cups)
- 1 package brown gravy mix
- ¼ cup water
- ¼ cup sliced green onions

Cut steak into serving pieces. Prepare with meat marinade, as directed on package. Drain marinade. In large fry pan, brown meat slightly on both sides. Reduce heat. Combine oyster stew, gravy mix and water. Add to meat. Simmer, covered, stirring occasionally, for 30–40 minutes until meat is tender. Stir in onions. Serve over rice.

SOUPER MEAT LOAF

- 2 pounds ground chuck
- 1 package dry onion soup mix
- 1 egg
- ½ cup ketchup
- ½ cup baked crumbs
- 4 slices American cheese

Mix all ingredients, except cheese; blend well. Divide mixture in half. Place half of meat in a ring mold. Place cheese strips over meat. Add remaining meat and seal well. Cover with waxed paper. Microwave on HIGH for 15 minutes. Rest 5 minutes or microwave at 50 percent for 25–30 minutes.

CHEESE-STUFFED MEAT LOAF
Serves 6-8

- 2 eggs, beaten
- ⅓ cup milk
- 1 tablespoon garlic salt
- ¼ teaspoon pepper
- ½ cup grated onion
- 2 cups cooked rice
- 1½ pounds lean ground beef
- 6 slices American cheese
- ½ cup barbecue sauce

Mix together eggs, milk, garlic salt, pepper, grated onion, cooked rice and ground beef. Press half of this mixture into a greased 9 x 5-inch loaf pan. Place cheese on top; spread rest of meat mixture over the top, pressing around edges to seal cheese in. Pour barbecue sauce over the top. Bake in 350-degree oven for 60–65 minutes.

CALIFORNIA MEAT ROLL

- 1½ pounds ground chuck
- ½ cup dry red table wine
- 1 egg, beaten
- ½ cup dry bread crumbs
- 1 teaspoon salt
- 2 tablespoons green pepper, finely chopped
- ¼ teaspoon sage
- ¼ teaspoon thyme
- ¼ teaspoon garlic powder
- 1 small onion, finely chopped
- 1 cup shredded cheddar cheese
- 1 cup fresh mushrooms, sliced

Combine all ingredients, except cheese and mushrooms, mixing thoroughly. Turn mixture onto 12-inch square heavy waxed paper. Pat or roll into 12-inch square. Sprinkle cheese and mushrooms over meat. Then roll as for jelly roll using paper to start well. Place seam side down in loaf pan. Bake at 350 degrees for 1½ hours. Can be served with tomato or mushroom sauce.

SOUR CREAM MEAT LOAF

2 pounds lean ground beef
½ medium onion, diced
¾ cup sour cream
¼ cup ketchup
2–3 slices bread, crumbled
Salt and pepper to taste
1 egg, beaten
Sour Cream Meat Loaf Sauce (recipe follows)

Bake at 350 degrees in loaf pan for 1 or 1½ hours until done. About halfway through cooking, baste with Sour Cream Meat Loaf Sauce.

Sour Cream Meat Loaf Sauce:
½ cup ketchup
⅛ cup brown sugar
1 teaspoon mustard

Mix all ingredients together.

LAYERED MEAT LOAF WITH MUSHROOM SAUCE

6 ounces herb-seasoned stuffing mix
1½ pounds lean ground beef
½ pound bulk pork sausage, with sage
1 egg, beaten
2 slices bread, crumbled
¼ cup milk
1 teaspoon garlic salt
2 teaspoons minced onion
1 teaspoon Worcestershire sauce
½ teaspoon pepper (No salt is needed as it is seasoned enough with other ingredients)
1 can mushroom soup
¼ cup water

Prepare the stuffing mix, using 1½ cups water and 3 tablespoons melted butter. Mix well and fluff lightly. Set aside.

Combine remaining ingredients, except soup and water, in a bowl; mix well. Spread half the meat mixture in bottom of a loaf pan. Spread stuffing over, patting it down evenly. Pat remaining meat mixture over stuffing. Preheat oven to 350 degrees. Bake loaf for 45 minutes, or until top is lightly browned. Combine mushroom soup with water and pour over meat loaf. Continue baking for 30 minutes longer.

MEXICAN MEAT LOAF

1½ pounds ground beef
1 medium onion, chopped
½ cup chopped mushrooms
¼ cup chopped green pepper
½ cup taco sauce
2 tablespoons barbecue sauce
1 egg, beaten
½ cup tortilla chips, finely crushed
½ teaspoon salt
Dash black pepper

Combine all ingredients; mix well. Pack into an oiled 8-inch loaf pan. Bake at 400 degrees for 1¼ hours, or until done.

You can use ground veal, pork or turkey if you like. Also may use ketchup instead of barbecue sauce.

MEAT LOAF CHOW MEIN

1 pound ground beef
1 package Chow Mein Oriental Seasoning Mix
¾ teaspoon garlic powder
½ teaspoon salt
½ teaspoon pepper
2 eggs
1 can crispy Chinese noodles (optional)

Mix all ingredients together, except crispy Chinese noodles. Mold into 2 loaves. Bake at 350 degrees for 1 hour. Arrange Chinese noodles around loaves for garnish before serving.

MEATBALL SUPREME
Serves 4

1 (10-ounce) can cream of vegetable soup
½ soup can of water
1 pound ground beef
1 egg
¼ teaspoon salt
2 tablespoons dry bread crumbs
2 tablespoons chopped onion
1 tablespoon chopped parsley
Dash of pepper
1 tablespoon shortening

Blend soup and water. Measure out ¼ cup of this mixture; combine with beef, egg, salt, bread, onion, parsley and pepper. Shape 12 meatballs; brown meat in shortening. Add remaining soup. Cover and simmer for 20 minutes. Stir now and then. If sauce is thin, remove cover and cook a few additional minutes.

SALISBURY STEAK

2 pounds hamburger
1 can onion soup
1 cup bread crumbs
2 eggs, beaten
1 can tomato soup
1 can celery soup

Mix the hamburger, bread crumbs, onion soup and eggs as for meat loaf. Add salt to taste. Add more bread crumbs, if needed. Make into patties; dip in flour and brown on each side.

Arrange in a greased baking dish. Make a gravy of 1 can celery soup, 1 can tomato soup and 1 can water.

Pour over the patties and bake in a 350-degree oven for 1 hour.

GREEN VEGETABLE MEAT LOAF
Serves 8

2 pounds lean ground meat
2 (10-ounce) boxes frozen chopped broccoli, thawed and drained
1 cup chopped onion
⅔ cup uncooked quick cooking oatmeal
2 large eggs
½ cup milk *or* water
1 (1.5-ounce) package meat loaf seasoning mix

Heat oven to 375 degrees. Lightly grease a 9 x 5 x 3-inch loaf pan. Put all ingredients into a large bowl. Mix with hands 3–4 minutes until well-blended. Press mixture into prepared pan. Bake 1 hour in the middle of oven. Remove from oven; cover loosely with foil and let stand 10–15 minutes. Drain off juice. This vegetable-laced meat loaf is delicious fresh from the oven, and even better the next day cold.

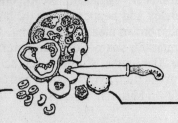

SWISS STEAK
Serves 4

¼ cup flour
¾ teaspoon salt
¼ teaspoon black pepper
1½ pounds round steak
3 tablespoons fat
1 medium onion, chopped
1½ cups stewed tomatoes
½ cup sliced carrots
½ cup sliced celery

Mix flour, salt and pepper. Dredge steak with flour; pound the flour into both sides of steak. In a Dutch oven, heat the fat; brown the steak well on both sides. Add vegetables; cover and simmer gently for 1½ hours.

SOUR CREAM SWISS STEAK
Serves 4

2 pounds round steak, 1 inch thick
¼ cup flour
1 teaspoon salt
¼ teaspoon pepper
2 tablespoons vegetable oil
2 onions, sliced
½ cup water
¼ tablespoon steak sauce
½ cup sour cream
2 tablespoons Swiss cheese, grated
⅛ teaspoon paprika

Dredge steak on both sides with flour seasoned with salt and pepper. Heat oil in skillet; brown steak on both sides. Add remaining ingredients, except cheese; cover skillet. Simmer 1 hour, or until meat is fork-tender; sprinkle Swiss cheese on steak while still hot.

FILET MIGNONETTES
Serves 6

1 (2–3-pound) flank steak
6 to 8 bacon strips
Meat tenderizer

Preheat broiler unit of oven or stove. Trim steak of any fat. Score 1 side of steak in a diamond pattern about ⅛ inch deep. Sprinkle with meat tenderizer. Starting at long end, roll up jelly roll fashion.

On flat surface, lay out bacon slices. Place rolled steak on slices and wrap bacon around. Secure with 6 toothpicks, equally spaced. With sharp knife, cut through between each piece to make 6 fillets.

Broil, cut side down, for 7 minutes. Turn and continue broiling for 10 minutes, or until desired doneness. (If crisp bacon is desired, stand on end for 2 minutes; turn and repeat.)

A definite man-pleaser steak without the price pinch of real fillet. Can be made up within ½ hour before dinnertime.

COLA ROAST
Serves 8–10

1 teaspoon salt
½ teaspoon pepper
½ teaspoon garlic powder
1 (4–5-pound) bottom-round roast
3 tablespoons vegetable oil
1½ cups cola-flavored soda
12 ounces chili sauce
2 tablespoons Worcestershire sauce
2 tablespoons hot sauce

Combine salt, pepper and garlic powder; rub over surface of roast. Brown roast on all sides in vegetable oil in Dutch oven. Drain off drippings. Combine remaining ingredients; pour over roast. Cover and bake at 325 degrees for 3 hours, or until tender.

BARBECUED FLANK STEAK

¼ cup soy sauce
3 tablespoons honey
2 tablespoons vinegar
1 green onion, chopped, *or* 2 teaspoons onion powder
½ to 1½ teaspoons garlic powder
1½ teaspoons powdered ginger
¾ cup salad oil
Flank steaks

Mix first 7 ingredients in large bowl; add steaks. Marinate at room temperature for 3–6 hours. Broil over hot coals until medium-rare or rare; slice diagonally, cutting in ½–¾-inch strips. Marinade will keep indefinitely in refrigerator if green onion is removed.

PEPPER STEAK
Serves 6

- 1½ pounds round steak, ½ inch thick
- 1 cup sliced onion
- 1 cup beef broth
- 2 stalks celery, chopped
- 1 tablespoon salt
- ½ teaspoon garlic powder *or* 1 garlic clove, minced
- ½ teaspoon ginger
- 2 green peppers, cut in strips
- 1 cup sliced mushrooms
- 1 (1-pound) can tomatoes, chopped
- 3 tablespoons soy sauce
- 2 tablespoons cornstarch
- 1 cup water

Cut round steak into thin strips and brown in Dutch oven in small amount of oil and margarine. Add beef broth, onion, celery, salt, garlic and ginger; simmer, covered, for 35–40 minutes, or until tender. Add green peppers, mushrooms and tomatoes; cook an additional 10 minutes. Mix soy sauce and cornstarch in 1 cup water until smooth. Slowly stir into sauce and cook, stirring constantly, until thickened. Serve over rice. This can be made the day before serving and reheated in the microwave.

BURGUNDY STEAK
Serves 2

- 1 cup burgundy wine
- 1 tablespoon Worcestershire sauce
- ½ teaspoon dried leaf basil
- ½ teaspoon dried leaf thyme
- ¼ teaspoon dry mustard
  Dash garlic powder
- 2 (8-ounce) beef rib-eye steaks
- ¼ cup butter *or* margarine
- 4 frozen french-fried onion rings
- ½ cup fresh mushroom slices

In a small bowl, mix burgundy, Worcestershire sauce, basil, thyme, mustard and garlic powder. Place meat in a plastic bag; put in a shallow baking pan. Pour marinade into bag; seal bag. Marinate in refrigerator 8 hours or overnight, turning bag over occasionally. Melt butter or margarine in a large skillet. Add onion rings. Cook over medium-high heat until golden brown. Remove onion rings and keep warm; reserve butter or margarine in skillet; Drain steak; reserve ½ cup marinade. Cook steaks in butter or margarine in skillet until done as desired, turning several times. Place steaks on a platter; reserve drippings in skillet. Cook and stir mushrooms in drippings until barely tender. Stir in reserved marinade. Cook and stir until heated through. Pour over steaks. Top with cooked onion rings.

SWISS STEAK
Serves 6

- 2 pounds round steak
- 6 tablespoons flour
- 1 teaspoon salt
- ½ teaspoon pepper
- 4 onions
- 6 tablespoons shortening
- ½ cup chopped celery
- ¾ cup chili sauce
- ¾ cup water
- 1 green pepper

Combine flour, salt and pepper; rub into both sides of steak; cut into 6 portions. Peel and slice onions. Preheat skillet; add half of shortening, then onions; brown lightly; remove from skillet. Add remaining shortening; brown steak on both sides. Reduce heat. Add celery, chili sauce and water. Cover; simmer 1 hour. Cut green pepper into slices. Add pepper and onions to meat. Continue cooking for 30 minutes.

BONELESS PRIME RIB ROAST
Serves 12

- 1 cup soy sauce
- 1 cup teriyaki sauce
- 1 cup dry sherry wine
- 1 cup water
- 2 tablespoons brown sugar
- 6 pounds rib-eye roast

- 1 package dry onion soup mix

Combine marinade ingredients, stirring to dissolve sugar. Place beef roast in large pan and marinate in mixture under refrigeration for 4 hours or more, turning occasionally. Place meat in a 350-degree oven and rub with onion soup mix. Cook, basting occasionally with marinade, until temperature reaches 120 degrees for rare, 130–140 degrees for medium or 160 degrees for well-done. Remove from oven and let stand 10 minutes before slicing.

BARBECUED LEMON CHICKEN

- 3 roasting *or* broiling chickens
- 1 cup salad oil
- ¾ cup fresh lemon juice
- 1 tablespoon salt
- 2 teaspoons paprika
- 2 teaspoons onion powder
- 1 teaspoon garlic powder
- 2 teaspoons crushed sweet basil
- 2 teaspoons crushed thyme

Have butcher split chickens and remove wings, backbone and tail. Clean well; place in shallow pan. Combine remaining ingredients; pour into jar. Cover; shake well to blend. Pour over chicken; cover tightly. Marinate overnight in refrigerator, turning chicken occasionally. Remove to room temperature 1 hour before grilling. Barbecue chicken over hot coals for 15–20 minutes on each side, basting often with marinade.

CHICKEN-VEGETABLE-FRENCH-FRY CASSEROLE
Serves 8

This provides meat, potatoes and vegetables in 1 dish. Put together ahead of time, and it is ready to eat 35 minutes after popping in the oven.

- 2 fryer chickens, cut up
- ¼ cup (½ stick) butter
- ¼ cup flour
- 1 teaspoon salt
- 2 cups reserved chicken broth
- 1 (10½-ounce) can cream of celery soup
- 1 (10-ounce) package frozen peas and carrots
- ½ cup (1 stick) butter
- 1 (1-pound) box frozen french fries
  Parmesan cheese

Cook, cool and bone chicken. Save 2 cups of broth. In a buttered 9 x 13-inch pan, put good-sized pieces of chicken. Melt butter; add flour, salt, broth and soup. Cook until thick and smooth. Cook peas and carrots for 3 minutes. Drain. Mix with sauce and pour over chicken.

Melt stick of butter; stir frozen french fries in butter until coated. Place on top of other ingredients. Sprinkle generously with Parmesan cheese. Bake, uncovered, at 450 degrees for 20–25 minutes. If it has been put together earlier and refrigerated, bake for 35 minutes.

CHICKEN AND BISCUITS
Serves 4

Filling:
- 2 tablespoons vegetable oil
- 1 small onion, peeled and chopped
- ½ green pepper, finely chopped
- ⅔ cup sliced mushrooms
- 2 tablespoons cornstarch
- 1½ cups milk
- 2 cups cooked chicken, cubed
  Salt and pepper

Biscuits:
- 2 cups flour
- 2½ teaspoons baking powder
- ⅓ cup margarine
- ⅔ cup milk

Heat oil in skillet. Add onion, green pepper and mushrooms. Sauté for a few minutes. Add cornstarch; cook 1 minute, stirring constantly. Add milk gradually; stir until boiling. Add chicken and seasoning. Turn into deep 9-inch pie plate. In bowl, sift flour and baking powder. Cut in margarine with pastry blender. Stir in milk with fork to make soft dough. Knead lightly on floured board; roll to about ½-inch thickness. With cookie, cut into 1½-inch rounds. Place rounds on top of chicken; brush with milk. Bake at 425 degrees for 10–15 minutes, or until biscuits are done.

CHICKEN NOODLE MEDLEY
Serves 6

- 10 ounces green noodles
- 1 medium-size onion
- 1 bay leaf
- 2 tablespoons butter
- 1 teaspoon onion salt
- ⅛ teaspoon pepper
- 3 pounds broiler-fryer chicken, cut up
- 1 (10¾-ounce) can cream of mushroom soup
- ¾ cup milk
- ⅔ cup grated Parmesan cheese
- 2 tablespoons chopped chives
- ½ teaspoon sage
  Paprika
- 1 (1-pound) package frozen baby carrots, drained and cooked

Preheat oven to 350 degrees. Cook noodles according to package directions, adding onion and bay leaf to cooking water. Drain noodles; discard onion and bay leaf. Toss together noodles, butter, onion salt and pepper. Spoon into buttered 13 x 9-inch baking dish. Sprinkle chicken pieces with salt and pepper; place on noodles. Combine soup, milk, ⅓ cup cheese, chives and sage; pour over chicken. Sprinkle with remaining cheese and paprika. Bake 45 minutes; add carrots. Bake additional 20 minutes, or until chicken is tender.

CHICKEN CHOLUPAS

- 4 chicken breasts, cooked, deboned and diced
- 3 cans cream of chicken soup
- 1 large can green chilies, diced
- 1 onion, finely diced
- 16 ounces sour cream
- ¾ pound Monterey Jack cheese, grated
- ¾ pound mild cheddar cheese, grated
- 12 small flour tortillas

Mix all ingredients together, except tortillas and only half the cheeses. Put 3 tablespoons mixture in each tortilla. Roll up and place in a greased baking dish. Pour rest of mixture over tortillas. Sprinkle remaining cheeses over all. Bake at 350 degrees for 45 minutes.

BAKED CHICKEN

- 2 chicken breasts
- 1 tablespoon butter *or* margarine, melted
- ½ cup Parmesan cheese
- 2 tablespoons butter *or* margarine

Preheat oven to 400 degrees. Dip chicken in melted butter and coat with cheese. Melt remaining butter in a pie plate and place chicken in pie plate, skin-side up. Bake at 400 degrees for 50 minutes. Baste with juice during baking. Cover with foil if chicken browns too quickly.

CRISPY SESAME CHICKEN
Serves 6–8

- 10 pieces chicken
- ½ cup butter
- ½ cup bread crumbs
- 1 cup grated Parmesan cheese
- 6 tablespoons sesame seeds

Preheat oven to 350 degrees. Rinse chicken and pat dry with paper towels. Combine bread crumbs, cheese and sesame seeds. Melt butter. Dip chicken into the butter and then the seasoned crumbs. Place chicken in a shallow pan (lining with foil helps with cleanup). Bake at 350 degrees for 1 hour.

BREADED PORK CHOPS
Serves 6

- 6 pork chops
- ¾ cup fine bread crumbs
- 1 teaspoon salt
- ⅛ teaspoon pepper
- 1 egg, beaten
- ¼ cup milk
- ¼ cup boiling water

Add salt and pepper to bread crumbs. Beat egg and add milk. Dip chops in liquid and roll in crumbs. Put 3 tablespoons fat into skillet; brown chops. Place chops in a baking pan or dish and add boiling water. Cover and bake at 400 degrees for about 50 minutes. (I take the cover off for about the last 10 minutes.) These are delicious and so easy to prepare, too. The chops turn out very tender. This is one of my favorite pork chop recipes.

BROILED SCALLOPS
Serves 3

- 1½ pounds scallops
- 6 tablespoons butter
- ½ teaspoon salt
- ⅛ teaspoon black pepper
- ⅛ teaspoon dry mustard

Wash; clean the scallops; pick them over for shells; season with the mixture of above seasonings. Place in drip-pan tray, with wire grill removed. Dot with butter. Broil at medium heat on 2nd shelf for 5 minutes. Turn the scallops with a broad spatula and broil for 2–3 minutes.

Melt additional butter to serve with the scallops.

QUICK CHICKEN BAKE
Serves 6

- 2 cups cooked chicken, cubed
- 1 can cream of chicken soup
- 1 cup sour cream
- ½ cup celery, diced
- ½ cup onion, chopped
- ½ cup water chestnuts, thinly sliced
- 1 cup cooked rice
- Bread crumbs

Mix together and place in a buttered 2-quart casserole. Sprinkle bread crumbs on top. Microwave on HIGH for 6–8 minutes.

If you prefer cream of mushroom soup or cheddar cheese soup—go for it. Do not be afraid to experiment.

PATIO LICKIN' CHICKEN
Serves 4 to 6

- 1 frying chicken, cut up
- 1 envelope dry onion soup mix
- 3/4 cup uncooked rice
- 1 can cream of mushroom soup or cream of chicken soup
- 1 soup can water
- 1 small can mushrooms, drained
- 1/2 teaspoon salt
- 1/4 teaspoon pepper

Season chicken; brown slightly in frying pan. Mix remaining ingredients together; place in 9 x 13-inch baking dish. Arrange chicken on top. Cover with foil; bake one hour at 350 degrees. Remove foil and bake 20 minutes longer.

TUNA AND CHEESE CASSEROLE

- ⅓ cup chopped onion
- 1 teaspoon butter *or* margarine
- 7 tablespoons (⅓ of a 10¾-ounce can) condensed cream of celery soup
- 2 teaspoons lemon juice
- ⅔ cup tuna, drained and flaked
- 1 cup cooked rice
- Salt to taste
- Black pepper to taste
- ¼ cup grated cheddar cheese

Preheat oven to 350 degrees. Cook onion in butter until tender, but not brown. Stir in remaining ingredients, except cheese. Turn into a buttered, shallow 6-inch casserole for 20 minutes, or until heated through. Top with cheese and bake 5 minutes longer.

GINGER AND RUM ROASTED CORNISH GAME HENS

- 4 Cornish game hens
- Salt and freshly ground pepper
- 1 large garlic clove, crushed
- ¼ cup honey
- ¼ cup chicken stock
- ¼ cup soy sauce
- ¼ cup rum
- 1 tablespoon peanut *or* vegetable oil
- 1 teaspoon ground ginger

Preheat oven to 375 degrees. Season Cornish hens well with salt and pepper, inside and out. Combine remaining ingredients in bowl. Spoon 2 tablespoons of the mixture into each hen cavity. Tie the legs together and fold the wings back. Place the hens in a roasting pan. Brush each hen with the sauce. Roast for 55 minutes, or until tender. Baste the hens twice during the cooking time with the sauce.

ROAST GOOSE
Serves 6

1 (6–8 pound) goose

Preheat oven to 400 degrees. Place goose, breast side up, on rack about 1 inch from bottom of roaster. After 30 minutes, turn down to 375 degrees and prick goose with fork around breast, back and drumsticks, letting excess fat escape. Let cook about 20 minutes per pound.

Apple Stuffing:
- 3 cups stale bread
- 1 egg
- ¼ cup chopped onion
- ½ cup melted butter
- ½ teaspoon salt
- ½ teaspoon poultry seasoning
- ¼ teaspoon sage
- ¼ teaspoon white pepper
- 1 cup chopped apples
  Chicken stock, enough to moisten

Sauté onions in butter until transparent. Cool. Add egg, bread, seasoning and apples; mix thoroughly, moistening with the stock until wet, but not soupy. Place in heavily buttered small baking dish and bake at 300 degrees for 1 hour 15 minutes.

Tangerine Sauce:
- 2 tablespoons sugar
- 1 lemon
- 1 orange
- ½ cup red current jelly
- ¼ cup wine vinegar
- ½ cup orange juice concentrate
- 1 pint brown gravy
- 2 tangerines

Grate peel from orange and lemon; save. Place sugar in heavy-bottomed saucepan and caramelize with lemon and orange split in two. Add jelly, orange juice and vinegar. Bring to a boil; remove lemon and orange. Add brown gravy and simmer for 15 minutes. Strain. Add tangerine segments and peel as garnish.

CHICKEN CHOW MEIN, AMERICAN-STYLE
Serves 4

- 1 tablespoon butter *or* margarine
- 4 tablespoons minced onion
- 1½ cups shredded, cooked chicken
- 1 cup celery, diced
- 1½ cups meat stock *or* water
- 2 tablespoons soy sauce
- 1½ tablespoons cornstarch
- 3 tablespoons cold water
  Chow mein noodles

Brown onion lightly in margarine. Add next 4 ingredients and simmer 15 minutes. Blend and stir into meat mixture; add cornstarch mixed in cold water. Cook until slightly thickened and clear. Serve hot on chow mein noodles.

CRUSTY BAKED CHICKEN
Serves 4

- 2 cups potato chips, finely crushed
- ¼ teaspoon salt
- ¼ teaspoon pepper
- ¼ teaspoon curry powder
- ⅛ teaspoon ginger
- 1 (3-pound) frying chicken, cut up
- 2 eggs, beaten
- ¼ cup milk
- ½ cup butter *or* margarine, melted

Mix potato chips, salt, pepper, curry powder and ginger. Combine eggs and milk; pour butter into shallow baking dish. Dip chicken in chips, then in egg mixture, then in chips again. Put pieces side by side in dish; bake at 375 degrees for 45 minutes.

FAVORITE CHICKEN LOAF
Serves 6

- 1 cup soft bread crumbs
- 2 cups milk
- 2 eggs, lightly beaten
- ½ teaspoon salt
- ¼ teaspoon paprika
- 3 cups cooked chicken, diced ¼ inch thick
- ½ cup cooked peas
- ¼ cup chopped pimiento
- 1 (10½-ounce) can condensed cream of mushroom soup for sauce

In a bowl blend bread crumbs, milk, eggs, salt and paprika. Stir in chicken, peas and pimiento. Turn into a well-greased loaf pan (9 x 5 x 3-inch). Bake in a moderate 325-degree oven until firm, about 40 minutes. Serve with mushroom sauce made from soup.

PATRICIA NIXON'S HOT CHICKEN SALAD
Serves 8

- 4 cups cold chicken, cut up into chunks (cooked)
- 2 tablespoons lemon juice
- ⅔ cup finely chopped toasted almonds
- ¾ cup mayonnaise
- 1 teaspoon salt
- ½ teaspoon monosodium glutamate
- 1 cup grated cheese
- 2 cups chopped celery
- 4 hard-cooked eggs, sliced
- ¾ cup cream of chicken soup
- 1 teaspoon onion, finely minced
- 2 pimientos, finely cut
- 1½ cups crushed potato chips

Combine all ingredients, except cheese, potato chips and almonds. Place in a large rectangular dish. Top with cheese, potato chips and almonds. Let stand overnight in refrigerator. Bake in a 400-degree oven for 20–25 minutes.

PIZZA MEATBALLS

1 cup ground beef
1 cup dried bread crumbs
1/2 cup milk
2 tablespoons instant minced onion
1 teaspoon garlic salt
1/2 teaspoon pepper
1/2 (8-ounce) package Mozzarella cheese cut into 12 bite size cubes
3 tablespoons flour
2 tablespoons salad oil
12 to 15-1/2 - ounce jar pizza sauce
4 cups hot cooked rice
Parsley for garnish

About 45 minutes before serving:
In medium brown with fork, mix well first 6 ingredients; shape mixture into 12 large meatballs with 1 cube of cheese in center of each, making sure that cheese is completely covered with meat mixture. On waxed paper, coat each meatball lightly with flour. In 12-inch skillet over medium heat, in hot salad oil, cook meatballs until browned on all sides. Spoon off fat. Add pizza sauce to meatballs in skillet; heat to boiling. Reduce heat to low; cover and simmer 10 minutes. Serve on rice

TEXAS ONE-DISH DINNER

2 pounds ground beef
1 chopped onion
1/2 cup chopped celery
1/4 teaspoon black pepper
1/2 teaspoon salt
1 (8 ounce) package noodles
1 can niblets corn
1 can tomato soup
1/2 cup grated Cheddar cheese

Brown beef, onion, celery, salt, and pepper. Cook noodles and drain. Place half the noodles in buttered casserole. Cover with meat mixture. Add corn and tomato soup. Add remaining noodles and top with grated cheese. Bake at 350 degrees for 25 minutes.

pizza sauce; pour over balls. Bake at 350 degrees for 45 minutes, covered with foil. Uncover; bake 15 minutes longer.

DELICIOUS SLOPPY JOES WITH CHEESE

1 large onion, chopped
2 cloves fresh garlic, chopped
1 pound ground beef
1/2 teaspoon seasoning salt
1 tablespoon margarine
2 teaspoons Worcestershire sauce
2 tablespoons brown sugar
2 tablespoons vinegar (white)
1-12 ounce bottle chili sauce
1/2 cup diced Cheddar cheese

Saute onion and garlic in melted margarine, lightly. Set aside. Brown ground beef, drain well.
Put meat in pot with all ingredients, except cheese. Cook slowly on top of stove, stir occasionally. Cook 30-45 minutes. During the last few minutes, add cheese, until melted. Serve on rolls. ENJOY.

PIZZA PORCUPINE BALLS

Serves 2-4

1 pound hamburger
1/4 to 1/2 cup uncooked rice
1/2 cup water
1/3 cup onion
1 teaspoon salt
15-1/2-ounce jar pizza sauce
1/8 teaspoon garlic powder
1/2 teaspoon celery salt
1/8 teaspoon pepper
2 teaspoons Worcestershire sauce
1 cup grated Mozzarella cheese
1/2 teaspoon chili powder

Mix meat, rice, water, onion, salts, garlic powder, pepper and Worcestershire sauce. Shape mixture into balls; place into ungreased baking dish. Mix together chili powder and

HAMBURGER CHOP SUEY

2 pounds ground beef
2 tablespoons oil
1-1/2 cups chopped onion
1-1/2 cups chopped celery
1 can water chestnuts, drained and sliced
1 can bean sprouts, drained
2 (10-1/2 ounce) cans cream of mushroom soup
1-1/2 cups warm water
1/2 cup rice (not instant)
1/4 cup soy sauce

Brown beef in oil. Drain off fat. Combine beef with rest of ingredients in large bowl. Mix well. Pour into 9x13 inch pan. Cover and bake in 350 degree oven for 1 hour, or until vegetables are done. Serve over heated chow mein noodles.

CHEESY CORNED BEEF LASAGNA

Serves 6-8

8 ounce package lasagna noodles
1-10 ounce package cream style corn
1-12 ounce can corned beef
2 - 10-1/2 ounce cans of condensed cream of chicken soup
1/2 cup chopped onions
1/2 cup chopped ripe olives
2 tablespoons chopped green pepper
2-1/2 cups of shredded American cheese

Cook noodles according to package directions; drain. Cook corn according to package directions. Crumble corned beef into a large bowl. Add soup, onions, olives, and green pepper. Stir in corn. Place 1/4 cup of sauce in a greased 11 x 7 inch baking dish. Alternate 3 layers of noodles, sauce and cheese, ending with cheese. Bake at 350 degrees for 45 minutes. Let stand 10 minutes before cutting.

STUFFED PORK ROAST

Serves 6-8

1 (4-5 pound) rolled pork roast
2 teaspoons poultry seasoning (divided)
2 teaspoons salt (divided)
3/4 teaspoon pepper (divided)
3 cups bread crumbs
3/4 cup chopped celery
1/2 cup chopped onion
1/2 cup butter or margarine

Season roast with 1 teaspoon poultry seasoning, 1 teaspoon salt, and 1/2 teaspoon pepper. Combine remaining ingredients for stuffing. Fill roast cavity with stuffing. Skewer edges. Place fat side up on roasting pan. Bake at 350 degrees for 1-1/2 to 2 hours, or until roast tests done.

well on all sides in hot fat in deep skillet or Dutch oven. Add chopped onion and saute until lightly browned and tender. Add 1-1/2 cups water, salt, pepper, parsley, and bay leaf; bring to boil. Cover and simmer until meat is tender, 3 to 4 hours, adding more water if necessary. Discard parsley and bay leaf. Add vegetables and cook 20 to 30 minutes or until tender. Remove meat and vegetables from skillet; keep warm. Measure drippings, add water to make 2 cups and return to skillet. Stir in flour mixture. Cook and stir until thickened and smooth; adjust seasonings. Slice meat and serve with vegetables and gravy.

SPECIAL PORK CHOPS

Serves 4

4 center cut pork chops
28-ounce can brick oven baked beans
2 teaspoons water
Cinnamon
1 tablespoon oil
2 tablespoons apple jelly
8 apple slices

In skillet, brown chops evenly in oil, about 10 minutes each side; drain chops on paper towels. Pour beans into 2-quart casserole; place chops on top of beans. Bake at 350 degrees for 45 minutes. In small bowl, combine jelly and water. Baste chops with mixture; arrange apple slices on top. Sprinkle with cinnamon. Return to oven and continue baking for another 15 minutes.

CRANBERRY CHOPS

Serves 6

6 pork chops, 1/2 inch thick
2 tablespoons butter
2 tablespoons oil
1 cup chopped onions
1/3 cup chopped carrots
1-1/4 cups chicken broth
2 tablespoons sugar
2 tablespoons red wine vinegar
1/2 cup cranberries

Trim chops, if necessary. Heat butter and oil in a heavy frypan. Brown chops on both sides; set aside. Sauté onions and carrots until brown and tender. Return chops to pan. Add chicken broth. Cover; cook 20 minutes until pork is done. Remove chops and keep warm. Add sugar, vinegar, and cranberries. Cook until cranberries pop. Heat chops in sauce before serving.

PORK CHOPS WITH HAWAIIAN RICE

Serves 4

4 lean pork chops
Salt and pepper
1 cup uncooked rice
3/4 cup chopped green pepper
1 (15 ounce) can tomato sauce
1 (13-1/4 ounce) can pineapple tidbits, undrained
1 tablespoon vinegar

Sprinkle chops with salt and pepper. Brown well on both sides in skillet, and pour off fat. Add 1 cup water, remaining ingredients, and salt to taste. Mix well. Simmer, tightly covered, for 45 minutes or until rice is tender.

PORK CHOP BAKE

Serves 4

4 pork chops
4 potatoes, peeled and sliced
2 onions, sliced
1 can lima beans
1 teaspoon sage

Parboil potatoes. In a lightly greased hot skillet, sear pork chops. In 2-quart baking dish, layer lima beans, potatoes and onions.

Lay pork chops on top; season with sage. Cover and bake at 350 degrees for 1 hour.

Note: Canned corn, sweet potatoes or apples can be substituted for lima beans.

BBQ PORK CHOPS

6 servings, 2 chops each

12 pork chops
3 medium onions cut in slices and separated into rings
2 cups tomato juices
2 tablespoons vinegar
1 teaspoons dry mustard
1 tablespoon Worcestershire sauce
1/2 cup finely chopped onion
1/2 teaspoon chili powder
1/2 teaspoon salt
Dash pepper

Brown chops on both sides. Arrange in roaster or large casserole. Cover each chop with sliced onion rings.

Sauce:
Combine all sauce ingredients together in medium size saucepan. Bring to boil. Simmer slowly for 10 minutes. Pour over chops in roaster, cover. Bake in 350 degrees oven for 30 minutes. Remove cover and bake for 15 minutes more.

MANDARIN CHICKEN

3 pounds chicken pieces
1/2 cup graham wafer crumbs
1 teaspoon salt
1/2 teaspoon garlic powder
1/2 teaspoon paprika
1/2 teaspoon pepper
2 eggs
1 tablespoon milk

Combine crumbs and spices in a plastic bag. Mix eggs and beat well with 1 tablespoon milk. Dip chicken pieces one at a time into egg mixture and then shake in the bag of crumbs and spices. Place chicken on lightly greased baking sheet. Bake at 425 degrees for 20 minutes. Turn and bake another 15 minutes or until done.

Mandarin Orange Sauce:
1 can mandarin oranges, drained (284 ml can), reserve liquid
2 tablespoons cornstarch
1 tablespoon sugar
1 teaspoon ketchup

Combine reserved mandarin juice with enough water to make 1 cup of liquid. Pour juice mixture into sauce pan. Add cornstarch, sugar, and ketchup, bring to a boil. Cook 2 minutes, stirring constantly. Add mandarin orange sections. Pour sauce over hot chicken on serving platter. Serve with white rice and broccoli.

BAKED CHOP SUEY
Serves 8

2 cups diced, cooked chicken
2 tablespoons margarine
1-1/2 cups chopped onion
1-1/2 cups chopped celery
1 cup chopped green pepper
3 tablespoons chopped pimiento
1/2 cup uncooked long grain rice
1 can mushroom soup
2 cups milk
2 tablespoons soy sauce
1 (3-ounce) can chow mein noodles

Sauté vegetables in margarine until golden. Add remaining ingredients, except noodles. Turn into

greased 13 x 9-inch casserole; cover. Bake in 350 degree oven for 1 hour, stirring occasionally. Add more milk, if needed. Sprinkle noodles on top and return to oven, uncovered, for 5 minutes.

WORKING GIRL'S CHICKEN

4 chicken legs
4 chicken breasts
1 teaspoon salt
1/2 teaspoon pepper
1/8 teaspoon garlic powder
1 can cream of mushroom soup
1 soup can milk

Season chicken with salt, pepper, and small amount of garlic powder. Dilute soup with milk. Place chicken in buttered casserole dish. Cover with soup. Bake at 400 degrees for 1 hour or until tender.

EASY PINEAPPLE CHICKEN

1 pound chicken breasts, cubed
1 can pineapple chunks
1 green pepper, cut in strips
1 red pepper, cut in strips
1 carrot, sliced thin
1/4 cup vinegar
2 teaspoons sugar (or substitute)
1 tablespoon cornstarch
2 tablespoons soy sauce
3/4 cup chicken broth

Bring broth to a boil; add chicken cubes. Simmer 10 minutes, stirring occasionally. Add undrained pineapple, green and red pepper slices, carrot slices, vinegar and sugar; bring to boil.

Stir cornstarch into soy sauce until smooth; stir into chicken mixture. Bring to boil, stirring constantly. Lower heat, cover and simmer 10 minutes. Serve with rice.

JEWELED CHICKEN SQUARES
Serves 6

1 cup chopped onion
1 cup chopped celery
1 tablespoon butter
2 tablespoons flour
1 cup double strength chicken broth or 1 cup chicken broth and 1 teaspoon chicken bouillon powder or 1 cube—dissolved in hot broth.
1 cup milk
3/4 teaspoon poultry seasoning
1/8 teaspoon pepper
2 cups chopped, cooked chicken
2 cups cooked rice
4 eggs, beaten
1 (8-ounce) can jellied cranberry sauce, diced
1/2 cup buttered soft bread crumbs

Sauté onions and celery in butter. Blend in flour. Add broth, milk, and seasonings. Cook until thickened. Add chicken and rice. Blend in eggs. Fold in cranberry sauce. Turn into greased shallow 2-quart casserole, sprinkle with crumbs. Bake 350 degrees for 30 minutes until firm in center. Cut into squares.

CHICKEN AND DRESSING

3/4 cup minced onion
1-1/2 cups chopped celery
1 stick butter
9 cups soft bread, cubed
2 teaspoons salt
1/2 teaspoon sage
1/2 teaspoon pepper

In a large skillet, cook and stir onion and celery in butter until onion is tender. Stir in about 1/3 of the bread cubes. Turn into large bowl. Add remaining ingredients. Add enough chicken broth to make mixing easy. Spoon over chicken. Bake in a 375 degree oven for 1 hour

CHICKEN SKILLET RATATOUILLE

Serves 8

1 small eggplant, pared and diced
1 small zucchini, pared and diced
1 onion, pared, halved, and thinly sliced
1 clove garlic, minced
2 cups canned tomatoes, undrained, broken up
Salt and pepper to taste
1/2 teaspoon oregano
1 pound chicken fillets, cut in cubes (2 skinless boneless breasts)

Spray a large non-stick skillet with cooking spray. Combine all ingredients, except chicken. Cover and simmer for 10 minutes, stirring frequently until vegetables are tender-crisp.

Meanwhile, cut chicken into cubes. Cook and stir in skillet, uncovered, until nearly all the liquid is evaporated, and chicken cubes are white, about 4 minutes. Good with cooked rice.

CHICKEN-ASPARAGUS-CHEESE BAKE

Serves 6

1 pound fresh asparagus, cut up and cooked, (or 1 package frozen cut-up asparagus, cooked)
2 cups sliced cooked chicken
1/2 teaspoon each marjoram and sage
1 cup unsifted Gold Medal flour
2 teaspoons baking powder
1 teaspoon salt
2 eggs, beaten
1/2 cup milk
1 cup grated Cheddar cheese
Cheese Sauce

Heat oven to 350 degrees (moderate). Line 11-1/2 x 7-1/2 x 1-1/2" baking dish with layer of asparagus. Place chicken atop asparagus. Sprinkle herbs over chicken. Stir flour, baking powder, and salt together in mixing bowl. Beat eggs, milk, and cheese; add to flour mixture. Beat batter well and pour over chicken, spreading evenly. Bake 25 to 30 minutes. Cut into squares and serve hot with Cheese sauce.

LO-CAL CHICKEN DIVAN

Serves 4, 235 calories per person

2 large chicken breasts, split and remove skin
3/4 cup sherry wine
3/4 cup lo-cal Caesar dressing
1 tablespoon dried parsley flakes

Place chicken in a nonstick shallow baking pan or lightly oil a shallow baking dish. Vigorously mix the wine, salad dressing and parsley together until well blended. Pour over the chicken. Bake 50 minutes in a preheated 350 degree over, basting occasionally. Serve the chicken with cooked frozen broccoli or you favorite vegetable. Pour the sauce the broccoli.

CHICKEN BREASTS WITH CHEESE

3 whole chicken breasts, skinned, boned, halved, and flattened
Salt and pepper
1/2 cup butter or margarine
2 tablespoons parsley
1 teaspoon marjoram
2 teaspoons thyme
1/4 pound mozzarella cheese
1/2 cup flour
2 beaten eggs
1 cup bread crumbs
1/2 cup dry white wine

Sprinkle chicken with salt and pepper and spread on half the butter. Blend remaining butter with parsley, marjoram, and thyme; set aside. Cut cheese into 6 sticks. Place one in the center of each breast. Roll up and tuck in ends. Roll breasts in flour and eggs; then roll in bread crumbs. Place in well buttered baking pan. Melt butter and herb mixture; pour evenly over breasts. Bake 30 minutes. Then pour wine into baking pan. Bake 25 minutes longer, basting frequently.

BAKED CHICKEN REUBEN

4 whole chicken breasts, halved and boned
1/4 teaspoon salt
1/8 teaspoon pepper
1 can (16 ounce) sauerkraut; drained
4 slices (4 x 6 inches square) natural Swiss cheese
1-1/4 cups bottled Thousand Island Salad Dressing. (Can use Weight Watchers for less calories)
1 tablespoon chopped fresh parsley

Place chicken in greased baking dish. Sprinkle on salt and pepper. Add sauerkraut over chicken; top with cheese. Spoon dressing evenly over cheese. Cover and bake in 325 degree oven about 1-1/2 hours. Sprinkle with chopped parsley to serve.

EASY CHICKEN MUSHROOM BAKE

2-1/2 to 3 pounds frying chicken, cut up or quartered
1-1/4 cups (10-1/2-ounce can) condensed cream of mushroom, celery or chicken soup
1/4 cup milk
1/2 cup (4-ounce can) drained mushroom stems and pieces
1/2 cup (1 envelope) dry onion chicken mix

Preheat oven to 375 degrees. Arrange chicken pieces in 13 x 9-inch pan. In medium mixing bowl, combine remaining ingredients; mix well. Pour over chicken. Bake at 375 degrees for about 1 hour until tender. Serve mushroom mixture as gravy.

MOCK CHICKEN - FRIED STEAK

Serves 8

1 beaten egg
1 cup corn flake crumbs
1/4 cup milk
1 teaspoon onion powder
1 teaspoon chili powder
1/2 teaspoon salt
1 pound beef
2 tablespoons cooking oil

Combine egg, 1/2 cup corn flake crumbs, milk, onion, chili powder, and salt; add ground beef and mix well. Shape into 8 patties. Coat with remaining corn flake crumbs. Cook in hot oil over medium heat for about 3-5 minutes on each side or until done.

CHICKEN CACCIATORE

Serves 4
159 calories per serving

4 chicken breasts, skinned
2 small green peppers, minced
1 clove garlic, minced
2 tablespoons chopped pimentos
1 bay leaf
1/8 teaspoon thyme
1 tablespoons dried parsley
1 cup mushrooms, chopped
2 cups stewed tomatoes

Combine all ingredients; simmer 45 minutes. Serve over cooked rice.

GOOEY CHICKEN

8-ounce bottle Russian dressing
10-ounce jar apricot preserves
1 package onion soup mix
2-1/2 to 3 pound chicken, cut up
Seasoned salt and freshly ground
    pepper to taste

Combine dressing, preserves and onion soup mix in bowl. Pour into 9 x

13-inch baking dish. Sprinkle chicken with seasoned salt and pepper. Place chicken, skin side down, in baking dish. Bake at 375 degrees for 45 minutes, basting occasionally. Turn chicken over and baste. Bake for 35 minutes more, basting occasionally.

An excellent main dish (when doubled) for a buffet dinner, served with wild rice and a green salad.

BANDIT WINGS

12-14 chicken wings
1/2 teaspoon salt
1/8 teaspoon pepper
8 tablespoons margarine
2 tablespoons vegetable oil
1/2 cup taco sauce
1/4 cup barbeque sauce
1/4 cup French dressing
1/8 teaspoon red pepper sauce
1/8 teaspoon Worcestershire sauce

Preheat oven to 300 degrees. Snip off wing tips at 1st joint. Cut apart two remaining parts at joint. Sprinkle with salt and pepper. Heat 2 tablespoons oleo and oil in large skillet. Cook half the wings until golden brown. Repeat with remaining wing parts. Melt remaining 6 tablespoons oleo in saucepan. Blend in remaining ingredients. Arrange wings in shallow baking pan, brushing enough sauce over wings to coat evenly. Bake until hot, 5-8 minutes. Arrange wings on platter. Pour remaining sauce into bowl and serve as a dip.

CHICKEN SHEPHERD'S PIE

Serves 4

1 (2-1/2 pound) broiler-fryer, cut up
1 stalk celery, cut up
5 peppercorns
4 large potatoes, pared and quartered
1 teaspoon salt
1 (10-ounce) package frozen mixed vegetables

1/4 cup minced onion
1/3 cup milk
3 tablespoons butter or margarine

Cook chicken in water to cover, with celery and peppercorns, until tender, about 45 minutes. Strain and reserve 2 cups broth. Cool chicken. Skin; bone; and cut up enough chicken to make 2 cups. Cook potatoes in large saucepan with salt and water to cover, until tender, about 30 minutes. Combine chicken broth, mixed vegetables, onion, and a sprinkle of salt in a large saucepan. Bring to a boil. Lower heat and simmer 5 minutes. Stir in chicken. Heat milk and margarine in a small saucepan. Drain and mash potatoes. Beat in hot milk mixture until potatoes are fluffy. Stir 1-1/2 cups mashed potatoes into the chicken mixture to thicken. Spoon into a 10-inch pie plate, quiche dish, or 6-cup shallow dish. Pipe remaining potatoes around edge of chicken mixture. Bake in a 400 degree oven for 20 minutes or until mixture is bubbly and potatoes are browned. Garnish with parsley, if desired.

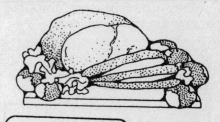

BUFFALO CHICKEN WINGS

15-20 chicken wings
Flour, salt and pepper
1 stick butter
1 tablespoon white vinegar
1/4 cup hot sauce (not Tabasco),
    more or less according to taste

Dredge wings in flour, salt and pepper. Deep fry until brown and crisp, about 12 minutes. (Wings may also be pan fried or baked). Keep hot.

Melt butter in saucepan. Add vinegar and hot sauce to taste. Put hot wings in a large bowl and pour sauce over wings. Toss until wings are well coated with sauce.

CHICKEN 'N NOODLES
Serves 4

4 tablespoons butter, divided
1 cup sliced fresh mushrooms
1/2 cup sliced carrots
1 cup light cream
1/4 teaspoon pepper
1/8 teaspoon nutmeg
1/2 cup grated Parmesan cheese
1/2 cup frozen peas
2 cups cooked chicken, diced
6 ounces broad noodles, cooked
   according to package directions
Additional Parmesan cheese (optional)

In large skillet on medium heat with 2 tablespoons of the butter, cook mushrooms and carrots until tender or until liquid is evaporated. Stir occasionally. Add cream, remaining butter, pepper, and nutmeg. Bring to simmer; gradually stir in cheese. Add peas and chicken; heat through. Toss chicken mixture with cooked noodles. Serve; sprinkle with additional cheese, if desired.

Easy "top-of-the-range" dish. Good way to use leftover chicken.

SAN DIEGO RATATOUILLE
Serves 6

2 (6-1/2-ounce) cans shrimp
1 large eggplant, cut into 1/2-inch
   cubes
1/4 teaspoon salt
2 green bell peppers, remove seeds
   and cut into chunks
2 fresh tomatoes, cut into 1/2-inch
   cubes
2 large onions, sliced and separated
   into rings
1 (29-ounce) can tomatoes, drained
1/2 cup chopped fresh parsley
1 tablespoon garlic salt
2 tablespoons basil, crumbled

Spread cubed eggplant in single layer on paper towel. Sprinkle with salt and let stand 20 minutes. Pat dry with paper towel. Mix all ingredients, except shrimp, in large skillet; simmer, uncovered, slowly for 25-30 minutes, or until volume is reduced. Stir in shrimp; continue simmering until mixture is very thick. Serve hot or cold. (140 calories per serving)

CRAB AND VEGETABLE FRITTATA
Serves 6

1 can crabmeat *or* 8 ounces fresh or
   frozen crabmeat
2 tablespoons butter or oleo
2/3 cup chopped onion
1/4 cup sliced mushrooms
1/4 teaspoon black pepper
1/2 cup non-fat milk
1 clove crushed garlic
1 cup chopped asparagus
1-1/2 teaspoons salt
3 eggs
1/2 cup grated Parmesan cheese

Drain and slice crab. Melt butter in large skillet. Add garlic, onion, asparagus, and mushrooms; sauté until tender. Add salt and pepper. Cook, covered, 5 to 7 minutes. Beat eggs, milk, and cheese. Combine crab and all ingredients in buttered casserole. Bake at 350 degrees for 20 minutes or until brown. Garnish with parsley.

BAKED HALIBUT WITH CHEESE SAUCE
Serves 4

2 halibut fillets (1-1/2 pounds)
1/2 teaspoon butter or margarine
1/4 pound grated cheddar cheese
1 egg, well-beaten
1-1/2 teaspoons salt, divided
1/4 teaspoon pepper, divided
1/4 teaspoon dry mustard
1 cup milk
4 sprigs parsley

Put halibut fillets in greased baking pan. Sprinkle with 1 teaspoon of the salt, 1/8 teaspoon pepper, and 1/2 teaspoon melted butter. Bake in very hot 450-degree oven until fish can be flaked with a fork. Mix grated cheese, beaten egg, dry mustard, 1/2 teaspoon salt, and 1/8 teaspoon pepper. Scald milk and slowly stir it into cheese mixture. Then cook this slowly in double boiler until smooth, thick sauce is made. Put fish on warm platter; pour on cheese sauce and garnish with parsley. Serve immediately.

SAVORY SPANISH TUNA LOAF
Serves 6-8

2 (12-1/2-ounce) cans tuna, drained
   and flaked
1-1/2 cups fresh bread crumbs
1/2 cup mayonnaise
1/4 cup celery, chopped
1/4 cup onion, chopped
1/4 cup bell pepper, chopped
3 tablespoons fresh lemon juice
2 eggs
2 tablespoons paprika
Spanish Sauce (recipe follows)

Combine all ingredients except Spanish Sauce. Place in a greased shallow baking dish; shape into loaf; dust with paprika across top of loaf. Bake at 350 degrees for 40 minutes or until golden brown. Serve with Spanish Sauce.

Spanish Sauce:
Makes 2 cups
1 (14-1/2-ounce) can stewed
   tomatoes
2 teaspoons cornstarch
3 tablespoons fresh lemon juice
1 teaspoon Worcestershire sauce
1/4 teaspoon sugar
1/8 teaspoon liquid hot pepper
   sauce

Combine tomatoes and cornstarch; add remaining ingredients. Over high heat bring to a boil; reduce heat; cook 5 minutes.

SPOONBREAD CHICKEN PIE

Serves 8

Chicken Filling:
6 tablespoons butter
1/4 cup chopped celery
6 tablespoons flour
2-1/2 cups chicken broth
1 teaspoon onion salt
1/2 teaspoon pepper
1 tablespoon dried parsley
3 cups chopped cooked chicken

Spoon Bread:
3 eggs
1 cup self-rising cornmeal mix
2 cups boiling water
1 cup buttermilk

Melt butter in saucepan. Sauté celery in butter. Add flour and stir well. Add chicken broth and stir until mixture thickens. Add onion salt, pepper, and parsley. Stir in chicken. Pour into 3 quart casserole and bake at 400 degrees for 10 minutes.

While casserole bakes, prepare spoon bread. Beat eggs; add cornmeal, boiling water, and buttermilk. Stir well after each ingredient is added. Pour mixture on top of hot chicken mixture and return to oven at 400 degrees. Continue to bake 30-40 minutes, or until brown.

MEXICALI CHICKEN

1 chicken, cut into pieces
1/2 cup shortening
1 small onion, chopped
1 clove garlic, mashed
2 stalks celery, chopped
1/2 green pepper, chopped
1 cup catsup
1 cup water
2 tablespoons brown sauce
2 tablespoons Worcestershire sauce
1 teaspoon salt
1/2 teaspoon cumin

Brown chicken pieces in shortening. Remove from pan and place in 9

x 13-inch baking dish, skin side down. Add onion and garlic to pan in which chicken was cooked; stir over low heat until onion is wilted. Add remaining ingredients; bring to a boil. Pour over chicken pieces in baking dish. Bake uncovered in 350 degree oven for 30 minutes. Turn chicken pieces over and continue to cook uncovered for another 30 minutes or until tender.

Good served with rice, cornbread, and green salad.

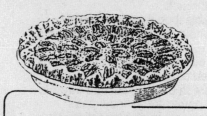

PICKLED CHICKEN GIZZARDS

1 quart chicken gizzards
1 cup water
1 cup cider vinegar
1 sliced onion
4 tablespoons pickling spice
1 tablespoon sugar

Cut chicken gizzards in half and cook thoroughly. Place in a quart jar and pour remaining ingredients over gizzards. Place a tight lid on jar and let set at least 8 hours, turning several times.

CHICKEN LIVERS

1/2-3/4 pound chicken livers
1/4 cup all-purpose flour
1 teaspoon salt
1/8 teaspoon pepper
1 teaspoon oregano, crushed
2 tablespoons vegetable oil
Lemon juice

Dredge livers in flour mixed with salt, pepper, and oregano. Heat oil in skillet. Add livers; fry 10 minutes, turning frequently. Squeeze fresh lemon juice over top before serving.

TURKEY MEATBALLS

1-1/2 to 2 pounds uncooked turkey
1 cup Italian style bread crumbs
1 teaspoon fennel seed
1/2 to 1 teaspoon crushed red pepper
1/2 teaspoon salt
1/2 cup finely chopped onion
Few shakes garlic powder
2 eggs (or 1/2 cup Egg Beaters)

Mix ingredients well; form into meatballs. Bake at 375 degrees on a cookie sheet sprayed with non-stick cooking spray for 20 minutes, turning once. Add to spaghetti sauce, continue to simmer until sauce is done.

TURKEY FRIED RICE

1 cup diced roasted turkey
1 tablespoon soy sauce
1/4 cup oil
1 cup uncooked rice
2 cups chicken bouillon (2 teaspoons instant bouillon or 2 bouillon cubes dissolved in 2 cups boiling water)
2 tablespoons chopped onion
1/4 cup sliced celery
1/4 cup minced green pepper
1 egg slightly beaten
1/2 cup finely-shredded head lettuce or Chinese cabbage

Pour soy sauce over turkey and let stand while starting to prepare rice. Heat oil in large skillet and add rice. Fry, stirring frequently, until rice is golden brown. Add bouillon and turkey. Cover and simmer until rice is almost tender and liquid is absorbed. Add onion, celery, and green pepper; cook uncovered a few minutes. Push rice to side of skillet and add egg. Stir slightly and cook until almost set. Then combine with rice mixture. Stir in cabbage or lettuce and serve immediately.

OVEN-FRIED CHICKEN PARMESAN
Serves 3-4

1/2 cup (2 ounces) grated Parmesan cheese
1/4 cup flour
1 teaspoon paprika
1/2 teaspoon salt
Dash of pepper
2-1/2- to 3-pound broiler-fryer, cut up
1 egg, slightly beaten
1 tablespoon milk
1/4 cup margarine, melted

Combine cheese, flour, and seasonings. Dip chicken in combined egg and milk; coat with cheese mixcook. Place browned meat in Crockpot. Add tomato sauce, onion, and green pepper. Cook on *low* for 6 to 12 hours, or on *high* for up to 6 hours.

DEVILED CHICKEN WITH CORN BREAD TOPPING
Serves 4

1 onion, chopped
3 tablespoons butter or margarine
1/4 cup flour
1 tablespoon chicken bouillon granules
1 cup milk
1/2 cup light cream
1 teaspoon Worcestershire sauce
1 tablespoon prepared mustard
1/4 teaspoon fresh lemon juice
4 cups cooked chicken, diced
2 cups frozen mixed vegetables, thawed
Salt and pepper to taste
1 package corn bread mix

Sauté onion in butter until soft; blend in flour and chicken bouillon granules. Stir in milk and cream; add Worcestershire sauce, mustard, and lemon juice; cook until mixture thickens. Add chicken, mixed vegetables, salt and pepper. Turn into 1-1/2-quart casserole. Prepare corn bread mix according to package directions. Carefully spoon corn bread mixture over top. Bake at 375 degrees for 30 minutes or until corn bread has risen and is golden brown.

ORIENTAL RAINBOW CHICKEN
Serves 4

2 tablespoons vegetable oil
1 tablespoon toasted sesame oil
1 small slice ginger root, cut into threads
1 tablespoon garlic, minced
2 whole chicken breasts, cut into 1-1/2-inch pieces
1 yellow pepper, cut into threads
1 red pepper, cut into threads
1 green pepper, cut into threads
1/2 pound fresh snow peas
1/2 pound fresh broccoli florets
1 cup green onion, sliced diagonally
2/3 cup teriyaki sauce
1 tablespoon cornstarch

Heat a wok or heavy skillet; add vegetable oil, toasted sesame oil, ginger threads, and garlic; stir-fry 10 seconds until fragrant. Add chicken; stir-fry 3 minutes. Add rainbow vegetables; stir-fry, stirring constantly, for 3 minutes. Combine teriyaki sauce and cornstarch; pour over chicken/vegetable mixture. Allow to thicken. Remove to a warmed platter; serve with cellophane noodles or hot rice.

YOGURT MARINATED CHICKEN

1 broiler chicken, cut into serving-size pieces
2 tablespoons lemon juice
1 cup plain yogurt
1/4 inch fresh ginger, minced
2 cloves garlic, minced
1/2 teaspoon ground cardamom
1/2 teaspoon chili powder
1/2 teaspoon cinnamon

Combine all the ingredients and marinate the chicken overnight. Bake at 375 degrees for 40-45 minutes, basting occasionally.

This chicken has a mild flavor and is very moist. It is just as delicious served cold as well.

CHICKEN KIEV

4 medium-size chicken breasts (split lengthwise, skinned and boned)
Salt
1 tablespoon chopped green onion
1 tablespoon chopped parsley
1/4 pound (1 stick) butter or margarine
2 beaten eggs
Flour and dry bread crumbs

Place each piece of chicken (skinned and boned) between two pieces of waxed paper. Pound with wooden mallet to form cutlets not quite 1/4 inch thick. Peel off paper and sprinkle with salt. Place a piece of butter at each end of cutlet. Sprinkle with parsley and onion. Roll meat as for jelly roll, tucking in sides and ends. Dust each roll with flour and dip in beaten egg, then roll in bread crumbs. Chill thoroughly at least one hour. Fry in hot fat about 15 minutes or until golden brown. Serve with mushroom sauce, if desired.

CHEESY CHICKEN SHORTCAKES
Makes 6

1/3 pound processed soft cheese
1/3 cup chicken broth
1-1/2 cups cubed cooked chicken
6 baking powder biscuits
Butter or margarine
Parsley (for garnish)

In the top of a double boiler melt cheese. Add chicken broth gradually, stirring constantly until sauce thickens. Add chicken. Split hot biscuits; spread with butter. Put biscuits together with a filling of hot chicken-cheese mixture; add parsley.

SALMON CIRCLE LOAF

Serves 6 to 8

2 cups or a pound salmon, flaked and deboned
1-1/2 cups cooked tomatoes
1-3/4 cups stale bread crumbs
2 tablespoons melted margarine
1 egg, well beaten
1 tablespoon lemon juice
1 teaspoon salt
1/4 teaspoon pepper

Mix ingredients lightly. Pour into well-greased circular mold. Bake in 425 degree oven for 20 minutes. Turn out onto round platter. Fill center with buttered peas and surround with tiny, whole beets.

TUNA BAKE ITALIAN STYLE

Serves 6

8 ounce package macaroni, cooked and drained
7 ounce can tuna, drained and flaked
15 ounce can tomato sauce
1/2 cup grated Parmesan cheese
1 tablespoon parsley flakes
1 teaspoon instant minced onion
1/2 teaspoon mixed Italian seasoning
1 chicken bouillon cube
1/4 cup boiling water
1 cup shredded Mozzarella cheese (4 ounces)

Combine macaroni, tuna, tomato sauce, Parmesan cheese, parsley, onion, and Italian seasoning. Dissolve bouillon cube in boiling water; add to macaroni mixture. Turn into greased 2-quart casserole. Bake in 350 degree oven for 30 minutes. Sprinkle with Mozzarella cheese. Continue baking 3 to 5 minutes or until cheese in melted.

A good family dish.

SHRIMP BARCELONA

Serves 6
259 calories per serving

1/2 cup finely chopped onions
2 cloves garlic, crushed
3 tablespoons vegetable oil
1 pound peeled, deveined raw shrimp
1 can (15-ounce) tomato sauce
1/4 cup sherry
1 cup fresh mushrooms, sliced, or use 1 (4-ounce) can sliced mushrooms
1 cup chopped green peppers
2 tablespoons snipped parsley
1 teaspoon chili powder
1/2 teaspoon salt
1/2 teaspoon thyme leaves, crushed
1/8 teaspoon ground black pepper
3 cups hot cooked rice

In large skillet cook onions and garlic in oil until tender crisp. Add remaining ingredients except rice. Simmer 10 minutes, or until shrimp are pink and vegetables are tender crisp. Serve over beds of fluffy rice.

BARBECUED SPICY SHRIMP

Serves 4

2 pounds raw, medium shrimp
1 cup olive oil
1/4 cup chili sauce
1 teaspoon salt
1 teaspoon oregano
1/2 teaspoon bottled red pepper sauce
2 garlic cloves, mashed
3 tablespoons lemon juice

Shell and devein shrimp, leaving tail attached. In bowl, mix shrimp with remaining ingredients until well blended; marinate at room temperature one hour. Spear shrimp on skewers; grill 8 inches above gray coals 5 minutes per side.

CRAB BARBECUE ON RUSKS

1 package (4 ounce) Holland round rusks (Zwieback)
1 package (3 ounce) cream cheese (more if desired)
1 pound crabmeat
1/3 cup bottled barbecue sauce
1/2 cup salad dressing or mayonnaise
12 thick tomato slices
6 slices sharp Cheddar slices

Spread 12 rusks with cream cheese. Combine crabmeat with barbecue sauce and salad dressing. Heap crab mixture on rusks. Top each with a slice of tomato. Cut cheese slices in 4 strips and cross over tomato. Bake in moderate oven at 350 degrees until cheese melts, about 15 minutes

CRAB RANGOON

1/2 pound fresh crab, drained and chopped
8 ounces cream cheese, room temperature
1/2 teaspoon Worcestershire sauce
1/4 teaspoon garlic salt
3 dozen wonton wrappers
3 cups cooking oil

Combine crab, cream cheese, Worcestershire sauce and garlic salt; mix until well combined. Place 1/4 teaspoon of filling in center of wonton wrapper (a large amount will only crack a wonton wrapper). Moisten top 2 ends of triangle and seal together with fork. Heat oil to 350 degrees; deepfry rangoon until golden brown. Dip in sweet and sour sauce and Chinese hot mustard. Uncooked crab rangoons may be frozen and deep-fried directly from the freezer.

They really taste just like those found on a Chinese Pu Pu Platter. We love them as a snack or with a meal.

Micro-
MAGIC

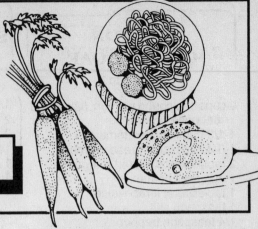

SAUSAGE WEDGES

½ pound bulk pork sausage
1 cup (4 ounces) shredded cheddar cheese *or* American
2 tablespoons diced onion
¾ cup milk
4 eggs, beaten
1 teaspoon dried parsley
2 tablespoons butter

Crumble sausage in a 9-inch pie plate. Cover with paper towel and microwave for 3–4 minutes on HIGH. Drain off fat; sprinkle cheese over sausage; stir in onion. In a medium bowl combine milk and eggs; add parsley and butter. Pour over sausage; cover with plastic wrap and microwave 4 minutes on HIGH. Stir; cover and microwave for 6–8 minutes on MEDIUM (50 percent). Let stand, covered, 5 minutes.

FISH CREOLE

1 pound sole or orange roughy fillets
1 (8-ounce) can tomato sauce
1 (2.5-ounce) jar sliced mushrooms
½ green pepper, diced
¼ teaspoon garlic powder
¼ teaspoon oregano
3 green onions, sliced
1 stalk celery, diagonally sliced
3 tablespoons water
1 teaspoon instant chicken bouillon

Rinse fish and pat dry. Arrange in 3-quart oblong baking dish with thicker portions toward outside of dish. Combine remaining ingredients in a 4-cup glass measure; pour evenly over fish. Cover with plastic wrap; microwave on HIGH for 8–10 minutes, or until fish flakes easily. Let stand 5 minutes.

CATFISH

4 (6-ounce) catfish fillets
2 tablespoons butter, melted
⅛ teaspoon garlic powder
¼ teaspoon dill weed
1 tablespoon lemon-pepper seasoning

Brush fillets with butter; arrange in a baking dish; place meatier portions toward outside edges of dish. Combine garlic powder, dill and lemon-pepper; sprinkle over fillets. Cover tightly with plastic wrap; fold back 1 corner to vent and microwave on MEDIUM-HIGH (70 percent) for 4½ minutes. Rotate dish and rearrange fish; cover and microwave on MEDIUM-HIGH (70 percent) for another 4½ minutes. Let stand, covered, 3–5 minutes.

SHRIMP STIR-FRY

1 head bok choy, sliced (about 8 cups)
1 large red pepper, chopped
1 tablespoon cooking oil
2 cloves garlic, minced
8 drops hot pepper sauce
1 teaspoon sesame seed
12 ounces uncooked fresh shrimp, well-drained
1 tablespoon water
2 teaspoons cornstarch

Combine bok choy and red pepper in a 2-quart bowl; microwave on HIGH, uncovered, for 5–6 minutes; stir once or twice; set aside. Combine oil, garlic, hot pepper sauce and sesame seed in casserole; microwave on HIGH, uncovered, for 2–2½ minutes, stir in shrimp; microwave on HIGH, uncovered, for 2–2½ minutes until shrimp are pink; stir once. Combine water and cornstarch in a 1-cup glass measure; mix well. Drain juices from vegetables and from shrimp into measure; blend well. Microwave on HIGH, uncovered, for 1–1½ minutes, or until mixture boils and thickens. Add to shrimp along with vegetables; toss lightly to coat. Microwave on HIGH, uncovered, for 1–2 minutes, or until heated through.

SALMON STEAKS

- 2 (8-ounce) salmon steaks
- 1 tablespoon butter
- ½ tablespoon lime juice
- 1 green onion, chopped
- ⅛ teaspoon ground pepper
- ⅛ teaspoon dill weed

Place salmon steaks on microwave-safe plate; place a paper towel over top of steaks and microwave on HIGH for 3–3½ minutes. Set aside. Combine butter, lime juice, onion, dill weed and pepper in small dish; microwave on HIGH for 30–45 seconds until melted. Pour over salmon. Garnish with lime slices.

PORK STIR-FRY

- 1 pound boneless pork, cut into thin strips
- 2 cloves garlic, minced
- 2 tablespoons soy sauce
- 2 tablespoons sherry
- ¼ cup apple juice
- 1 tablespoon cornstarch
- 3 green onions, sliced
- 2 cups broccoli pieces
- 1 cup shredded carrots
  Dash pepper
- 2 cups fresh bean sprouts

Combine pork, garlic, soy sauce and sherry in a 2-quart casserole. Stir to coat evenly; let stand 10 minutes. Blend together apple juice and cornstarch; stir into pork mixture. Cover with casserole lid. Microwave on HIGH for 4–5 minutes; stir once. Add onion, broccoli, carrots and pepper; do not stir; cover, microwave for 3–4 minutes, or until vegetables are tender-crisp. Add sprouts; cover and microwave for 1½–2 minutes. Toss to mix.

VEGETABLE STIR-FRY

- 1 tablespoon oil
- 1 clove garlic, minced
- 1 small onion, sliced
- 1 cup sliced mushrooms
- 2 cups sliced cauliflower pieces
- ¾ cup thinly sliced carrot
- ½ cup sliced green pepper pieces
- 3 tablespoons teriyaki sauce
- ½ tablespoon cornstarch
- 3 tablespoons cashews *or* peanuts

Combine oil, garlic, onion and mushrooms in a microwave casserole. Microwave on HIGH, uncovered, for 1½–2 minutes; stir in cauliflower, carrot and green pepper; cover with lid. Microwave for 3½–4 minutes. Stir once. Combine teriyaki sauce and cornstarch in 1-cup glass measure. Drain juices from vegetables into cup and mix well. Microwave on HIGH, uncovered, for 1–1½ minutes; stir once. Pour over vegetables; sprinkle with nuts; toss lightly.

HEARTY MINESTRONE
Serves 6–8

- 5 cups water
- 1 can condensed beef bouillon
- 5 teaspoons instant beef bouillon granules
- 1 clove garlic, finely minced
- 1 small onion, finely chopped
- 1 (16-ounce) can tomatoes, undrained
- 1 cup broken spaghetti pieces, uncooked

- 1 teaspoon salt
- ⅛ teaspoon pepper
- ¼ teaspoon oregano
- ¼ teaspoon basil
- 1 cup frozen peas
- 1 (16-ounce) can kidney beans, undrained
- 1–2 cups cooked beef, cubed

Combine water, bouillon, garlic, onion, tomatoes, spaghetti, beef, salt, pepper, oregano and basil in 3-quart casserole. Cover and microwave on HIGH for 22–30 minutes, or until spaghetti is tender. Add peas and beans; cover and return to microwave to cook for 8 more minutes on HIGH. Sprinkle with grated mozzarella cheese.

TUNA VEGETABLE CHOWDER

- 1½ cups water
- 1 medium potato, diced
- 2 tablespoons chopped onion
- ¼ cup diced carrot
- ¾ teaspoon salt
- ¼ teaspoon celery salt
  Dash pepper
- 1 teaspoon chopped chives
- 1 teaspoon Worcestershire sauce
- ⅔ cup fresh *or* frozen corn
- 1 (6½-ounce) can tuna, drained
- 1 cup half-and-half

In 2-quart container combine water, potato, onion, carrot, salt, celery salt, pepper, chives and Worcestershire sauce. Cover and microwave on HIGH for 7–15 minutes, or until vegetables are just about tender. Add corn; cover and return to microwave; heat for 5–8 minutes on HIGH, or until corn is tender. Stir in tuna and cream; cover and microwave for 2–4 minutes until heated through

FRIED RICE

3 tablespoons butter
3 eggs, well beaten
4-5 cups cooked rice
2 tablespoons chopped green onion
1/2 teaspoon salt
1 teaspoon sugar
3/4 tablespoons soy sauce
1 cup cooked, diced ham, chicken, or salami

Melt butter; microwave on HIGH, for 40 seconds. Add eggs; cover; microwave for 1-1/2 minutes. Stir; re-cover and microwave for 1 additional minute. Add remaining ingredients; stir gently to blend and microwave for 3-5 minutes on HIGH.

RICE PILAF

1 cup regular rice, long grain
1 cup pearl barley
¼ cup butter
8 green onions, chopped
3 cubes beef bouillon
4 cups water
½ pound fresh mushrooms, sliced
2 large cloves garlic
1 teaspoon salt

Combine rice, barley and melted butter; microwave for 5 minutes on HIGH; stir twice. Add remaining ingredients; cover and microwave on HIGH for 6 minutes, then 16–18 minutes on 70 percent power.

SHALIMAR SALAD

4 stalks broccoli
1 large head cauliflower
2 bell peppers, thinly sliced
1 can water chestnuts, drained and sliced
½ pound fresh mushrooms, cut in large pieces
1 (8-ounce) jar Indian chutney

3 tablespoons curry powder
1½ to 2 cups mayonnaise
1 cup chopped pecans

Break broccoli florets into bite-size pieces, discarding heavy stalks. Microwave fon HIGH or 2 minutes; rinse immediately in cold water; drain and repeat with cauliflower. Mix broccoli and cauliflower with peppers, water chestnuts and mushrooms. Cover and refrigerate.

To make dressing: Thoroughly mix chutney, mayonnaise and curry powder; refrigerate. One hour before serving, toss vegetables well with the dressing. Refrigerate until needed. Just before serving, sprinkle with nuts.

SURPRISE SLAW

Combine in large bowl:
4 cups shredded cabbage
1 cup finely chopped celery
1 green pepper, chopped
1 medium onion, chopped

Combine for dressing:
½ cup mayonnaise
½ cup sour cream
½ teaspoon salt
⅛ teaspoon pepper
½ cup dry-roasted peanuts, chopped
1 tablespoon butter
¼ cup Parmesan cheese

Brown in microwave on HIGH for 3–6 minutes; stir twice. Add ¼ cup grated Parmesan cheese; sprinkle on top of slaw mixture.

MICROWAVE POTATOES

Peel and dice 3 or 4 large potatoes. Place in microwave casserole dish; dot with 1/2 stick margarine. Return to microwave and cook 3-5 minutes more, or until potatoes are done. Season with salt, pepper, and parsley flakes.

ASPARAGUS A LA GREENBRIAR

1 pound fresh asparagus spears
1 tablespoon butter *or* margarine
1 tablespoon flour
2 teaspoons chicken bouillon
1 teaspoon dry mustard
¼ cup dry white wine
¾ cup half-and-half
4 baked croissants
8 ounces thinly sliced turkey

Snap off tough ends of asparagus; arrange spears in 10 x 6-inch dish; add butter; cover with plastic wrap. Microwave for 5–6 minutes. Drain liquid into 2-cup class measure; set asparagus aside. Blend the flour into liquid in measure; stir in bouillon, mustard and wine until smooth. Microwave on HIGH, uncovered, for 1–1½ minutes; stir once. Stir in half-and-half. Microwave on HIGH, uncovered for 1–1½ minutes. Slice the croissant in half; place turkey and asparagus on bottom half, then sauce; add top.

ASPARAGUS APPETIZERS

12 ounces fresh asparagus spears
1 tablespoon water
6 ounces cream cheese
2 ounces blue cheese
1 teaspoon lemon juice
Assorted crackers

Snap off tough ends of asparagus and discard. Cut each spear into 1-inch pieces; combine asparagus and water in 2-cup glass measure; cover with plastic wrap; microwave 4–5 minutes; drain. Save ⅓ cup of asparagus pieces and set aside. Combine remaining ingredients in food processor; process until smooth. To serve, spread cheese mixture on crackers; garnish with asparagus piece.

ORANGE ASPARAGUS

1½ pounds fresh asparagus
1 tablespoon water
1 tablespoon honey
2 teaspoons cornstarch
½ cup orange juice
1 tablespoon margarine

Snap off tough ends of asparagus spears; place in a 10 x 6-inch pan; add water; cover with plastic wrap and vent. Microwave on HIGH for 5–6 minutes; drain and set aside. Combine honey, cornstarch and orange juice in a 1-cup measure; microwave on HIGH, uncovered, for 1–1½ minutes; stir once. Stir in margarine; spoon sauce over asparagus.

FRESH SPEARS

1 pound fresh asparagus spears
2 tablespoons water

Snap off tough ends of asparagus spears; arrange in a 10 x 6-inch dish; add water; cover with plastic wrap. Microwave on HIGH for 6–7 minutes; drain. Serve with butter or sauce.

SUPREME RICE CASSEROLE

1 stick butter, cut into pieces
1⅓ cups uncooked instant rice
1 can onion soup
⅓ pound fresh mushrooms, sliced, or 1 (4-ounce) can
½ teaspoon pepper

Combine all ingredients in baking dish; cover tightly and microwave 5 minutes on HIGH. Stir and microwave 5 additional minutes on 50 percent power. Let stand several minutes before serving.

BROCCOLI ONION CASSEROLE

2 (10-ounce) packages frozen broccoli cuts
1 (8-ounce) can pearl onions, drained
1/4 cup cracker crumbs
2 tablespoons water
1 can cream of mushroom soup
1/2 cup shredded Cheddar cheese

Place broccoli and water in casserole; microwave on HIGH for 10 minutes. Drain; stir to break up. Stir in onions and soup. Top with cracker crumbs and microwave on HIGH for 7 minutes. Sprinkle with cheese; microwave for 1 minute on HIGH until cheese is melted.

CELERY WITH CARROTS
A microwave recipe
Serves 4

6 sticks celery, cleaned and cut into julienne (match stick size) strips
1/2 pound carrots, scraped and cut into julienne (match stick size) strips
2 tablespoons butter
1 tablespoon snipped chives
1 teaspoon marjoram
Dash salt
Dash pepper
1 teaspoon chopped parsley

The total weight of the vegetables should be about 12 ounces. Arrange the celery and carrots in 3-3/4 cup oval or round casserole dish. Flake butter over vegetables. Sprinkle with chopped chives and marjoram; season well with salt and pepper. Spoon over 2 tablespoons water. Cover with plastic wrap and pierce. Microwave on HIGH for 10 minutes. Vegetables should be stirred half way through cooking, to make sure they cook evenly. Allow to stand 5 minutes, covered. Sprinkle with parsley before serving. Total Microwave cooking time: 10 minutes.

I make this often. It is delicious and quick to fix.

FRUIT DELIGHT

Prepare this ahead of time to allow flavors to develop.

1 (20-ounce) can pineapple chunks, juice pack
2 (11-ounce) cans mandarin orange sections, drained
½ to 1 cup seedless grapes, halved
2 kiwis, halved lengthwise and sliced
½ cup orange juice
¼ cup honey
1 tablespoon lemon juice

Drain pineapple; reserve juice. In a large bowl combine pineapple, mandarin oranges, grapes and kiwi. Combine pineapple liquid, orange juice, honey and lemon juice. Pour over fruit. Cover and chill until ready to serve.

CARROTS WITH VINEGAR

1½ pounds carrots, peeled and cut into ½-inch cubes
¼ cup minced onion
3 tablespoons red wine vinegar
1 bay leaf
¼ teaspoon salt
Dash pepper

Mix carrots and onion in 2-quart casserole. Add vinegar and bay leaf; cover with lid and microwave on HIGH for 10 minutes; stir at halftime. Stir and cover with paper towel; microwave on HIGH for 5 minutes, until almost all liquid evaporates and carrots are tender. Add salt and pepper to taste. Let stand covered for 3 minutes.

CORN-ON-THE-COB
Serves 4

4 medium ears of corn (in husk)
8 paper towel sheets

For each ear, hold 2 connected paper towel sheets under running water until soaked, but not dripping. Squeeze gently to remove excess water. Spread paper towel sheets flat on counter. Place corn (in husk) lengthwise in center of 2 connected paper towel sheets. Fold one long side over corn. Fold both ends toward center. Roll up over corn. Place loose edge of packet down on microwave-safe platter. Microwave on HIGH for 9 to 15 minutes, or until tender, rearranging ears once. Let stand for two minutes. Remove and discard paper towels. If desired, place corn in husks on edge of grill to keep warm, turning ears once or twice.

FRESH MUSHROOM SOUP
Serves 4–5

2 cups fresh mushrooms, sliced
1 tablespoon onion, finely chopped
¼ cup butter *or* margarine
¼ cup all-purpose flour
1 tablespoon beef bouillon granules
   Dash pepper
2 cups water
2 tablespoons dry white wine
1 cup half-and-half

In 1½-quart casserole combine butter, mushrooms and onions; microwave, uncovered, on HIGH for 3½–5 minutes, or until mushrooms are just about tender. Stir once; add flour, bouillon and pepper; stir well. Gradually add water; stir until smooth. Microwave on HIGH for 7–10 minutes, or until mixture boils and thickens, stirring 3 times. Add wine and half-and-half; microwave 2–3 minutes, or until heated through.

MICROWAVE CAULIFLOWER WITH LEMONY BUTTER

1 pound whole cauliflower
2 tablespoons butter
1 tablespoon lemon juice
1/8 teaspoon salt
1 teaspoon parsley, finely chopped
1/2 to 1 teaspoon paprika

Cut off cauliflower's heavy stems, close to the base; rinse in cold water. With sharp knife, make X cuts in base of stem. Place whole cauliflower on glass pie plate. Cover; bake on HIGH power for 10 to 12 minutes. Let stand covered for 4 minutes; drain. Melt butter; add lemon juice and salt; mix. Pour over whole cauliflower; sprinkle with parsley and paprika. Serve hot.

STUFFED ONION

4 large onions, peeled
1/4 cup water
1/2 pound ground beef
1 (8-ounce) can tomato sauce
1 cup cooked rice
1 teaspoon chili powder
1/2 teaspoon salt
Dash pepper
1/2 cup shredded Cheddar cheese

Place onions and water in 2-quart casserole. Cover; microwave on HIGH for 8 minutes or until onions are about tender. Drain. Scoop out centers of onions, leaving walls about 1/3 inch thick. Chop enough onion pulp to make 2 cups. Combine with ground beef in 1-quart casserole. Cover and cook on HIGH for 3 minutes. Drain off fat. Stir in half of tomato sauce and all remaining ingredients, except cheese. Stuff onions with beef-rice mixture, mounding high on top. Spoon any remaining mixture in dish around onions. Pour remaining tomato sauce over all. Cook on HIGH for 6 minutes. Sprinkle cheese on top. Continue to microwave on HIGH for 1-2 minutes or until cheese melts.

PLAN AHEAD BRUNCH
Serves 9

1 package (12 ounces) frozen hash brown potatoes
6 eggs
1/3 cup whipping or light cream
1 cup (4 ounces) shredded Cheddar cheese
2 tablespoons chopped chives
1/4 teaspoon salt
Dash of pepper
1 cup (4 ounces) diced ham, or Canadian bacon

Place potatoes in 8-inch square baking dish; cover with plastic wrap and microwave on HIGH 6-7 minutes until steaming, stir once. Combine eggs, cream, chives, salt, pepper, cheese, and ham. Add mixture to potatoes, cover with waxed paper, and microwave 12 minutes at MEDIUM (50%) stirring twice. Then finish cooking for 3-4 minutes on HIGH or until set. Let stand 5 minutes, cut into squares.

APRI-ORANGE SAUCE
Makes 2 cups

1/2 cup apricot jam
1 tablespoon cornstarch
1/2 cup orange juice
1/8 teaspoon ground cloves

Combine jam, cornstarch, and orange juice in a 2-cup glass measure; mix well. Microwave on HIGH, uncovered, 2 to 2-1/2 minutes or until mixture boils and thickens; stir once. Stir in cloves.

LOW COUNTRY EGG PIE

- 4 slices firm-textured white bread, no crusts
- 1 cup milk
- ⅔ cup half-and-half
- 1 cup coarsely shredded sharp cheddar cheese
- ¼ cup grated Parmesan cheese
- 2 tablespoons finely grated onion
- 3 eggs, lightly beaten
- 2 tablespoons Dijon mustard
- ½ teaspoon salt
- ¼ teaspoon ground hot red pepper
- ⅛ teaspoon white pepper
- 1 tablespoon *each* parsley flakes and paprika
- 2 hard-cooked eggs, peeled and coarsely chopped

Soak bread in milk and half-and-half for 5 minutes. Combine with cheeses, onion, eggs, mustard, salt, hot red pepper and white pepper; fold in hard-cooked eggs. Spoon into 9-inch round, 1½-quart casserole; sprinkle with paprika and parsley. Microwave, uncovered, on MEDIUM (50 percent) for 18–21 minutes. Rotate casserole every 4 minutes, or until set. Cover pie with foil and let stand 5–7 minutes; cut into wedges and serve warm.

EGGS VERDI

- ½ cup butter *or* margarine
- 1 tablespoon lemon juice
- ⅛ teaspoon ground red pepper
- 3 large egg yolks, beaten
- 1 (12-ounce) package frozen spinach soufflé, thawed
- 4 large eggs
- 2 English muffins, split and toasted

In a 1-quart bowl combine butter, ¼ cup water, lemon juice and pepper; microwave, uncovered, on HIGH for 2½ minutes or until boiling. With a wire whisk beat in egg yolks a little at a time. Cook, uncovered, on HIGH for 15 seconds (will be thin). Let stand 5 minutes; stir twice.

Place soufflé in custard cups divided evenly; microwave on HIGH for 4 minutes; stir once. Crack an egg into each cup over soufflé mixture; with wooden pick puncture yolk. Cover the cups with waxed paper; microwave on HIGH for 3–4 minutes. Rearrange the cups in oven after 2 minutes. Let stand, covered, for 3 minutes. Reheat sauce on HIGH for 1 minute. Run spatula around edge of soufflé mix in each cup; turn out each onto a muffin half. Spoon sauce over. Serve immediately.

BACON AND SWISS CHEESE QUICHE

- 1 (9-inch) single crust pie shell
- ½ pound bacon (9–11 strips)
- 2 tablespoons flour
- ¼ teaspoon salt
- ½ teaspoon ground nutmeg
- ⅛ teaspoon cayenne pepper
- ¼ cup chopped onion
- 2 cups half-and-half
- 4 eggs
- ⅓ cup grated Swiss cheese
  Paprika
  Parsley flakes

Microwave pie shell in a glass pie plate on HIGH for 5–7 minutes; rotate ½ turn after 2½ minutes. Cool. Arrange bacon in single layer on microwave bacon rack; top with paper towels. Microwave on HIGH for 9 minutes, or until crisp. Cut into bite-sized pieces and sprinkle over bottom of crust.

In a 1½-quart casserole combine flour, salt, nutmeg, cayenne and onion; whisk in half-and-half to blend well. Microwave on HIGH for 4–6 minutes, whisking every minute until hot and thick. Meanwhile in small bowl beat eggs to blend; add about ¼ of half-and-half mixture to eggs and whisk well. Then add mixture back to warm half-and-half; microwave on MEDIUM HIGH (70 percent) for 3–5 minutes. Pour into pie shell. Distribute cheese evenly over top, then sprinkle with paprika and parsley; microwave at MEDIUM (50 percent) for 6–9 minutes. Let stand 15 minutes.

GOLDEN SPICE MARBLE CAKE
Serves 6

- 1 package microwave yellow cake mix
- ⅔ cup buttermilk
- ⅓ cup oil
- 1 egg
- 1 tablespoon molasses
- ½ teaspoon cinnamon
- ¼ teaspoon nutmeg

Frosting:
- 1 cup confectioners' sugar
- 1 tablespoon margarine *or* butter
- ½ teaspoon lemon juice
- 1–2 tablespoons milk

Use solid shortening; grease a 7-inch round pan. In a medium bowl, combine all cake ingredients; beat with a spoon until well-blended. Pour half of batter (about 1 cup) into second bowl. Stir in molasses, cinnamon and nutmeg. Spoon yellow and spice batter alternately into prepared pan. Pull knife through batter in wide curves; turn pan and repeat for marble effect.

Microwave on HIGH for 5 minutes. Cake is done when it pulls away from the sides of the pan. If any additional time is necessary, add it in 30-second intervals. Immediately invert onto serving plate. In a small bowl combine confectioners' sugar, margarine and lemon juice; gradually add milk until desired spreading consistency.

MEXICAN CHOCOLATE CAKE

1 package microwave chocolate cake mix with pan
⅔ cup water
⅓ cup oil
1 egg
1 teaspoon cinnamon

Topping:
1 (6-ounce) package (1 cup) semisweet chocolate chips
¼ cup amaretto *or* 2 teaspoons almond extract *and*
2 tablespoons water
½ cup whipping cream
1½ teaspoons confectioners' sugar
½ teaspoon vanilla
¼ cup sliced almonds

Using solid shortening, grease a 7-inch round pan. In a medium bowl, combine all cake ingredients. Beat with a spoon for about 75 strokes; pour into a prepared pan; microwave on HIGH for 6½ minutes. Cake is done when it pulls away from sides of pan. If cake is not done, add additional time in 30-second intervals. Immediately invert onto serving plate. Cool completely.

In small microwave-safe bowl, combine chocolate chips and amaretto; microwave on MEDIUM (50 percent) power for 1½–2½ minutes; stir once partway through cooking, beating until smooth. Cool 20 minutes; spread on top of cake.

In small bowl, beat whipping cream until soft peaks form. Blend in confectioners' sugar and vanilla; beat until stiff peaks form. Spread over chocolate mixture; top with almonds. Store in refrigerator.

BREAD PUDDING

¼ cup butter *or* margarine
4 slices bread, cubed

½ cup sugar
2 tablespoons lemon juice
1 cup milk
3 eggs
Cinnamon

Microwave butter on HIGH in a 1-quart casserole for about 1 minute; add bread, sugar and lemon juice; toss to lightly mix. Combine milk and eggs; beat until smooth; pour over bread mixture. Sprinkle with cinnamon. Place casserole in an 8-inch square glass baking dish; add 1 cup warm water to baking dish. Microwave on HIGH, uncovered, for 11–13 minutes, or until center is just about set. Serve with Rum Custard Sauce.

Rum Custard Sauce:
1½ cups milk
½ cup light cream
⅓ cup sugar
⅛ teaspoon salt
3 large eggs, lightly beaten
3 tablespoons rum

Combine milk, cream, sugar and salt in a 2-quart glass measure. Place in microwave and cook for 4 minutes on 70 percent power. Stir ½ cup milk mixture into eggs; gradually stir eggs into milk mixture and microwave on 50 percent power for 2½ minutes.

Stir, then microwave for 2½ minutes on 30 percent power. Let stand until cooled; stir in rum. Serve over Bread Pudding.

MICROWAVE DATE BARS
Makes 30

Date Filling (recipe follows)
½ cup butter-flavored shortening
1 cup brown sugar, packed
1 egg
½ teaspoon vanilla
¼ cup water
2 cups flour

¾ teaspoon baking soda
¼ teaspoon salt
Confectioners' sugar

Prepare Date Filling; cool. Cream together shortening and brown sugar. Mix in egg, vanilla and water. Stir together flour, soda and salt; blend into shortening mixture. Spoon half into greased 8 x 8-inch baking dish. Carefully spread date mixture. Top with remaining dough. Microwave on 50 percent power (MEDIUM) for 5 minutes; rotate once if necessary. Then microwave on HIGH for 5–7 minutes. Top will no longer be doughy looking. Let stand on flat surface until cool. Dust with confectioners' sugar. Cut into squares.

Date Filling:
¼ cup granulated sugar
1 tablespoon flour
⅓ cup water
¾ cup (¼ pound) pitted dates

In a 2-cup measure stir together sugar, flour and water until smooth. Add dates. Cover with plastic wrap. Microwave on HIGH for 2–3 minutes, stirring after each minute, until thick. Stir until dates are softened. Cool to room temperature before using.

ELEGANT KRISPIE BARS

6 ounces white chocolate coating
1 cup peanut butter
4 cups rice cereal
1 cup salted peanuts

Combine coating and peanut butter in a 2-quart bowl and microwave on HIGH for 2½–3 minutes until coating is melted; stir twice. Add cereal and peanuts. Press into 13 x 9-inch baking dish. Refrigerate until set, about 1 hour. Cut into squares.

BAKED CUSTARD

2 cups milk
4 eggs, beaten
⅓ cup sugar
1 teaspoon vanilla
Dash of salt
Dash ground nutmeg

In a 4-cup glass measure, heat milk on HIGH for 4 minutes until very hot, but not boiling. Meanwhile, combine beaten eggs, sugar, vanilla and a dash of salt. Beat until well-blended; gradually add hot milk to beaten egg mixture; beat well. Divide egg mixture evenly between 6 (6-ounce) cups. Place in a 13 x 9 x 2-inch baking dish; sprinkle with nutmeg. Pour about ½ cup boiling water around cups in dish; cover with waxed paper. Microwave on medium power (50 percent) for 8½ minutes; rearrange cups every 3 minutes. Remove any that are soft-set. Rearrange the remaining custards in dish; microwave on medium power (50 percent) for 5 minutes. Let stand 10 minutes.

MOCHA CREAM PUDDING

⅔ cup sugar
2 tablespoons cornstarch
¼ teaspoon salt
1⅔ cups milk
1½ (1-ounce) squares unsweetened chocolate
1 egg, beaten
2 tablespoons butter *or* margarine
1 teaspoon instant coffee crystals
1 teaspoon vanilla

In a 1½-quart bowl combine sugar, cornstarch and salt. Stir in milk and chocolate; mix well; microwave on HIGH for 6 minutes, stirring after 3 minutes, then every minute.

Gradually stir small amount of the

hot milk mixture into the beaten egg; return all to bowl and mix well; microwave on HIGH for 30 seconds; stir after 14 seconds; add butter, coffee crystals and vanilla. Stir until butter melts. Cover with waxed paper. Cool, then chill.

PEANUT BUTTER PIECES

2 sticks butter
1 pound powdered sugar
1 cup graham cracker crumbs
1 cup peanut butter
1 (12 ounce) package chocolate chips

Place butter in large bowl and microwave on HIGH for 2-3 minutes. When butter is melted, add sugar, crumbs, and peanut butter. Mix until smooth; press into 8x8 dish; microwave on HIGH for 2 minutes. Put chocolate chips in large bowl and microwave 50% for 3-4 minutes; stir several times while cooking.

When melted, spread over peanut butter layer; chill. Cut into squares and store in airtight container.

LEMON BARS

½ cup butter
1 cup flour
¼ cup confectioners' sugar
1 cup sugar
2 eggs
3 tablespoons *each* lemon juice and rind
2 tablespoons flour
2–3 tablespoons confectioners' sugar

Melt butter; add flour and confectioners' sugar; blend well. Spread in an 8 x 8 x 2-inch pan. Microwave on 70 percent power (MEDIUM HIGH) for 3½–4 minutes, or until bubbling over entire surface.

Beat together sugar, eggs, lemon juice, grated rind and 2 tablespoons flour. Pour over hot

bottom layer. Microwave on 70 percent (MEDIUM HIGH) for 5–6 minutes, or until center is firm. Sprinkle with confectioners' sugar. Cool. Cut into bars.

CHOCOLATE CHIP BARS

½ cup butter
¾ cup brown sugar
1 egg
1 tablespoon milk
1 teaspoon vanilla
1¼ cups flour
½ teaspoon baking powder
⅛ teaspoon salt
1 (6-ounce) package chocolate chips, divided
½ cup nuts (optional)

Mix all together, using only half of the chips in the batter. The other half goes on top. Using an 8- or 9-inch square dish, microwave on HIGH for 6½ minutes.

CARAMEL O'S BAR

14 to 16 ounces caramel candies
¼ cup water
½ cup peanut butter
4 cups Cheerios cereal
1 cup salted peanuts

Topping:
1 cup chocolate chips
¼ cup peanut butter
2 tablespoons margarine

Combine caramels, water and peanut butter in large mixing bowl. Microwave for 3–5 minutes, or until melted; stir every minute. Stir in cereal and peanuts; press into buttered 13 x 9-inch pan. Melt topping ingredients in a 2-cup glass measure by microwaving them for 2 minutes on 50 percent power (MEDIUM). Stir, then microwave 2 more minutes on 50 percent power; blend well. Spread over bars. Cool before cutting.

PARMESAN POTATO SLICES

1 small onion, chopped
1/2 cup chopped celery
2 tablespoons butter or margarine
3 medium unpeeled potatoes, cleaned
1/2 teaspoon garlic salt
Dash pepper
1/4 cup Parmesan cheese, or to taste
1/4 teaspoon poultry seasoning
1/2 teaspoon dried parsley flakes
Paprika

Combine onion, celery, and butter in an 8-inch square baking dish. Cover with waxed paper. Microwave on HIGH 2-1/2 to 3 minutes or until vegetables are just about tender. Thinly slice potatoes into baking dish; mix lightly. Cover and microwave on HIGH 10-12 minutes or until potatoes are tender; stir once. Add garlic salt, pepper, cheese, seasonings; mix lightly. Sprinkle with paprika. Microwave on HIGH for 1-2 minutes, uncovered.

LIME-THYME POTATOES

1/4 cup melted margarine or butter
1 teaspoon grated lime peel
1 tablespoon lime juice
1 teaspoon dried thyme leaves
3 medium baking potatoes
1/4 cup grated Parmesan cheese
Paprika, salt and pepper

In a pie plate combine butter, thyme leaves, lime peel, and juice. Cut each potato lengthwise into eighths; toss in butter mixture. Arrange skin side down on paper-towel-covered plate; sprinkle with cheese, paprika, salt, and pepper. Microwave on HIGH for 13 minutes, covered with waxed paper; rotate dish halfway through.

SESAME-SPRINKLED BRUS-SELS SPROUTS

Serves 4

1 pound brussels sprouts
1 tablespoon water
2 tablespoons butter or margarine
2 teaspoons sesame seed
1 tablespoon soy sauce
1 teaspoon sesame oil
1/8 teaspoon lemon pepper

Combine brussels sprouts and water in a 1-quart casserole; cover; microwave on HIGH for 8-9 minutes or until tender. Drain and set aside. Place butter and sesame seeds in uncovered small glass dish and microwave on HIGH for 3-4 minutes, until toasted; stir twice. Mix in the soy sauce and sesame oil; spoon over the brussels sprouts; sprinkle with lemon pepper. Mix lightly.

PEA PODS ORIENTAL

1 (10-ounce) package frozen pea pods
1 tablespoon oil
1 tablespoon soy sauce

Remove wrapping from box of frozen pea pods. Place box on paper towel in microwave. Microwave on HIGH 3-4 minutes, or until heated through. Place in a bowl; toss lightly with oil and soy sauce. Microwave on HIGH 1-2 more minutes. These are served tender crisp. Do not overcook. Leftovers can be refrigerated and tossed into a salad for another use.

BROCCOLI AND MUSHROOMS

1 pound fresh mushrooms
1 pound fresh broccoli flowerets
1/4 cup hot water
2 cups Italian dressing

In a 3-quart casserole combine broccoli and water; cover and microwave for 1 minute on HIGH. Drain and rinse in cold water. In a bowl or plastic bag combine broccoli, mushrooms, and dressing.

Refrigerate at least 8 hours. If using a bowl stir several times, with a bag just turn bag over several times. Remove vegetables to serving platter with slotted spoon.

CHEESE-STUFFED MUSHROOMS

10 medium large mushrooms
1 tablespoon butter or margarine
1 (3-ounce) package cream cheese
2 tablespoons Parmesan cheese
1/8 teaspoon garlic salt
1/8 teaspoon hot pepper sauce
Paprika

Remove stems from mushrooms by gently twisting them. Place caps, open side up, on microwave-safe plate; set aside. Chop stems; combine stems and butter in a 1-quart casserole. Microwave (HIGH), uncovered, 2-3 minutes or until tender. Add cheeses; mix until softened and creamy. Stir in garlic salt and pepper sauce. Spoon cheese mixture into each cap, mounding mixture. Microwave (HIGH), uncovered, 2-3 minutes or until mushrooms are heated through. Sprinkle with paprika and/or parsley flakes.

PITA CHIPS
Makes 24

1 tablespoon margarine
Dash garlic powder
Dash paprika
1 pocket-bread pita round

Microwave the margarine on HIGH for 30 seconds or until melted. Stir in garlic powder and paprika. Cut pocket bread in half horizontally. Brush inner side with margarine; cut rounds into strips. Place on paper-towel-lined plate. Microwave on HIGH, uncovered, for 1 min. 30 seconds to 1 min. 45 seconds, or until bread is crisp. Serve plain or with favorite dip. (10 calories each)

ULTIMATE NACHOS
Serves 4

Paper towel
24 large tortilla chips
1 cup shredded Monterey Jack, Cheddar or Colby cheese
6-7 tablespoons canned refried beans
2 tablespoons chopped onions, optional
1 medium tomato, chopped
1-2 cups shredded lettuce
1/4 cup sour cream, optional
1/4 cup sliced black olives
1 tablespoon jalapeño pepper, fresh or canned, optional
Taco sauce

Place towel on microwave-safe plate; arrange tortilla chips on the paper towel-lined plate. Spread chips with refried beans; top with shredded cheese and chopped onions. Microwave 2-5 minutes at 50% (medium). Before serving, after cheese has melted, top with shredded lettuce, chopped tomato, olives, jalapeño pepper, taco sauce, and small dollops of sour cream.

OUTRAGEOUS SPINACH DIP

1 (10-ounce) box frozen chopped spinach
1 (8-ounce) can water chestnuts, finely chopped
1-1/2 cups sour cream
1 cup mayonnaise
1 package dried vegetable soup mix
2 green onions, finely chopped
1/4 teaspoon garlic powder
1/2 teaspoon seasoning salt

Remove paper from box of spinach; place box on paper towel in microwave oven. Microwave on HIGH for 6 minutes. In mixing bowl combine remaining ingredients; drain and squeeze spinach before adding to cream mixture. Refrigerate for 2 hours before serving. Serving suggestion: Take a round un-sliced loaf of pumpernickel bread and cut a circle in the top and remove. Gently pull bread from inside to be later used to dip. When ready to serve, pour dip into bread.

PUMPERNICKEL SURPRISE MUFFINS

1 cup milk
1/3 cup oil
1 egg
2 tablespoons molasses
3/4 cup whole wheat or white flour
1/2 cup rye flour
1/4 cup packed brown sugar
1/4 cup unsweetened cocoa powder
2 teaspoons baking powder
1 teaspoon caraway seeds
1/2 teaspoon salt
1 (3-ounce) package cream cheese
1/2 teaspoon grated orange rind

Beat together milk, oil, egg, and molasses in 2-cup measure. Combine flours, brown sugar, cocoa, baking powder, caraway seeds, and salt in a bowl. Add milk mixture; stir just until moistened. Cut cream cheese into 12 equal cubes; roll grated orange rind in as you roll into a ball. Line the muffin cups with paper liners; spoon a little batter into each cup, filling 1/4 full. Place a cream cheese ball in the center of each muffin. Top with remaining batter; fill 3/4 full. Microwave, uncovered, on HIGH for 2 to 2-1/2 minutes for 6 muffins.

VEGETABLE CORN MUFFINS

Makes 12 muffins
(Microwave - Diabetes Exchange)

1 cup all-purpose white flour
1/2 cup cornmeal
1 tablespoon sugar
1 tablespoon baking powder
1/2 teaspoon salt
3/4 teaspoon Italian seasoning
1/8 teaspoon garlic powder
2 eggs, beaten
1 tablespoon vegetable oil
1/2 cup corn, drained
1/3 cup skim milk

1/3 cup chopped green pepper
1/4 cup finely chopped onion

Combine all ingredients in mixing bowl. Stir just until blended. Line each muffin or custard cup with 2 paper liners. Fill 1/2 full. Microwave on HIGH as directed below or until top springs back when touched, rotating and rearranging after 1/2 the time.

Cooking time:
1 muffin = 1/4 to 3/4 minutes
2 muffins = 1/2 to 2 minutes
4 muffins = 1 to 2-1/2 minutes
6 muffins = 2 to 4-1/2 minutes

OATMEAL APPLE MUFFINS

1/4 cup water
1/2 cup quick cooking oats
3 tablespoons butter or margarine
2 tablespoons oil
1 egg
1/2 cup packed brown sugar
1/2 cup whole wheat or white flour
1 teaspoon baking powder
1/4 teaspoon salt
1/2 teaspoon cinnamon
1/4 teaspoon nutmeg
3/4 cup chopped apple

Topping:
1 tablespoon butter or margarine
2 tablespoons brown sugar
1 tablespoon flour
1 tablespoon chopped nuts
1/4 teaspoon cinnamon

Microwave water in mixing bowl for 2-3 minutes or until boiling. Stir in oats; let stand 5 minutes. Add butter and oil; stir until butter is melted. Beat in egg and brown sugar; add flour, baking powder, salt, cinnamon, nutmeg; stir until moistened; stir in apple.

Line 12 microwave-safe muffin cups with paper liners; spoon batter into cups, filling 2/3 full. Combine topping ingredients in small bowl; mix with fork until crumbly; spoon mixture evenly onto muffin batter. Microwave on HIGH, uncovered, 2 to 2-1/2 minutes. Repeat with remaining muffins.

CORN MUFFINS

1/2 cup buttermilk
3 tablespoons oil
1 egg
3/4 cup cornmeal
1/2 cup whole wheat or white flour
3 tablespoons sugar
2 tablespoons baking powder
1/2 teaspoon soda
1/2 teaspoon salt
1 (4-ounce) can green chilies
1 cup fresh or canned corn, drained
1/2 teaspoon dried minced onion
1 teaspoon jalapeno peppers
   (optional)

Beat together buttermilk, oil, and egg in a 2-cup measure. Place cornmeal, flour, sugar, baking powder, and soda and salt in mixing bowl. Add buttermilk mixture; stir just until moistened. Mix in chilies, corn, minced onions, and jalapeno peppers. Line muffin cups with paper liners; spoon batter into cups, fill 3/4 full. Microwave 6 muffins at a time on HIGH, uncovered, 2 to 2-1/2 minutes.

CARAMEL TOPPED RICE CUSTARD

(Microwave Method)

Combine caramels and 1/4 cup milk in 2-cup glass measure. Cook on HIGH (maximum power) 2 minutes, or until caramels melt, stirring every minute. Pour equal amounts into 6 buttered cups. Spoon 1/3 cup rice into each cup. Blend remaining ingredients; pour evenly into each cup. Place cups in shallow micro-proof dish, containing 1 inch water. Cook at 70% power for 15 minutes, or until almost set, rotating dish 1/4 turn every 5 minutes. Let stand 10 minutes. Loosen custard with knife and invert onto dessert plates Garnish with chopped nuts or coconut, if desired. Serve warm.

CHOCOLATE AMARETTO MOUSSE

2 ounces cream cheese
2 tablespoons semisweet chocolate pieces
1/2 tablespoon Amaretto liqueur
1/2 cup whipping cream
2 tablespoons sugar

Combine cream cheese and chocolate pieces in 1-cup glass measure. Microwave on HIGH, uncovered, 30-45 seconds or until chocolate is soft. Stir to melt chocolate; blend in liqueur; set aside.

Beat cream and sugar until thick; fold in chocolate. Spoon into individual dishes. Refrigerate until set, about 2 hours. Top with shaved chocolate or chocolate jimmies.

CARAMEL NUT POPCORN CLUSTERS

1 (14-ounce) bag approximately 40 caramel squares
2 tablespoons light cream
2 quarts popped popcorn, lightly salted
1 cup salted, roasted peanuts

Combine caramel squares and cream in small bowl. Microwave 2 minutes, 30 seconds to 3 minutes on MEDIUM HIGH, stirring several times or until caramel is smooth. In large bowl, mix popcorn and peanuts together, adding caramel sauce gradually. Stir until combined. Drop by spoonfuls onto wax paper. Let cool.

LEMONY BARBECUE SAUCE

Makes 1 cup

2 tablespoons butter or margarine
1/2 cup chopped onion
1 clove garlic, minced
1/2 cup catsup
1/4 cup lemon juice
2 tablespoons molasses
1 tablespoon Worcestershire sauce
1/4 teaspoon dry mustard
1/4 teaspoon salt
1/4 teaspoon pepper
1/4 teaspoon ground cumin
5 thin slices lemon, seeded and quartered

Place butter in a 1-1/2-quart casserole. Microwave on HIGH for 45 seconds or until melted. Add onion and garlic; cover with lid; microwave on HIGH for 2 minutes. Add remaining ingredients; cover and microwave on HIGH for 3-4 minutes; stir once. Use as a basting sauce for beef, pork, or chicken.

ALMOND VANILLA CUSTARD SAUCE

Makes 1 cup

1 egg, beaten
3/4 cup half-and-half
2 tablespoons sugar
1/2 teaspoon vanilla extract
1/4 teaspoon almond extract

Combine all ingredients in a 2-cup measure; mix well. Microwave on MEDIUM (50%) power for 4-7 minutes or until thickened. Stir with whisk after 2 minutes and every minute thereafter. Stir well; cover and chill. Serve over pound cake or fruit.

SWEET AND TANGY BARBECUE SAUCE

Makes 1-1/2 cups

1 cup chopped onion
3 cloves garlic, minced
2 tablespoons oil
1/2 cup brown sugar, packed
1/2 cup red wine vinegar
1/3 cup water
1 (6-ounce) can tomato paste
2 tablespoons soy sauce
1 teaspoon instant beef bouillon
1 teaspoon prepared mustard

Combine onion, garlic, and oil in 1-quart casserole; cover with lid. Microwave on HIGH for 2 to 2-1/2 minutes or until tender. Stir in remaining ingredients. Cover. Microwave on HIGH, 5-6 minutes. Sauce can be covered and refrigerated for up to 2 weeks.

FROSTY PUMPKIN PRALINE PIE

Crust:
1/4 cup butter or margarine
1-1/4 cups graham cracker crumbs
2 tablespoons sugar

Praline pieces:
1/4 cup firmly packed brown sugar
1/4 cup sliced or slivered almonds
1 tablespoon butter or margarine
1 teaspoon water

Filling:
1 cup canned pumpkin
1/2 cup firmly packed brown sugar
1/4 cup milk
1 teaspoon cinnamon
1/2 teaspoon nutmeg
1/4 teaspoon ginger
1/4 teaspoon salt
1 pint (2 cups) vanilla ice cream

Topping:
1 cup whipping cream
2 tablespoons sugar
1 teaspoon vanilla

In bowl microwave butter on HIGH 1/2-1 minute or until melted; stir in crumbs and sugar until combined. Press mixture into bottom and up sides of a 9-inch pie plate; microwave uncovered 1-1/2 to 2-1/2 minutes or until heated through. Rotate twice, if necessary. Cool.

In an 8-inch round glass baking dish, combine all ingredients for praline pieces; microwave on HIGH, uncovered, 2-3 minutes or until bubbly and nuts are lightly toasted, stirring several times. Cool; break into pieces.

Combine in glass mixing bowl, all ingredients for filling, except ice cream. Microwave on HIGH for 3-4 minutes, uncovered; stir once. Stir in ice cream; let stand until ice cream can be easily mixed in. Pour into crust. Freeze until firm. Beat cream until thickened; beat in sugar and vanilla. Spread over pie; sprinkle with praline pieces. Freeze until served. You can use crushed gingersnaps for cracker crumbs.

SPECIAL CHOCOLATE PIE

Yield 1-9 inch pie

24 large marshmallows
1/2 cup of half & half
1-6 ounce package of semi-sweet chocolate chips (it must be real chocolate, not the food type)
2 tablespoons creme de cacao
2 tablespoons Kahlua
1 cup whipping cream
1-9 inch chocolate wafer crust; (recipe on page 50)

Microwave marshmallows, milk (half & half), and chocolate, in a 3 quart casserole at MEDIUM, 3-4 minutes; stir and cool slightly. Add the creme de cacao and Kahlua to the half & half mixture. Chill 20-30 minutes. Whip the cream until stiff. Fold into chocolate mixture. Pour filling into the chocolate wafer crust and freeze. Remove from freezer 5-10 minutes before serving.

ONE MINUTE CHOCOLATE WAFER PIE CRUST

Makes one pie crust

7 tablespoons butter
1-1/2 cups chocolate wafers crushed crumbs
2 tablespoons walnuts, crushed crumbs.

Microwave butter in a 9 inch glass pie plate at HIGH for 1 minute. Stir in the wafer and walnut crumbs. Press mixture evenly in the pie plate. Chill, pour pie filling into shell and freeze.

LO -CAL COCOA

1 cup nonfat dry milk powder
2 teaspoons unsweetened cocoa

2 - 4 packets Equal

Combine the dry milk and cocoa. Store at room temp. Makes enough for 4 cups of cocoa. Fill mug with 3/4 cup water. Microwave on HIGH for 1 minute or until hot. Stir in 1/4 cup Cocoa mix and 1/2 - 1 packet of Equal.

MICROWAVE APRICOT CRISP

Serves 4

1-14 ounce can apricot pie filling
1 tablespoon sugar
2 oranges, grated rind and juice
1/4 cup soft margarine
3/4 cup raw oats
1/3 cup light brown sugar
3 tablespoons flour
4 gingersnaps, crushed

Mix together pie filling, sugar, orange rind, and juice in a shallow, oven-proof dish. Combine margarine, oats, brown sugar, and flour, until crumbly. Spoon evenly over fruit mixture and sprinkle with the crumbs. Place in microwave and cook about 10 minutes or until fruit juices begin to bubble through crisp crust.

Serve warm with whipped cream.

SEASONED SEEDS

1 cup pumpkin seeds
1 tablespoon butter or margarine
1/2 teaspoon Worcestershire sauce
1/4 teaspoon garlic salt
1/4 teaspoon onion salt or seasoned salt

Remove membrane from seeds. If seeds are washed, pat dry. Place in a 9-inch glass pie plate; add remaining ingredients; microwave on HIGH for 8-10 minutes until lightly toasted, stirring 4-5 times. Cooking time will depend on size of seeds and moistness.

BARBECUED LAMB SHANKS
Serves 4

12 thin lemon slices
4 lamb shanks (about 3-1/2 pounds)
Barbecue sauce
8 paper towel sheets

For each lamb shank, place 2 paper towel sheets, one on top of the other, on the counter. Place three lemon slices diagonally across center of paper towel sheets. Place lamb shank on lemon slices. Fold three corners toward center, covering lamb like an envelope. Roll up over remaining corner. Hold under running water until soaked, but not dripping. Place loose corner down on microwave-safe plate.

Microwave on HIGH for 5 minutes. Rotate plate half turn. Microwave on MEDIUM (50 per cent power) for 5 minutes per pound, rotating plate once. Remove and discard paper towel sheets. Brush lamb shanks with barbecue sauce. Place lamb on hot grill. Grill to desired doneness, 20 to 30 minutes, turning and brushing occasionally with barbecue sauce.

CRAB AND CORN BISQUE
8 servings

2 tablespoons butter or margarine
1 small onion, chopped
1 small red pepper, chopped
1 large celery stalk, chopped
1/4 teaspoon dried thyme leaves
1/8 teaspoon ground red pepper
1 can condensed cream of potato soup, undiluted
2 cups milk
1 (17-ounce) can cream-style corn
1 (12-ounce) package fish and crab blend (surimi)

In 3-quart casserole, melt butter on HIGH one minute; add chopped onion, pepper, celery, thyme and ground red pepper; cover with plastic wrap; turn back one corner to vent. Cook on HIGH for 5 minutes, stirring once. Stir in soup, milk, corn and surimi; cover and vent; microwave on HIGH for 7 minutes or until boiling.

CHEDDAR FISH BUNDLES
Serves 4

1-1/2 cups shredded cheddar cheese'
1-1/2 cups fresh bread crumbs
2 tablespoons mayonnaise
2 teaspoons horseradish
1 pound sole fillets
1 tablespoon margarine, melted

Combine 1 cup cheese, crumbs, mayonnaise, and horseradish; mix lightly. Spoon mixture over fish; roll up; secure with wooden toothpicks. Place fish, seam side down, in baking dish, drizzling with margarine. Microwave on HIGH for 5-6 minutes or until fish flakes easily; turn dish after 3 minutes. Sprinkle with remaining cheese; microwave 1-1/2 to 2 minutes or until melted.

QUICK AND LIGHT FISH PLATTER
Serves 1

2 carrots, cut into 2 inch x 1/8 inch strips
1 stalk celery, cut into 1" slices
1 tablespoon water
Parsley flakes
1 tablespoon butter or margarine
4 to 6 ounces defrosted flounder fillets
2 teaspoons lemon juice
Paprika
1 tablespoon sliced green onion
2 tablespoons almonds, toasted

Place carrot strips around edge of a dinner plate; top with celery, water and parsley; dice 1 teaspoon of butter and place on vegetables. Cover with plastic wrap; turn back one edge to vent. Microwave on HIGH for 2 minutes. Uncover; place fish on center of plate. Top with lemon juice, remaining butter, paprika, and onion. Re-cover with plastic wrap; microwave on HIGH for 2 minutes. Let stand 2 minutes. Sprinkle with toasted almonds.

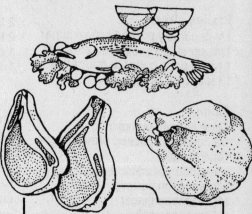

ITALIAN CHICKEN SUPREME

2 medium carrots, cut in thin strips
1 medium zucchini, cut in thin strips
1 medium onion, thinly sliced
2 whole boneless chicken breasts, skinned and cut in half (about 1 pound)
1 teaspoon Italian seasoning
4 pats butter
Salt and pepper

Divide carrots, zucchini, and onion evenly among the 4 paper towels. Place a pat of butter, salt, and pepper over assembled vegetables. Cover vegetables with boneless chicken breast. Sprinkle with Italian seasoning. Fold towel around chicken and vegetables to completely enclose. Moisten under running water. Place paper towel bundles in a round glass baking dish. Microwave on HIGH for 9-10 minutes, or until chicken is cooked. Remove from microwave and let stand 1 minute before serving.

Makes 4 servings of 1 chicken breast and 1/2 cup vegetables each.

For 2 servings: 6 minutes on HIGH
For 1 serving: 3 minutes , 30 seconds on HIGH
Calories per serving: 167

CHICKEN SAVORY CASSEROLE

1/2 cup uncooked long grain rice
1-1/2 cups water
1 teaspoon salt
1 skinned and boned chicken breast
1 package frozen chopped broccoli
2 tablespoons butter or margarine
2 tablespoons flour
1/2 teaspoon salt
1/8 teaspoon pepper
1 cup milk
3/4 cup shredded Cheddar cheese
2 tablespoons dry sherry or white wine
1/2 cup sour cream
2 tablespoons dry bread crumbs
2 tablespoons Parmesan cheese
1/4 teaspoon paprika
1/2 teaspoon poultry seasoning
1 teaspoon dried minced onion

Combine rice, water, and 1 teaspoon salt in 1-1/2 quart casserole; cover. Microwave HIGH for 3-4 minutes, cut chicken into bite size pieces, add to rice mixture, cover. Microwave 50% (MEDIUM) for 15-17 minutes. Stir once. Set aside.

Microwave broccoli in package for 3 to 4 minutes, add to rice, set aside. Microwave butter HIGH 30-45 seconds in a 4 cup glass measure. Blend in flour, 1/2 teaspoon salt and pepper; stir in milk until smooth. Microwave on HIGH uncovered 3-1/2 to 4 minutes until it thickens; stir once during last part of cooking time. Stir in cheddar cheese and sherry. Add to rice mixture along with sour cream, mix lightly, cover. Microwave on HIGH for 3-4 minutes; stir once. Combine bread crumbs, Parmesan cheese, and paprika; mix well. Spoon over casserole. Microwave HIGH 3-4 minutes, uncovered.

CHICKEN A LA KING
For Microwave

3 tablespoons butter
5 tablespoons flour
1 teaspoon salt

1-3/4 cups clear chicken stock
3 cups cooked, cubed chicken
1 (4 ounce) can mushrooms, drained

Put the butter in a deep 2 quart heat-resistant bowl. Blend in the flour and salt. Gradually stir in the chicken stock. Cook uncovered on HIGH for 4 minutes until thickened and smooth. Stir occasionally. Add the remaining ingredients and cook uncovered on HIGH for 3 minutes until heated through. Serve hot over toast or a bed of rice.

QUICK CHICKEN IN A SPUD - WHAT COULD BE EASIER

1 large baking potato
1 package (4 ounces) frozen chicken a la king

Scrub and prick the potato with fork. Place in microwave and cook on HIGH for 3 minutes; turn potato over. Remove cooking pouch from the package of chicken a la king. Snip corner of pouch and place in oven next to potato; microwave HIGH 3-4 minutes. Cut almost through potato lengthwise, press ends to open potato. Sprinkle potato with salt and pepper. Spoon chicken mixture into potato. Sprinkle with paprika.

QUICK NOODLES AND HAM

1-1/2 cups water
1/2 cup milk
2 tablespoons butter
1 package (4.5 ounces) Parmesan noodles and mix
1-1/2 cups cubed cooked ham
1 package (6 ounces) frozen pea pods

Microwave 1-1/2 cups water for 6-7 minutes until boiling. Stir in milk,

butter, noodles and sauce mix, and ham. Cover with lid, or plastic wrap and microwave on HIGH 5-6 minutes; stir once. Add the package of pea pods, cover. Microwave for 2-3 minutes on HIGH, stir once. Let stand about 5 minutes before serving.

MICROWAVE MEATBALLS
Makes 24

1 pound ground beef
2 cups soft bread crumbs
2 eggs
1/2 cup finely chopped onion
1 tablespoon steak sauce
1 clove garlic, crushed
1/2 teaspoon paprika
1/4 teaspoon pepper

Mix all ingredients together; shape into 1 inch balls. Arrange in microwave-safe pan. Cover with wax paper and microwave on HIGH for 20 minutes.
Good hot or cold.

Here is a recipe for barbecue sauce. It yields about 1-1/2 cups. Refrigerate unused portion in a covered container.

BARBECUE SAUCE

1-1/2 cups chopped onion
1 tablespoon vegetable oil
1 cup beef broth
3/4 cup tomato paste
1/3 cup red wine vinegar
3 tablespoons dark brown sugar
2 tablespoons prepared mustard
1 teaspoon salt
1/2 teaspoon pepper

In a medium bowl, combine onion and oil; microwave on HIGH for 1-2 minutes, or until onion is tender. Stir in remaining ingredients; microwave on HIGH 4-5 minutes. Reduce power to 50% (MEDIUM) and continue to microwave for 5 minutes until thickened. Use at once or transfer to container; cool and refrigerate.

EGG HAMLET FOR ONE

1 egg
1 slice of American cheese
1 slice of ham
1 hamburger roll

Break egg into small bowl; blend well. Cover with wax paper; microwave for 1-1/2 to 2 minutes on MEDIUM HIGH (70%), stir once. Assemble sandwich by putting together slice of cheese, ham, cooked egg, and salt and pepper. Wrap sandwich in paper napkin and microwave 30-40 seconds on 70% to heat roll and melt cheese.

POTATO PICK-UPS
Makes 24
(a microwave finger food)

12 small red potatoes
1/2 teaspoon chicken-flavor instant bouillon
1/2 cup pimiento-stuffed olives
3 tablespoons mayonnaise
2 tablespoons chopped parsley

Cut each potato in half lengthwise. In 3-quart casserole, cook potatoes, bouillon, and 1/2 cup hot tap water, covered, on HIGH in microwave for 10 to 12 minutes until potatoes are tender, stirring once; drain. Rinse potatoes under cold water; drain; refrigerate about 1 hour or until chilled.

Meanwhile, chop olives. In small bowl, stir olives, mayonnaise, and parsley. Onto cut side of each potato half, spoon a rounded teaspoonful of olive mixture. (35 calories per serving)

POTATO SALAD
Serves 6

1/2 cup low–calorie Italian dressing
2 cups hot cooked, cubed potatoes

1/2 cup bias-sliced celery
1/2 cup thinly sliced red onion, separated into rings
1/4 cup sliced radishes
2 tablespoons chopped green pepper
1/2 teaspoon salt
1/4 teaspoon dried dill weed
2 tablespoons snipped parsley

In a large bowl pour the Italian dressing over the hot cooked potatoes; mix gently to coat. Cover and marinate in the refrigerator for at least 2 hours. Add celery, onion, radishes, green pepper, salt, and dill. Toss gently to combine. Sprinkle with parsley. (46 calories)

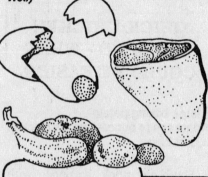

HEARTY GERMAN POTATO SALAD

3 slices bacon, cut up
1 small onion, chopped
2 tablespoons flour
1 tablespoon sugar
1 teaspoon salt
1/2 teaspoon caraway or celery seed
1/8 teaspoon pepper
1/2 cup water
1/4 cup vinegar
2 (16-ounce) cans sliced white potatoes, drained
1 package hot dogs, cut into 1/2 inch pieces

Combine bacon and onion in microwave-safe casserole; cover with paper towel and microwave for 4-5 minutes on HIGH or until bacon is crisp. Stir in flour, sugar, salt, caraway, pepper, water and vinegar until blended. Microwave on HIGH, uncovered, 2-3 minutes; stir twice. Stir in potatoes and hot dogs; mix lightly. Cover with casserole lid. Microwave 6-7 minutes on HIGH or until heated through.

SWEET POTATO SOUFFLÉ

1 (18-ounce) can sweet potatoes
1/4 cup granulated sugar
1/4 cup dark brown sugar
1/4 cup margarine, melted
2 eggs
3/4 cup evaporated milk
1/2 teaspoon cinnamon
1/2 teaspoon nutmeg
1/4 teaspoon vanilla

Topping:
6 tablespoons margarine, melted
1/2 cup brown sugar
1/2 cup walnuts, chopped
1 cup crushed crackers, Ritz® or Townhouse®

Combine potatoes with next 8 ingredients and mix well. Pour into a 2-quart casserole and microwave on 70% for 13-16 minutes. Rotate dish once, if necessary. Combine topping ingredients and spread over potatoes. Microwave on 70% for 2-4 more minutes.

SOUPER CHEESE POTATOES

4 large potatoes, peeled and cubed
1/4 cup water
1/2 can condensed Cheddar cheese soup
1/2 cup sour cream
1/2 cup half-and-half
1 tablespoon snipped chives
1/2 teaspoon garlic salt
1/2 cup (2 ounces) shredded Cheddar cheese
Paprika
1 teaspoon parsley
1/8 teaspoon pepper

Combine potatoes and water in a casserole; cover with lid and microwave on HIGH for 12-14 minutes; stir once. Stir in soup, sour cream, half-and-half, chives, and garlic salt. Microwave on HIGH for 4-5 minutes, uncovered; stir once. Sprinkle with cheese and paprika. Let stand, covered, about 5 minutes or until cheese is melted. Sprinkle with paprika, parsley, and pepper.

MICROWAVE TOMATOES

4 large ripe tomatoes
3/4 cup mayonnaise
1/4-1/2 teaspoon curry powder
One-half of a 6-ounce package ranch dressing

Halve the tomatoes and arrange in a circle, cut side up, in a 9-inch pie plate. Mix remaining ingredients and spread over the top of the tomatoes. Microwave for 3-5 minutes on HIGH, turn around halfway through the cooking time. Do not cover. Let stand one minute.

SCALLOPED CORN MICROWAVE

1 (17-ounce) can whole kernel corn
1 (17-ounce) can cream style corn
1/2 cup Ritz Cracker crumbs
1 (5-ounce) can evaporated milk
1 egg, slightly beaten
1/8 teaspoon dry mustard
1 tablespoon dry onion flakes (or 1/4 cup chopped onion, sauted in butter)
1 (2-ounce) jar chopped pimiento
3 tablespoons grated Parmesan cheese
3 tablespoons margarine, cut into small pieces
1 teaspoon paprika

Combine all ingredients, except cheese, butter, and paprika; mix well. Put into a greased 1-1/2 quart casserole. Place cheese on top of casserole and dot with butter. Cover and microwave 10 minutes on Level 8 or until set. Let stand, covered, 3-5 minutes. Sprinkle with paprika before serving.

HOT CHEESE DIP

1/4 green pepper (finely chopped)
1/2 bunch green onions (finely chopped)
1-5 ounce jar of sharp Old English cheese
1- 8 ounce jar Cheese Whiz
1-7 ounce can minced clams, drained
Garlic powder to taste

Combine all ingredients in a 1-1/2 quart glass casserole dish. Heat uncovered on full power for 2 minutes; stir after one minute. Serve hot with corn chips. This is a very tasty cheese dip!

PUMPKIN SOUP
Serves 5-6

1 can chicken broth
3 cups water
1 tablespoon chicken bouillon or granules
1 small onion, chopped
1/2 cup chopped celery
1/2 cup chopped carrot
1 can (16-ounce) pumpkin
1/3 cup dry white wine (optional)
2 tablespoons butter
1/4 teaspoon thyme
Dash pepper
1/8 teaspoon garlic powder
Sour Cream

Combine chicken broth, water, bouillon, onion, celery, and carrots in 2-quart casserole; cover; microwave 15-30 minutes or until vegetables are tender. Let stand 10 minutes. Transfer vegetable mixture to food processor or blender. Process at medium or until smooth; add pumpkin; process until smooth. Return mixture to casserole; stir in wine, butter, salt, thyme, and garlic powder. Microwave on HIGH, uncovered, for 5-8 minutes, or until heated through, stirring 2 or 3 times. Serve in bowls; top with a spoonful of sour cream.

ICED FRESH TOMATO SOUP

2 tablespoons vegetable oil
6 medium tomatoes, chopped
1/4 cup catsup
1 tablespoon dry dillweed
Dash of Tabasco sauce
1 cup chopped onion
1 (10-ounce) can beef broth
3 cups crushed ice
1 teaspoon salt
1/2 cup heavy cream

Place oil, onion, and tomatoes in 8-cup measure, microwave on HIGH 2-3 minutes to make onion tender. Stir in beef broth and catsup. Microwave on HIGH for 2 minutes, cool slightly, and pour into blender and process until smooth. Return to 8-cup measure; stir in ice and seasonings. Chill until cold. Whip cream, and top each bowl of soup with it.

TACO PORK STRIPS
Serves 4

1 boneless pork chop 1/2 inch thick
2 teaspoons taco breading

Cut pork chop in 1/2-inch thick strips. Coat strips with breading; place in dish; cover with plastic wrap. Microwave on 30% power or MEDIUM LOW or 2 minutes. Turn strips over and rearrange; cover; microwave 2-1/2 minutes on MEDIUM LOW (30%).

Taco Breading:

1/2 cup cornflake crumbs
1-1/2 tablespoons taco seasoning mix

Combine. Makes 1/2 cup for enough for 4 chops.

BACON STICKS
Makes 10

10 thin bread sticks (any flavor)
5 slices of bacon (cut lengthwise)
1/2 cup Parmesan cheese

Dredge one side of bacon strip in cheese. With cheese side out, roll bacon around bread stick diagonally.
Place sticks on microwave dish or paper plate lined with paper towels. Microwave on HIGH 4-1/2 - 6 minutes. When done, roll again in cheese.

Salad
BOWL

FROZEN WALDORF SALAD

- ¹/₂ cup sugar
- ¹/₂ cup pineapple juice
- ¹/₈ teaspoon salt
- ¹/₄ cup lemon juice
- ¹/₂ cup diced celery
- ¹/₂ cup crushed pineapple, drained
- 2 medium apples, diced with skins left on
- ¹/₂ cup walnuts *or* pecans, broken in small pieces
- 1 cup heavy cream, whipped

Combine sugar, pineapple juice, salt and lemon juice in saucepan. Cook over medium heat, stirring until thick. Let cool. Stir in celery, pineapple, apples and nuts. Fold in whipped cream.

Spoon into an 8-inch square pan or individual molds. Freeze. Garnish with maraschino cherries. Allow salad to be at room temperature for about 20 minutes before serving.

ORANGE-CREAM SALAD
Serves 10

- 1 (20-ounce) can pineapple chunks, drained
- 1 (16-ounce) can peach slices, drained
- 1 (11-ounce) can mandarin orange sections, drained
- 3 medium bananas, sliced
- 2 medium apples, cored and chopped
- 1 (3-1/3 to 3-3/4 ounce) package vanilla instant pudding mix
- 1-1/2 cups milk
- 1/2 of a 6-ounce can (1/3 cup) frozen orange juice concentrate, thawed
- 3/4 cup dairy sour cream
- Lettuce

In a large bowl combine pineapple chunks, peaches, orange sections, bananas, and apples; set aside. In small bowl combine dry pudding mix, milk, and orange juice concentrate. Beat with rotary beater 1 to 2 minutes or until well blended. Beat in sour cream. Fold into fruit mixture. Cover and refrigerate several hours. Serve salad on lettuce leaves.

YOGI BERRY SALAD

- 1 Red Delicious apple, cored and chopped
- 1 cup halved, seedless green grapes
- 1 cup sliced strawberries
- ½ cup sliced celery
- ¼ cup raisins
- ½ cup lemon yogurt
- 2 tablespoons sunflower seeds
- Lettuce

In a bowl, combine apple, grapes, strawberries, celery and raisins. Toss gently. Fold in yogurt. Cover and chill. Just before serving, stir in sunflower seeds. Serve on lettuce leaves.

PASTA AND VEGETABLE SALAD
Makes 5 quarts

- 1 pound mostaccioli noodles *or* other large pasta
- 2 tablespoons chicken soup mix
- 1 or 2 cucumbers, diced
- 1 large tomato, diced
- 1 small onion, finely chopped
- 1 green pepper, finely diced
- Sweet Herb Dressing (recipe follows)

Cook mostaccioli according to package directions, except substitute chicken soup mix for salt; drain and cool. Add cucumbers, tomato, onion and green pepper. Pour enough Sweet Herb Dressing over salad to moisten. Refrigerate several hours.

Sweet Herb Dressing:
Makes 2 cups
- 1 cup salad oil (or less)
- 1 cup vinegar
- ½ cup sugar
- 1 tablespoon parsley
- 2 teaspoons seasoning salt
- 2 teaspoons sweet 'n hot mustard
- 2 teaspoons minced green onion
- 1 teaspoon garlic powder
- ¾ teaspoon black pepper
- ½ teaspoon celery seed

Combine all ingredients in covered jar; shake well.

EGGNOG CHRISTMAS SALAD
Serves 8–10

- 2 cups crushed pineapple with juice
- 1 envelope unflavored gelatin
- 3 tablespoons fresh lime juice
- 1½ cups eggnog
- ¾ cup chopped celery
- 1 (3-ounce) package raspberry gelatin
- 1½ cups boiling water
- 1 (10-ounce) package frozen cranberry orange relish
  Salad greens

Drain pineapple juice into saucepan; heat to boiling. Soften gelatin in lime juice; dissolve in boiling pineapple juice. Cool. Add eggnog; chill until partially set. Fold in pineapple and celery. Pour into mold; chill until firm. Dissolve raspberry gelatin in boiling water; add cranberry-orange relish, stirring until relish is thawed. Chill until slightly thickened; pour over eggnog mixture. Chill until firm. Unmold on salad greens.

YUM YUM SALAD

- 1 (3-ounce) package lime gelatin
- 1 (8-ounce) package cream cheese, softened
- 1 cup boiling water
- 1 cup whipping cream *or* 1 package whipped topping mix, prepared
- 1 small can crushed pineapple
- ¹/₂ cup chopped pecans
  Toasted coconut

Place gelatin, hot water and cream cheese in pan and stir over low heat until cheese is blended well into mixture. Remove from heat; add crushed pineapple and pecans. Place in refrigerator until it begins to thicken. Add whipped cream and let set until firm. Sprinkle with toasted coconut before serving.

CHEESE-LIME SALAD
Serves 10

- 3 cups boiling water
- 2 (3-ounce) packages lime-flavored gelatin
- 1 cup pineapple juice
- 1 teaspoon vinegar
- ½ teaspoon salt
- 2 cups creamed cottage cheese
- 1 teaspoon onion, finely chopped
- 1 teaspoon green pepper, finely chopped
- ½ cup cucumber, coarsely chopped
- ½ cup celery, coarsely chopped

Pour boiling water on gelatin in bowl; stir until gelatin is dissolved. Stir in pineapple juice, vinegar and salt. Pour 1 cup of the gelatin mixture into an 8-cup mold. Refrigerate until firm.

Refrigerate remaining mixture until slightly thickened, but not set; beat with beater until light and fluffy. Mix in remaining ingredients and pour on gelatin layer in mold. Refrigerate until firm. Unmold on serving plate.

ORANGE DELIGHT

- 2 cups small-curd cottage cheese
- 2 cups crushed pineapple, drained
- 2 small *or* 1 large package orange-flavored gelatin
- 2 cups whipped topping

Fold all ingredients together; chill before serving. For fewer calories, use low-fat cottage cheese, unsweetened pineapple and sugar-free gelatin.

Yummy any way you fix it! Different flavors of gelatin are great too.

ARTICHOKE RICE SALAD

- 1 package chicken rice combination mix (cooked as directed)
- 3 green onions, chopped
- ½ green pepper, chopped
- 8 to 10 pimiento green olives, chopped
- 2 jars marinated artichoke hearts in oil (dice and reserve liquid)
- ¼ teaspoon curry powder
- ⅓ cup mayonnaise
  Oil from 1 jar artichokes
  Salt and pepper to taste

Mix onion, pepper, olives and artichokes with cooled rice combination mix. In separate bowl, mix mayonnaise, oil and curry powder. Pour this dressing over rice mixture. Add salt and pepper. Mix and refrigerate overnight.

PEPPERONI SALAD
Serves 6–8

- 1 medium onion, thinly sliced
- 8 ounces pepperoni, thinly sliced
- ¼ cup crumbled bleu cheese
- ⅔ cup salad oil
- ⅓ cup cider vinegar
  Salt and freshly ground pepper to taste
- 10 ounces fresh spinach, washed thoroughly, dried and chopped
- ½ head iceberg lettuce, chopped

One day before serving, separate onion slices into rings and place in large bowl; add pepperoni slices and bleu cheese. Add oil, vinegar, salt and pepper. Toss in the spinach and lettuce. Chill salad overnight in covered bowl.

HARVEST CARROT SALAD
Serves 6–8

3 cups shredded carrots
1 (17-ounce) can apricot halves, drained and chopped
½ cup sliced celery
⅔ cup raisins
¼ cup chopped walnuts, toasted
½ cup salad dressing *or* mayonnaise

Combine all ingredients, tossing well. Cover and refrigerate before serving.

ARTICHOKE GRAPEFRUIT SALAD
Serves 4
(Pastel and picture pretty)

1 (15-ounce) can artichoke hearts
¼ cup salad oil
2 tablespoons vinegar
1 teaspoon Worcestershire sauce
½ teaspoon salt
⅛ teaspoon pepper
1 tablespoon chopped parsley
Lettuce, romaine, endive
2 pink grapefruit, sectioned

Drain artichoke hearts and cut in halves. Combine oil, vinegar, salt, Worcestershire sauce, pepper and parsley, mixing well. Pour over artichokes in bowl and chill for several hours. Combine greens; add artichoke mixture and grapefruit; toss and serve.

BURGUNDY BEET SALAD
Serves 7

1 pound cooked beets, skinned and diced
½ cup walnuts, finely chopped
1 tablespoon prepared horseradish
⅓ cup unflavored yogurt
1¼ teaspoons mayonnaise
¼ cup half-and-half *or* cream
⅓ cup orange juice
¼ teaspoon salt
⅛ teaspoon pepper
2 tablespoons parsley, chopped

Place beets and walnuts in a salad or serving bowl; stir in horseradish, yogurt, mayonnaise, half-and-half and orange juice. Mix thoroughly; season with salt and pepper. When serving, sprinkle each serving with the chopped parsley.

TOMATO CHEESE SALAD
Serves 8

1½ cups hot condensed tomato soup, undiluted
½ cup cream cheese
1 tablespoon butter
¼ teaspoon salt
1 tablespoon onion juice
1 tablespoon unflavored gelatin
¼ cup cold water
½ cup mayonnaise
½ cup heavy cream *or* evaporated milk
¼ cup stuffed olives, chopped

Heat soup, cheese, butter, salt and onion juice until cheese has softened. Soften gelatin in cold water and dissolve in hot mixture; cool until mixture starts to thicken. Whip cream and add with mayonnaise and stuffed olives. Turn into mold and chill. When firm, unmold on lettuce and garnish with stuffed olives, sliced. Serve with mayonnaise sprinkled with paprika.

ORANGE CHICKEN SALAD
Serves 2

2 cups cooked, cubed chicken
1 cup sliced celery
¼ cup chopped walnuts
1 teaspoon grated onion
½ teaspoon salt
⅓ cup orange juice
¼ cup mayonnaise
2 oranges, peeled and sectioned
¼ cup dry bread crumbs
¼ cup grated Parmesan cheese

Combine chicken, celery, walnuts, onion, salt, orange juice and mayonnaise in mixing bowl; mix well. Cover and refrigerate for 1 hour. Stir in orange sections. Spoon mixture into casserole; sprinkle with bread crumbs and Parmesan cheese. Bake in a preheated 350-degree oven for 25 minutes, or until mixture is heated through and cheese is lightly browned. Serve with rolls.

SANTA'S RED RASPBERRY RING
Serves 8–10

1 (10-ounce) package frozen red raspberries, thawed
2 (3-ounce) packages raspberry-flavored gelatin
2 cups boiling water
1 pint vanilla ice cream
1 (6-ounce) can (¾ cup) frozen pink lemonade concentrate, thawed
¼ cup pecans

Drain raspberries, reserving syrup. Dissolve gelatin in boiling water. Add ice cream by spoonfuls, stirring until melted. Stir in lemonade concentrate and reserved syrup. Chill until partially set. Add raspberries and pecans. Turn into a 6-cup ring mold. Chill until firm.

GAZPACHO SALAD MOLD

- 1 envelope unflavored gelatin
- ¼ cup chicken broth
- 1¾ cups tomato juice
- ¼ cup minced green pepper
- ¼ cup chopped celery
- ¼ cup sliced green onion
- ¼ cup chopped cucumber
- 1 tablespoon Worcestershire sauce
- ¾ teaspoon lemon juice
  Dash celery salt
- 2 small tomatoes, chopped
  Lettuce

In small bowl sprinkle gelatin over chicken broth. Soften for 10 minutes. In medium saucepan combine tomato juice, green pepper, celery, green onion, cucumber, Worcestershire sauce, lemon juice and celery salt. Simmer 5 minutes. Remove from heat and stir in gelatin. Stir until dissolved. Set saucepan in cold water and stir until cool. Fold in tomatoes. Pour mixture into a small, shallow rectangular-shaped pan. Chill, covered, for 4 hours or overnight. Cut in squares or rectangles and serve on lettuce leaves.

BING CHERRY SALAD

- 1 (3-ounce) package cherry gelatin
- 1 cup boiling water
- 1 large can black bing cherries
- ½ pint sour cream
- ½ cup chopped pecans

Dissolve gelatin in bowl with boiling water. Drain cherry juice and add to water. Refrigerate until gelatin begins to form, about 70 minutes. Beat sour cream into gelatin; add cherries and pecans. Pour mixture into a 9 x 9 x 2-inch square pan and refrigerate until firm. This is nice to serve guests for lunch *or* dinner.

FRESH SPINACH SALAD

- 1 package fresh spinach
- 1 (No. 2) can bean sprouts, rinsed and drained
- 1 (8-ounce) can water chestnuts, drained and sliced
- 4 hardcooked eggs, sliced
- 1 medium onion
- ½ package bacon, fried and crumbled

Dressing:
- ¾ cup sugar
- ¾ cup vinegar
- ¼ cup oil
- ⅓ cup ketchup
- 2 teaspoons salt
- 1 teaspoon Worcestershire sauce

Tear clean, crisp, well-drained spinach leaves in a large bowl. Add other ingredients. Mix dressing ingredients and pour over salad. Toss well and serve immediately.

GREEN AND WHITE VEGGIE SALAD

- 1 cup salad dressing
- ½ cup sour cream
- 1 tablespoon vinegar
- 1 tablespoon granulated sugar
- 1 small onion
- ⅛ teaspoon Worcestershire sauce
  Dash hot sauce
  Salt and pepper to taste
- 1 head cauliflower, pulled into florets
- 1 bunch broccoli, washed and cut up

Place the onion in food processor and process until finely chopped. Add remaining ingredients, except veggies, and process until well-blended. Pour over the broccoli and cauliflower.

FROZEN SEAFOOD SALAD MOLD
Serves 4–6

- 2 teaspoons unflavored gelatin
- ⅓ cup cold water
- 2 cups flaked cooked seafood (crab, shrimp *or* lobster)
- ⅔ cup tomato ketchup
- 2 tablespoons lemon juice
- 3 tablespoons vinegar
- 1 teaspoon prepared horseradish
- ¼ teaspoon salt
- ½ cup mayonnaise
  Tomatoes *or* lettuce

Soften gelatin in cold water and dissolve over hot water. Combine with seafood, ketchup, lemon juice, vinegar, horseradish and salt. Fold in mayonnaise. Freeze in refrigerator tray until firm, about 2 hours. Cut into cubes and arrange on slices of tomatoes or lettuce.

Note: Serve Frozen Seafood Salad in hollowed-out tomatoes or in cucumber boats ... or serve as a loaf on watercress with border of overlapping cucumber and tomato slices.

THANKSGIVING MINCEMEAT MOLD
Serves 10–12

- 2 large packages cherry gelatin
- 3½ cups hot water
- ½ cup walnuts, finely chopped
- 2 cups moist mincemeat

Dissolve cherry gelatin in hot water. Pour ¾ cup mixture into 1½-quart mold; chill until firm. Chill remaining gelatin until slightly thickened; fold in nuts and mincemeat. Turn into mold over firm gelatin; chill again until firm; unmold. Garnish with sweetened whipped cream, maraschino cherry halves and mint leaves.

THREE-FRUIT MOLDED SALAD

2 envelopes unflavored gelatin
½ cup grapefruit juice
½ cup sugar syrup*
¼ cup orange juice
1 teaspoon lemon juice
2 cups ginger ale
Pinch of salt
½ cup cherries, drained
1 cup grapefruit sections
1 cup orange sections
Lettuce

In top of double boiler over medium heat, combine gelatin with the grapefruit juice and stir to dissolve the gelatin. Remove from heat. Add sugar syrup, orange and lemon juices, ginger ale and salt. Stir well. Chill until slightly thickened. Add cherries, grapefruit and orange sections. Pour and spoon into a lightly oiled 6-cup mold or 6 individual (1-cup) molds. Chill until firm, about 1–2 hours. Unmold and serve on a bed of lettuce. Top each serving with a dollop of mayonnaise.
*To make sugar syrup, combine ½ cup sugar and ½ cup boiling water.

BROCCOLI SALAD

1 large bunch broccoli, finely cut (may use frozen)
2 cups grated mozzarella cheese
½ pound bacon, fried and crumbled
1 small red onion, finely cut

Mix together and add dressing (recipe follows).

Dressing:
1 cup mayonnaise
2 tablespoons vinegar
¼ cup sugar

Refrigerate several hours.

CUCUMBERS WITH YOGURT
Serves 8

2 medium cucumbers, peeled, seeded and diced
Salt
1 garlic clove, mashed *or* minced
2 cups yogurt
2 tablespoons fresh lemon juice
1 teaspoon chopped dill
2 tablespoons olive oil
1 tablespoon chopped fresh mint *or* 1 teaspoon dried mint

Sprinkle cucumbers with salt; let stand 15 minutes and pour off liquid. Mash garlic in bowl with lemon juice; add yogurt, dill and cucumbers; mix well and chill. When serving, sprinkle with oil and mint.

SPINACH SOUFFLÉ SALAD

1 (10-ounce) package frozen, chopped spinach
1 envelope unflavored gelatin
½ cup sugar
¾ teaspoon salt
1 cup cold water
¼ cup lemon juice
⅓ cup mayonnaise *or* salad dressing
1 cup cream-style cottage cheese, drained
¼ cup celery, finely chopped

Cook spinach according to package directions. Press against sides of a sieve to drain very thoroughly. Cool. In small saucepan soften gelatin in ½ cup cold water. Heat and stir until gelatin dissolves. Add sugar, salt, remaining water and lemon juice. Mix well. Place mayonnaise in a small bowl. Gradually stir in gelatin mixture. Chill until mixture begins to set. Beat gelatin mixture until fluffy. Fold in spinach, cottage cheese and celery. Turn into a 5-cup mold. Chill 4 hours or overnight.

LEMON-LIME VEGETABLE SALAD
Serves 5–6

2 medium carrots, grated
1 stalk celery, thinly sliced
1 medium green pepper, seeded and finely chopped
½ small onion, finely chopped
2 tablespoons lemon juice
Dash paprika
1 tablespoon water
1 envelope gelatin
1½ cups lemon-lime–flavor soda

Prepare vegetables and set aside. In small saucepan, mix lemon juice, paprika and water; heat almost to boiling point. Remove from heat and add gelatin, stirring until thoroughly dissolved. Add soda and stir until well-mixed. Add vegetables and pour into small, rectangular dish. Chill for several hours or overnight until set. Cut into squares and serve. Top with a dollop of mayonnaise, if desired.

CHRISTMAS TREE SALAD

1½ cups canned fruit cocktail
1 package lime gelatin
2 tablespoons lemon juice
Whipped cream

Drain fruit cocktail, reserving syrup. Add enough hot water to syrup to make 2 cups liquid. Dissolve gelatin in hot liquid; stir in lemon juice. Cool until slightly thickened; fold in 1 cup fruit cocktail. Set cone-shaped paper cups lined with waxed paper into small glasses. Fill with thickened gelatin mixture. Chill until firm. Unmold onto individual dessert plates, gently pulling off paper. Trim trees with whipped cream festoons piped on with cake decorating tube; decorate base of tree with remaining fruit cocktail.

This is bound to get raves and compliments from your guests!

LETTUCE STUFFED SALAD

1 medium head iceberg lettuce, washed and well-drained
1 (1¼-ounce) package blue cheese
2 (3-ounce) packages cream cheese
2 tablespoons mayonnaise
2 tablespoons minced green onion
6 sliced pimiento-stuffed olives
2 teaspoons sweet relish
Salt and pepper to taste
½ teaspoon Worcestershire sauce
Dash hot pepper sauce
2 slices crisp-fried bacon, well-drained
Sliced apples for bed

Hollow out the heart of lettuce, leaving a 1½-inch shell. Beat cheeses and mayonnaise together until smooth. Add remaining ingredients and mix well. Fill lettuce shell; wrap well in a clean towel and chill 1–2 hours, or until cheese is firm. Cut into crosswise slices ¾-inch thick. To serve, layer a platter with sliced apples. Set the sliced lettuce over apples and serve.

RUBY RASPBERRY MOLD
Serves 4

1 (3-ounce) package raspberry gelatin
1 cup white grape juice
1 cup whole raspberries

Dissolve gelatin in 1 cup hot water; cool. Add white grape juice; chill until syrupy. Fold in raspberries and turn into mold. Chill until firm; unmold. Serve plain or with whipped cream.

BROCCOLI-RAISIN SALAD

3 heads broccoli, cut in small pieces
½ cup chopped onion
4 slices bacon, cooked and crumbled
¾ cup raisins

Toss ingredients together.

Dressing:
1 cup mayonnaise
2 tablespoons sugar
2 tablespoons white vinegar

Dressing should be tangy in flavor. Pour over salad. Again, toss lightly.

CUCUMBER DELIGHT

1 (3-ounce) package lime gelatin
¾ cup boiling water
1 package unflavored gelatin
¼ cup cold water
1 cup salad dressing
1 tablespoon finely minced onion
1 cup cottage cheese
1 cucumber, peeled and chopped
⅛ to ¼ teaspoon Tabasco sauce
1 clove garlic, minced
½ cup slivered almonds
Green food coloring

Dissolve lime gelatin in boiling water, then unflavored gelatin in cold water. Put salad dressing, onion, cottage cheese, cucumber, Tabasco sauce, garlic and almonds in blender; blend well. Then add lime and unflavored gelatins; blend again. Add green food coloring for a more vivid color. Mold and chill overnight.

OLIVE WREATH MOLD

1 (20-ounce) can crushed pineapple
1 (3-ounce) package lime gelatin
¼ teaspoon salt
½ cup grated cheddar *or* American cheese
½ cup chopped pimientos, drained
½ cup chopped celery
⅔ cup chopped pecans
1 cup whipping cream
Stuffed green olives

Drain pineapple into saucepan. Reserve pineapple. Heat juice; add gelatin and dissolve thoroughly. Let cool in refrigerator until it starts to thicken. Stir in salt. Add cheese, pimientos, celery, pecans and reserved pineapple. Whip cream and fold into gelatin mixture. Line bottom of a 4-cup mold with sliced green olives. Carefully spoon mixture into mold. Chill until firm. Unmold and serve.

BEST PEA SALAD

1 (14-ounce) can small-kernel white corn
1 can small-size peas
1 can French green beans
1 cup diced celery
1/4 cup fresh onion
1 green pepper, chopped
Sliced olives as desired for taste

Dressing:
1 cup sugar
3/4 cup white vinegar
1/2 cup oil
1/2 teaspoon salt
1/4 teaspoon pepper

Boil together dressing ingredients for about 3 minutes—then cool.

Put vegetables in bowl. Pour dressing over vegetables and marinate in refrigerator for about 24 hours before serving.

HOLIDAY DELIGHT
Serves 10–12

2 large packages lime gelatin
½ pint whipping cream, whipped
1 small can crushed pineapple, drained
1 small jar maraschino cherries, drained and sliced
1 cup miniature marshmallows

Prepare gelatin in large bowl according to package directions. Place gelatin bowl on ice. Beat with rotary beater until fluffy and firm. Fold in whipped cream. Combine pineapple, cherries and marshmallows with gelatin. Pour into lightly greased mold. Refrigerate overnight.

CELEBRATION SALAD
Makes 16 squares

1 large package raspberry gelatin
1 cup boiling water
1 (20-ounce) can pineapple, undrained
1 pint raspberry sherbet
2 cups vanilla ice cream, softened

Prepare gelatin in boiling water. Allow to cool before adding pineapple and sherbet. Fold in ice cream. Place in an 8 x 8-inch glass cake dish. Allow to set.

SANTA FE SALAD
Serves 4–6

1 head iceberg lettuce
2 cups cooked pinto beans
¼ pound grated longhorn cheese

2 tablespoons chopped green chili
6½ ounces tortilla chips, crushed
4 ounces prepared herb oil and vinegar salad dressing
1 avocado, sliced
2 tomatoes, cut in wedges
Ripe pitted olives

Tear crisp lettuce into bite-size pieces. Toss with beans, grated cheese, green chili and tortilla chips. Toss salad lightly with dressing. Garnish with avocado slices, tomato wedges and ripe olives. Serve chilled.

CONGEALED FRUIT SALAD

2 (3-ounce) packages strawberry gelatin
2 cups boiling water
1 (10-ounce) package frozen strawberries, thawed
2 ripe bananas
1 (8-ounce) can crushed pineapple, not drained
1 cup sour cream

Mix strawberry gelatin with boiling water; add strawberries, mashed bananas and pineapple. Chill until set. Top with sour cream.

SWEET AND SOUR PINEAPPLE COLESLAW

1 (1 pound, 4½-ounce) can crushed pineapple, drained
3 cups crisp cabbage, shredded
½ cup celery, chopped
¼ cup green pepper, chopped
1 cup miniature marshmallows
½ cup heavy cream
4 tablespoons wine vinegar
¼ teaspoon salt
⅛ teaspoon pepper

Combine first 5 ingredients. Beat cream until stiff; fold in vinegar, salt and pepper. Continue beating until well-blended; mix with salad; chill.

QUICK MACARONI SALAD
Serves 10

1 box macaroni and cheese dinner
1 can tuna, drained
4 eggs, hard cooked
5 tablespoons mayonnaise
1/4 cup chopped pickles

Cook macaroni and cheese dinner as directed on package. Then add and mix all additional ingredients; refrigerate.

FRUIT WALDORF
Serves 4

2 cups diced apples (small)
1 cup diced pineapple
2 tablespoons (or less) honey
½ cup chopped walnuts
½ cup coconut

Combine and mix all ingredients together well. Chill thoroughly before serving on a bed of lettuce.

CELERY AND ORANGE SALAD
Serves 6

3 medium oranges
2 ribs celery
2 shallots, chopped
4 tablespoons oil
1 tablespoon lemon juice
Salt and pepper
Chopped parsley

Peel oranges, cutting just beneath the pith. Hold the fruit in one hand and cut out each segment, freeing it from its protective membranes as you cut. Cut the celery into 1½-inch julienne strips. Put the shallots, oranges and celery into a bowl; add the remaining ingredients and toss. Allow salad to rest for 1–6 hours before serving.

PEACH GELATIN SALAD

1 (8-ounce) container whipped topping
1 (6-ounce) box peach gelatin *or* any flavor gelatin
2 (7-ounce) cans *or* 1 (15-ounce) can crushed pineapple
2 cups buttermilk

Heat pineapple with juice; add gelatin and stir thoroughly; let cool. In large bowl beat (whisk) whipped topping and buttermilk. Add cooled gelatin mixture. Pour into mold and allow to congeal, or set.

RED AND GREEN HOLIDAY SALAD
Serves 4

2 cups torn lettuce leaves, rinsed and patted dry
2 cups fresh broccoli florets
½ pint cherry tomatoes
⅓ cup olive oil
2 tablespoons lemon juice
¼ teaspoon mustard
¼ teaspoon salt
Pinch of pepper
½ cup croutons, seasoned with herbs and cheese

Line salad bowl with lettuce. Arrange broccoli and tomatoes on top. Combine oil, lemon juice, mustard, salt and pepper in a small bowl. Mix well; pour over salad. Sprinkle with croutons.

CRANBERRY-PLUS RELISH
Makes 7½ cups

4 cups (1 pound) fresh *or* frozen cranberries

4 oranges, peeled, sectioned and seeded
2 cups sugar (add less for tart taste)
1 apple, unpeeled and cut up
½ teaspoon almond flavoring
1 (8½-ounce) can crushed pineapple, undrained

Chop cranberries in a food processor, then add oranges and chop. Add remaining ingredients; pulse for several seconds to blend. Chill several hours before serving.

FRUIT AND COTTAGE CHEESE MOLD
Serves 4

2 teaspoons unflavored gelatin
3 tablespoons canned pineapple juice
2½ cups cottage cheese
Lettuce *or* other greens
Sliced pineapple
Strawberries
French dressing

Soften gelatin in pineapple juice and dissolve over hot water. Stir into cottage cheese. Pour into 1 large or 6 individual oiled molds and chill until firm. Unmold on lettuce or other greens and garnish with sliced pineapple and halved strawberries. Serve with French dressing.

LOW-CALORIE PINEAPPLE SALAD
Serves 8

2 (8-ounce) packages lemon gelatin
2 cups boiling water
1 (1-pound) can grapefruit sections, drained
1 (8-ounce) can crushed pineapple, drained
2 cups (1 pint) plain low-fat yogurt

In bowl, combine the gelatin and boiling water. Stir until dissolved. Add drained fruits; mix until blended. Chill until mixture is syrupy. Add the yogurt and mix well. Turn into a 1½-quart mold and chill until firm.

24-HOUR SALAD

1 can Eagle Brand sweetened condensed milk (not evaporated)
1 cup large grapes, seeded and halved
1 cup nuts, coarsely broken
1 (8-ounce) can crushed pineapple, including juice
½ pound small marshmallows
1 package Dream Whip (whipped) *or* equal amount of Cool Whip
¼ cup vinegar
1 teaspoon prepared mustard

Mix milk, vinegar and mustard together, then add all other ingredients. Make the day before, if needed.

BROCCOLI AND MUSHROOMS ELEGANT SALAD

2 bunches (stalks) fresh broccoli
1 pound fresh mushrooms
1 bottle Zesty Italian dressing

Cut broccoli into flowerets. Add thickly sliced mushrooms. Pour Italian dressing over broccoli and mushrooms. Add tight-fitting cover. Refrigerate several hours or overnight, turning occasionally. This is very good and is really elegant-looking when served in a pretty dish. Perfect for potluck dinners and church suppers.

SALAD BY CANDLELIGHT
Serves 2

2 lettuce leaves
1 banana, cut in half crosswise
2 pineapple rings
1 cherry *or* red grape, cut in half

On two small plates, place lettuce leaves. Place pineapple in center of leaf. Stand ½ banana in hole of each pineapple ring. Attach cherry half on top of each banana to represent a flame. Now doesn't that look like a candle?

CHINESE COLD PLATE
Serves 6

4 cups shredded lettuce
⅔ cup cooked rice, chilled
1 cup frozen peas, thawed
¾ cup lean pork, cooked and diced
½ cup water chestnuts, sliced
¼ cup Miracle Whip salad dressing
¼ cup sour cream
½ teaspoon celery seed
Salt to taste

Toss first 5 ingredients together. Combine next 4 ingredients for dressing. Pour over vegetable-meat mixture and toss.

Chill until served. Garnish with pineapple slices and fresh strawberries.

CAULIFLOWER PEA SALAD

2 heads cauliflower, finely chopped

---

1 (10-ounce) package frozen peas
¼ cup green onions, chopped
1 cup cheddar cheese, cubed
8 slices bacon, fried crisp and cut up
Pepper to taste
2 cups mayonnaise (regular *or* light)
½ teaspoon seasoned salt
¼ teaspoon garlic salt

Combine all ingredients. Refrigerate for 3 hours, or overnight before serving.

RASPBERRY-WINE MOLD
Serves 4–6

1 (16-ounce) can raspberries
½ cup red wine
Water
2 (3-ounce) packages raspberry-flavored gelatin

Drain raspberries into 2-cup measure; add ½ cup red wine and water to make 2 cups. Prepare raspberry gelatin, using berry-wine-water mixture. Pour into individual molds. Add raspberries to molds when gelatin has cooled. When firm, invert onto serving plates.

FAMOUS FRUIT-SALAD DRESSING
Makes 2 cups

1 cup sweet cream
½ cup brown sugar
¼ cup vinegar
½ cup granulated sugar
Salt to taste

Beat cream until slightly thickened; add remaining ingredients and mix well. Refrigerate overnight to thicken. Delicious on spinach salad, too!

BAKED MACARONI SALAD
Serves 4

2 pounds macaroni salad
½ pound baked *or* boiled ham, diced
¼ pound sliced cheddar cheese, cut up
1 tablespoon melted margarine
¼ cup seasoned bread crumbs

Preheat oven to 350 degrees. In greased 1¼-quart casserole, combine macaroni salad, ham and cheese. In cup combine melted margarine and bread crumbs. Sprinkle over top of macaroni salad. Bake for 20–25 minutes.

FABULOUS ROQUEFORT DRESSING
Makes 1 quart

1 (3-ounce) package Roquefort cheese
2 cups mayonnaise
3 teaspoons chives *or* green onion, finely chopped
1 teaspoon black pepper
1 teaspoon garlic powder
½ teaspoon Worcestershire sauce
1 cup sour cream
½ cup buttermilk

Blend all ingredients, mixing in sour cream and buttermilk last. Chill. If dressing is too thick, thin with additional buttermilk at serving time. We use this recipe as a dip with corn chips and potato chips, as well as salad dressing.

SEAFOOD SALAD
Serves 6-8

1/2 small cabbage (about 1 pound) washed and pulled apart
1 small onion, peeled and sliced
4 tablespoons sweet pickles, finely chopped
1 cup mayonnaise
3 tablespoons sugar
12 fish sticks
12 popcorn shrimp

Combine cabbage, onion, and pickles, and chop until fine, using a hand chopper. Mix mayonnaise and sugar, and add to cabbage salad. Fry fish sticks and shrimp until golden brown; drain on paper towels. Cut six fish sticks and six shrimp into chunks. Mix into cabbage salad. Place in serving bowl. Place remaining fish sticks and shrimp on top

SHRIMPLY GREAT MOLD
Serves 8

1-1/2 tablespoons unflavored gelatin
1/4 cup cold water
1 (10-ounce) can tomato soup
1 (8-ounce) package cream cheese, softened
20 salad shrimp, cooked, peeled and coarsely chopped
1 cup mayonnaise
1 small onion, grated
3/4 cup celery, diced finely
1 tablespoon prepared horseradish

Dissolve gelatin in cold water; set aside. In a saucepan, heat soup; add gelatin mixture; stir until dissolved. Add cream cheese; remove from heat; beat until well blended. Add remaining ingredients. Pour into a well-oiled 1-quart mold; chill until firm. Serve portion on a crisp lettuce leaf; garnish with a lemon twist.

SKILLET HAM SALAD
Serves 4

1/4 cup chopped green onions
1/4 cup chopped green pepper
2 cups diced cooked ham
1 tablespoon fat
3 cups potatoes, cooked and diced
1/4 teaspoon salt
Dash pepper
1/4 cup mayonnaise
1/2 pound sharp, processed American cheese, diced (1-1/2 cups)

Cook onions, green pepper, and meat in hot fat, stirring occasionally until meat is lightly browned. Add potatoes, salt, pepper, and mayonnaise. Heat, mixing lightly. Stir in cheese; heat just until it begins to melt. Garnish with green onions, if desired.

SUPER SUPPER SALAD
Makes 6-1/2 cups

1 (8-ounce) package chicken-flavored rice mix
2 (5-ounce) cans Swanson Mixin' Chicken
1-1/2 cups (about 2 medium) diced tomatoes
1/2 cup chopped fresh parsley
1/2 cup chopped green onion
2 tablespoons vinegar
3/4 cup undiluted evaporated milk
1/2 cup mayonnaise
1/2 teaspoon Italian seasoning

Cook rice mix according to package directions. Cool. Mix rice with chicken, tomatoes, parsley, and onion. Stir vinegar into evaporated milk until milk thickens. Add mayonnaise and Italian seasoning. Stir into rice mixture. Chill thoroughly.

CRANBERRY TURKEY SALAD
Serves 4-6

1 can whole cranberry sauce
2 cups cooked diced turkey
1 cup finely diced celery
1/2 cup chopped walnuts
1/4 cup mayonnaise
2 tablespoons lemon juice
Lettuce leaves

Combine all ingredients except lettuce leaves and mix well. Arrange salad on lettuce leaf. Garnish with additional reserved walnut pieces, if desired.

CHUNKY CHICKEN SALAD

1 cup raw carrot, shredded
1/2 cup Miracle Whip, thinned slightly with cream
1 cup chicken, cooked and diced
1/4 cup minced onion
1 cup diced celery
1 tablespoon pickle relish
1 small can shoestring potatoes or 2 cups sesame sticks

Combine vegetables with dressing and relish. Add chicken and potato sticks or sesame sticks just before serving.

POPCORN SALAD
Serves 6-8

6 cups popped popcorn
1/2 cup green onion, sliced
1 cup celery, diced
3/4 - 1 cup mayonnaise
3/4 cup chopped cooked bacon (reserve some for top)
1 cup grated cheese (reserve some for top)
1/2 cup sliced water chestnuts

In bowl, combine popcorn, sliced onion, diced celery, mayonnaise, bacon, cheese, and water chestnuts. Chill. Top with reserved bacon and grated cheese. Best when used within 3-4 hours.

EASTER CROWN SALAD

3 (3-ounce) packages cream cheese
1/2 teaspoon salt
2 cups grated cucumber, drained
1 cup mayonnaise
1/4 cup minced onion
1/4 cup minced parsley
1 clove garlic
1 tablespoon unflavored gelatin
1/4 cup cold water
1 head lettuce
2 hard-cooked egg yolks, sieved

Mix first 6 ingredients in a bowl that has been rubbed with garlic. Soften gelatin in cold water and dissolve over hot water. Cool to lukewarm and combine with cheese mixture. Beat thoroughly and pack into a deep spring-form pan. Chill until mixture is firm. Remove from mold onto a bed of lettuce and sprinkle sieved egg yolks over top. Garnish with radish roses, if desired.

BEAN AND TOMATO SALAD

1 (15-1/2 ounce) can garbanzo beans
3 tablespoons vegetable oil
1 tablespoon wine vinegar
Salt and pepper
1 pound tomatoes, peeled and sliced
1 medium-size onion, sliced into thin rings
2 teaspoons fresh chopped basil or 1 teaspoon dried basil

Drain beans; rinse under cold water. Beat oil and vinegar together; season with salt and pepper. Add the beans and mix until well coated, being careful not to break up the beans. Arrange tomato and onion slices in a shallow dish; sprinkle with basil, salt, and pepper. Spoon beans on top. Serve chilled.

ZESTY MEXICAN BEAN SALAD

2 medium limes
1/2 of a 12-ounce jar chunky salsa (about 3/4 cup)
1/3 cup salad oil
1-1/2 teaspoons chili powder
1 teaspoon salt
1 (16-ounce) can black beans, drained
1 (15 to 19-ounce) can red kidney beans, drained
1 (15 to 19-ounce) can garbanzo beans, drained
2 celery stalks, thinly sliced
1 onion, sliced
1 medium tomato, diced

Squeeze lime juice into bowl; stir in salsa, oil, chili powder, and salt. Add beans, celery, onion and tomato. Toss to mix well. Serve at room temperature or cover and refrigerate, to serve chilled later. Many ingredients may be purchased in the Ethnic Department of your food store.

CARROT SALAD
Serves 6

1 pound carrots
1 bunch chives, chopped
1 cup mayonnaise (homemade or commercial variety)
2 tablespoons vinegar
Salt and pepper

Peel and finely grate carrots. Combine chives, mayonnaise, and vinegar; season with salt and pepper; blend with a whisk. Pour over carrots and let stand 15 minutes. Serve.

RAISIN-CARROT SALAD
Serves 8

1 cup seedless raisins
1-1/2 cups shredded carrots
1/2 cup celery, finely chopped
1/2 cup chopped walnuts
Pinch of salt
Dash cayenne
4 tablespoons mayonnaise

Rinse raisins in hot water; drain; cool and combine with remaining ingredients. Chill and serve on crisp lettuce.

CARROT-RAISIN SALAD

1/2 cup shredded carrots
1/2 cup seedless (or seeded) raisins
4 tablespoons lemon juice
1/4 cup mayonnaise
6-12 lettuce leaves or 1-1/2 cups shredded cabbage

Shred carrots. Soak raisins in lemon juice. Combine ingredients; mix with dressing. Serve in lettuce cups.

PICNIC SALAD BOWL
Serves 6

1 (No. 2) can asparagus tips
Mustard French Dressing (recipe follows)
3 hard-cooked eggs
1/3 cup deviled ham
Hearts of lettuce
2 strips pimiento
6 wedges Swiss cheese

Marinate asparagus in dressing; chill. Cut eggs lengthwise and remove yolks. Stuff with deviled ham and mashed egg yolks which have been moistened with dressing. Toss lettuce hearts in salad bowl with dressing. Arrange asparagus tips in center (held together with pimiento strips); surround with cheese; border with stuffed egg halves. May substitute cooked green beans for asparagus tips.

Mustard French Dressing:

1 cup olive or salad oil
1/4 cup vinegar
1/2 teaspoon salt
Few grains cayenne
1/4 teaspoon white pepper
2 tablespoons chopped parsley
2 teaspoons prepared mustard

Combine; beat or shake thoroughly before using. Makes 1-1/4 cups dressing.

SPINACH-ORANGE TOSS
Serves 6

1 small onion, thinly sliced
Boiling water
6 cups (8 ounces) fresh spinach, torn
1 (11-ounce) can mandarin oranges, drained
1 cup fresh mushrooms, sliced
3 tablespoons salad oil
1 tablespoon lemon juice
1/4 teaspoon salt
Dash pepper
3/4 cup almonds, slivered

Place onions in bowl and cover with boiling water; allow to stand 10 minutes; drain, and dry on paper towels. Place spinach, which has been torn into pieces, in large salad bowl. Add onions, mandarin orange slices, and mushrooms. Toss lightly with hands; cover with plastic wrap and chill thoroughly.

For dressing, place salad oil, lemon juice, salt and pepper in a screw-top jar and shake well. Chill. Before serving, shake again and pour over spinach-orange mixture. Toss lightly until ingredients are coated. Sprinkle almonds over top and serve immediately. This is a very good side dish with Chinese food.

SPINACH SALAD
Serves 6

1/2 pound spinach
1/2 head iceberg lettuce
1 small red onion, thinly sliced and separated into rings
1 slivered hard-cooked egg white (yolk saved for vinaigrette)
Vinaigrette (recipe follows)

Tear spinach and lettuce into bite-size pieces and layer with onion and slivered hard-cooked egg white in a salad bowl. Add vinaigrette and toss well.

Vinaigrette:

In a small bowl mash saved hard-cooked egg yolk; add 1 teaspoon salt, 1/4 teaspoon pepper, 1/4 teaspoon paprika, 1/4 teaspoon dry mustard, 1/4 cup red wine vinegar,

1/2 cup vegetable oil, and 2 tablespoons finely chopped parsley; whisk well.

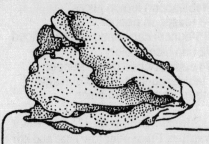

GREEN VEGETABLE SALAD

1 small can English peas, drained
1 can French style green beans, drained
1 can shoe peg corn, drained
1 cup chopped celery
1 cup chopped green pepper
1 cup chopped onion
1 small jar pimientos, chopped

Mix together 1/2 teaspoon salt, 1/2 cup vinegar, 1/2 cup salad oil and 1/3 cup sugar; stir until dissolved. Pour over vegetables; mix well and chill 4-5 hours before serving. Will keep for several days in refrigerator.

FRESH VEGETABLE SALAD

1 bunch broccoli, broken into flowerettes
1 head cauliflower, broken or sliced
1 bunch celery, sliced
1 box mushrooms, sliced
1 box cherry tomatoes, halved
1 can ripe olives, pitted and drained
1 bag radishes, sliced
3 or 4 carrots, sliced

Toss with one large bottle Italian dressing mixed with one package dry Italian dressing mix. Can prepare several hours ahead of time before serving.

GREEN VEGETABLE SALAD

1 can English peas, drained
1 can French-style green beans, drained
1 can shoe peg corn, drained
1 cup diced celery
1 cup diced green peppers
1 cup chopped green onions or regular onions
1 small can pimientos, diced

Mix together:
1/2 teaspoon salt
1/2 cup sugar
1/2 cup vinegar
1/2 cup salad oil

Stir until sugar is dissolved. Pour over vegetables. Chill overnight. Will keep for several days.

MUSHROOM SALAD
Serves 4

1 tablespoon butter
1/2 pound mushrooms, cleaned and stems trimmed
3 ounces champagne
1 teaspoon clear Karo syrup
2 tablespoons catsup
2 tablespoons raisins
1 teaspoon pine nuts (pignoli)
Coarsely shredded lettuce

Soak raisins in 1 tablespoon of champagne for 5 minutes. Drain well and set aside. Melt butter in a saucepan. Add mushrooms, and gently sauté for 2 minutes over medium heat, stirring constantly. Add the Karo syrup; mix well a few seconds. To this add champagne, catsup, pignoli, and raisins. Simmer only 1 minute. Pour mixture into a bowl and chill thoroughly. When ready to serve, be sure to serve on a bed of shredded lettuce.

CHERRY FROZEN SALAD
Makes 32-34 small cups

1 (16-ounce) can cherry pie filling
1 large can crushed pineapple, drained
1 can sweetened condensed milk
1 large carton Cool Whip
2 cups miniature marshmallows
1 cup chopped pecans

Mix all together in order given. Spoon into paper cups. Freeze.

This is delicious and can also be used as a dessert.

SPRINGTIME SALAD
Serves 6

1 (1-pound) can grapefruit sections
4 green onions, thinly sliced
1/2 cup sliced radishes
1/2 cup cucumber, sliced or greens of your choice

Drain grapefruit. Wash and dry greens (of your choice) and tear into bite-size pieces. Add grapefruit sections, onions, radishes, and cucumber. Toss and serve with a Roquefort dressing, before serving.

MOUNTAIN DEW SALAD

1 large package lemon gelatin
1-2/3 cups boiling water
1 cup small marshmallows
1 cup Mountain Dew soda
1 (#303 can) crushed pineapple, drain
1 can lemon pudding or pie filling
1 medium container Cool Whip

Mix gelatin in boiling water with marshmallows until dissolved. Add Mountain Dew and drained pineapple. Chill until set. Mix pudding and Cool Whip. Spread on top of gelatin which has set.

SILHOUETTE SALAD
Serves 4

1 envelope Knox unflavored gelatin
1 cup water, divided
1 (10-1/2 ounce) can condensed cream of chicken soup
1 tablespoon lemon juice
1/8 teaspoon pepper
1 (5-ounce) can boned chicken, diced
1/2 cup diced celery
1/4 cup chopped green pepper
2 tablespoons chopped pimiento
2 teaspoons grated onion

Sprinkle gelatin on 1/2 cup water to soften. Place over low heat and stir until gelatin is dissolved. Remove from heat; stir in soup until well-blended. Add other 1/2 cup water, lemon juice, and pepper. Chill until the consistency of unbeaten egg white. Fold in chicken, onion, green pepper, and pimiento. Turn into a 3-cup mold and chill until firm.

MOUNTAIN DEW SALAD

1 (6-ounce) package lemon gelatin
1 cup boiling water
1 can cold Mountain Dew beverage
1 (15-ounce) can pineapple chunks or tidbits, drained and juice reserved
1 package lemon pudding (cooked type)
1 cup whipping cream (whipped) or Cool Whip
1 cup colored mini marshmallows

Dissolve gelatin in boiling water; add Mountain Dew and juice drained from pineapple; chill until it begins to thicken. Cook pudding according to package instructions; cool.

Mix gelatin, lemon pudding, and whipped cream, beating together. Add drained pineapple and marshmallows. Pour into a large bowl and chill.

COTTAGE CHEESE DELIGHT

1 quart cottage cheese
1 can crushed pineapple, drained
1 (6-ounce) box orange gelatin
1 small package miniature marshmallows
1 large container Cool Whip

Mix cottage cheese, pineapple, and gelatin powder together. Blend in marshmallows and Cool Whip; chill before serving.

SHAMROCK SALAD

First Layer:
1 (3-ounce) package lime gelatin
1 small can undrained crushed pineapple

Dissolve gelatin in one cup hot water, then cool. Add pineapple. Pour mixture into large mold and chill until set.

Second Layer:
1 (3-ounce) package lemon gelatin
2 (3-ounce) packages cream cheese
10 marshmallows
2 cups whipping cream

Dissolve lemon gelatin in one cup hot water. Mix one package cream cheese with one cup whipping cream. Pour mixture on top of set lime gelatin. Chill until set. Mix remaining cream cheese with one cup whipped cream and the marshmallows cut into small pieces. Turn out mold on lettuce green and top with this mixture. You may decide to serve this creation as a dessert.—Whip 1/2 cup cream; add drained maraschino cherries and drained pineapple slices, arranged, to form an attractive circle on top.

St. Patrick's Day is a special one, not only because it is the beginning of spring, but because of the teasing, elfish nature of this man who makes "everything come up green" on this day. Special foods are your way of contributing to a genial atmosphere for both children and adults. On this day, we are all the same age—Happy St. Patrick's Day!

FRUIT COCKTAIL SALAD

1 (5-5/8 ounce) package vanilla flavored Jello instant pudding mix
1-1/3 cups buttermilk
1 (8-ounce) container Cool Whip
1 (30-ounce) can fruit cocktail, well-drained
2 cans mandarin oranges, well-drained
1 cup miniature rainbow-colored marshmallows (optional)

Blend buttermilk into pudding mix using medium speed of mixer. When smooth, blend in Cool Whip. If consistency of mixture seems too thick, add a little more buttermilk. Fold in fruit cocktail and mandarin oranges, reserving half a can of oranges for garnish. Swirl a design on top of salad with a tablespoon. Gently arrange balance of mandarin orange slices in swirled design on top of salad.

Add colored marshmallows to mixture before garnishing, if desired.

GOLDEN FRUIT SALAD

2 large Golden Delicious apples, diced
2 large Red Delicious apples, diced
4 large bananas, sliced
2 (20 ounce) cans pineapple chunks, drained (reserve juice)
2 (16 ounce) cans Mandarin oranges, drained
Whole green grapes, optional

Mix Together:
1 cup sugar
4 tablespoons corn starch
Reserved pineapple juice
2 tablespoons lemon juice
2/3 cup orange juice

Stir and boil 1 minute. Pour hot mixture over fruit. Leave uncovered until cool.

SHORTCUT FROZEN SALAD

1 small package *instant* lemon pudding
1 pint whipped topping, thawed
1/2 cup mayonnaise
2 tablespoons lemon juice
1 (1-pound) can fruit cocktail, drained
1 cup miniature marshmallows
1/4 cup chopped pecans

Prepare pudding according to package directions; blend in whipped topping, mayonnaise, and lemon juice. Fold in remaining ingredients. Turn into a 9x5x3-inch loaf pan and freeze until firm. Slice to serve.

GUM DROP FRUIT SALAD

Serves 8

1 (#2 can) pineapple tidbits
1/4 cup sugar
2 tablespoons flour
1/4 teaspoon salt
3 tablespoons lemon juice
1-1/2 teaspoons vinegar
2 cups seedless grapes, halved
2 cups miniature white marshmallows
2/3 cup gumdrops, halved (do not use black drops)
1 (4-ounce) bottle maraschino cherries, drained and halved
1/4 cup chopped pecans
1 cup whipping cream, whipped

Drain pineapple, reserving 1/3 cup of syrup. Combine sugar, flour, and salt. Add reserved pineapple syrup, lemon juice, and vinegar. Cook over medium heat, stirring constantly until thick and boiling. Continue cooking 1 minute. Set aside and cool. Combine pineapple and remaining ingredients, except the whipped cream. Fold the cooked dressing into the whipped cream. Cover and refrigerate for 12-24 hours.

BANANA BAVARIAN CREAM

1 (6-ounce) package lemon-flavored gelatin
2 cups hot water
1/4 teaspoon salt
2/3 cup sugar
1/2 cup heavy cream
5 bananas

Dissolve gelatin in hot water. Add salt and sugar. Chill until cold and syrupy. Fold in cream, whipped only until thick and shiny, but not stiff. Crush bananas to pulp with fork, and fold at once into mixture. Chill until slightly thickened. Turn into mold. Chill until firm. Unmold. Serve with Strawberry Sauce. (Recipe below)

Strawberry Sauce:
1/3 cup butter
1 cup powdered sugar
1 egg white
2/3 cup strawberries

Cream butter and sugar, gradually add crushed strawberries and egg whites. Beat well.

BUNNY SALAD

Serves 6-8

1 (3-ounce) package orange gelatin
1 cup boiling water
1 cup pineapple juice and water
1 teaspoon grated orange rind
1-1/3 cups crushed pineapple, drained
1 cup grated raw carrots

Dissolve gelatin in boiling water. Add pineapple juice/water mixture and orange rind. Chill until slightly thickened. Then fold in pineapple and carrots. Pour into 6-8 individual round molds. Chill until firm. Unmold on crisp lettuce. Add carrot strips to form ears, a large marshmallow for the head, and half a marshmallow for the tail. Serve plain or with mayonnaise, if desired.

Soups & STEWS

HOT LEEK SOUP

- 4 thick leeks, washed and trimmed
- 4 medium-size potatoes
- 2 tablespoons butter
- 4 cups stock (chicken *or* veal)
  Yolk of 1 egg
- 2 cups coffee cream
- ⅛ teaspoon nutmeg
  Salt and pepper to taste
- 1 tablespoon chopped chives, for garnish

Slice cleaned leeks, crosswise, and sauté in butter. Thinly slice the potatoes; add to leeks and cook together. (Do not let potatoes fry.) Cover with the stock and cook, covered, until both are soft. Drain and sieve; then combine with hot stock for purée. Beat egg yolk lightly and gradually combine with some of the stock; then add to rest of soup. Check for seasonings. Add nutmeg; pour in the cream and heat, but do not boil. Garnish with chives and serve.

OLD-FASHIONED BEEF STEW

- 2–3 tablespoons shortening
- 2 pounds stewing beef (cut in 1½-inch cubes)
- 1 large onion, sliced
- ½ teaspoon garlic powder
- 4 cups boiling water
- 1 tablespoon salt
- 1 tablespoon lemon juice
- 1 teaspoon sugar
- 1 teaspoon Worcestershire sauce
- ½ teaspoon pepper
- ½ teaspoon paprika
- 1–2 bay leaves
- ¼ teaspoon allspice
  Carrots and potatoes, cut in cubes *or* bite-size pieces

Heat shortening in large pot or Dutch oven. Brown stewing beef for about 20 minutes. Add onion and garlic along with all remaining ingredients, except for carrots and potatoes. Cover and simmer for about 1½–2 hours. Add carrots and potatoes; cook until tender. Thicken with a mixture of flour and water.

Variation: Try adding a small can of sliced mushrooms and desired amount of egg noodles, instead of carrots and potatoes, for terrific beef and noodles. Do not forget to discard the bay leaves before serving.

WASHDAY SOUP
Serves 6–8

- 2 cups dried beans, any kind
- ½ cup dried split peas
- 2 tablespoons rice (not instant)
- 2 tablespoons barley
- 2 quarts cold water
- 2 large ribs celery, sliced
- 2 medium onions, peeled and sliced
- 2 medium potatoes, peeled and cubed
- 1 cup diced turnip
- 2 cups canned tomatoes, undrained
- 1 teaspoon salt
- ¼ teaspoon pepper
- 1 ham bone (with some meat left on it)

Cover beans, peas, rice and barley with cold water and let stand overnight. Bring to a boil, in the same water. Add vegetables, salt and pepper. Simmer about 1 hour. Add ham bone and simmer for another hour. If water cooks away, add a bit more from time to time. Remove ham bone; pick off bits of meat and add to soup.

CHILI WITH YELLOW BEANS

- 1 pound lean ground beef
- ¼ cup chopped onion
- 1 (16-ounce) can tomatoes
- 1 (16-ounce) can cut wax beans, drained
- 1 (10¾-ounce) can condensed tomato soup
- ¼ teaspoon pepper
- 1 teaspoon salt
- 1 teaspoon chili powder

Cook and stir meat and onion in large skillet until meat is brown. Drain off fat and stir in remaining ingredients. Heat to boiling. Reduce heat and cover; simmer meat mixture for 25–30 minutes.

DEER (VENISON) CAMP CHILI

1 pound dried pinto beans
2 teaspoons ground cumin
2 pounds venison, cut into ¼-inch cubes
1½ teaspoons salt
2 cloves of garlic, chopped
4 large onions, chopped
2 tablespoons chili powder
1 (28-ounce) can crushed tomatoes
1 (28-ounce) can peeled tomatoes

Wash beans and place in a pot with salt and water to cover well. Bring to a boil. Remove from heat and soak for about 1 hour. Add more water, if necessary, just to cover the beans; simmer while preparing rest of chili, for about 1 hour. In a large, heavy iron pot, brown the salted venison cubes with 3 or 4 tablespoons of bacon fat or oil. Add garlic, onions and spices. Cook, covered, until onions and garlic are soft. Add both cans of tomatoes and heat until simmering. Then add beans, including bean juice. (Two cans of cooked pinto beans may be substituted.) Bring to a slow boil then lower heat and simmer for 3–4 hours. It is better if served reheated the next day.

Ladle into serving bowls and sprinkle with chopped raw onions or coarsely shredded sharp cheddar cheese. Serve with crusty fresh-baked bread or hot corn bread and butter.

COWBOY STEW
Serves 8

6 slices bacon
1 cup diced onion
1/2 cup chopped green pepper
1 clove garlic, crushed
1-1/2 pounds ground beef
2 (1-pound, 13-ounce) cans tomatoes
1 teaspoon salt

1/4 teaspoon pepper
1 tablespoon chili powder
1 (12-ounce) can whole-kernel corn, drained
1 (1-pound) can red kidney beans, drained
2 cups cubed potatoes, cooked
2 cups sliced carrots, cooked

Cook bacon until crisp; drain on paper towels; crumble and reserve. Sauté onion, green pepper, and garlic in bacon drippings until tender.

Add ground beef; cook until well-browned, breaking up with fork as it cooks. Add tomatoes, salt, pepper, and chili powder. Cover; simmer 30 minutes. Add vegetables; simmer 15 minutes. Sprinkle with bacon.

CREAM OF ASPARAGUS SOUP
Serves 6

4 tablespoons butter, divided
2 tablespoons all-purpose flour
1 bunch (10 ounces) fresh asparagus*
1 small onion, finely chopped
1 quart chicken stock or broth
½ cup heavy cream, warmed
Salt and pepper

Melt 2 tablespoons butter in small saucepan; stir in flour. Cook 3 minutes over low heat, stirring constantly. Cool. Wash and cut asparagus into ½-inch pieces, reserving ¼ cup tips for garnish. Sauté onion in remaining 2 tablespoons butter in large saucepan until tender. Stir in asparagus; cover. Cook for 3 minutes. Stir in stock/broth; heat to simmering. Stir in small amount of asparagus/stock mixture into butter/flour mixture until smooth; return blended mixture to saucepan, stirring until smooth. Simmer, covered, until asparagus is tender, about 20 minutes. Remove from heat; cool slightly. Purée in small amounts in container of electric blender; return to saucepan. Blend cream into soup. Taste; add salt and pepper, if needed. Steam asparagus tips in microwave, or on stove until tender-crisp. Spoon soup into individual bowls; garnish with tips.

*You may substitute about 2 cups of broccoli or cauliflower for asparagus.

BLUE NORTHER' CHILI
Serves 8–10

¼ cup olive oil
1 large onion, chopped
1 tablespoon chopped parsley
2 (8-ounce) cans tomato paste
1 (15-ounce) can tomato sauce
1 (1½-ounce) can chili powder
Dash of pepper
2 cloves garlic, minced
4 stalks of celery with leaves, chopped
2 pounds ground beef, cubed or ground coarsely
5–6 cups water
1¼ teaspoons salt
1 cup cooked red beans (optional)

Heat olive oil in a 5-quart Dutch oven. Add garlic, onion, celery and parsley; sauté just until tender, about 5 minutes. Add ground beef, and brown, stirring occasionally. Drain off pan drippings, reserving 3 tablespoons. Add reserved pan drippings to meat mixture. Stir in tomato paste, tomato sauce, water, chili powder, salt and pepper. Bring to a boil; reduce heat and simmer for 1 hour. Add red beans during last 15 minutes, if desired.

FRESH CORN SOUP
Serves 4–6

12 ears corn
Boiling water
1 quart milk
Salt and pepper
1 tablespoon butter

Cut kernels from 12 large ears of fresh corn and cover them with boiling water. Simmer for 30 minutes, then slowly stir in a quart of milk. Season with salt, pepper and butter.

CHILI CON CARNE IN A HURRY
Makes 3 cups

¼ pound ground beef
½ cup chopped onion
1 medium clove garlic, minced
   Generous dash ground cumin seed
1 (16-ounce) can pork and beans
½ cup tomatoes and green chilies

In saucepan, brown beef and cook onion with garlic and cumin until tender (use shortening if necessary). Stir to separate meat. Add remaining ingredients. Bring to boil; reduce heat. Simmer 10 minutes; stir occasionally.

CHILI
Serves 4–6

2½ pounds beef brisket, cut in 1-inch cubes
1 pound lean ground pork
1 large onion, finely chopped
2 tablespoons oil
   Salt and pepper to taste
2–3 cloves garlic, minced
2 tablespoons diced green chilies
1 (8-ounce) can tomato sauce
1 beef bouillon cube
1 (12-ounce) can beer
1¼ cups water
4–6 tablespoons chili powder
2½ tablespoons ground cumin
⅛ teaspoon dry mustard
⅛ teaspoon brown sugar
   Pinch of oregano

In a large iron kettle or Dutch oven, brown beef, pork and onions in heated oil. Add salt and pepper to taste. Add remaining ingredients. Stir well. Cover and simmer 3–4 hours, until meat is tender and chili is thick and bubbly. Stir occasionally.

GIBLET SPINACH SOUP WITH DUMPLINGS
Serves 4–6

   Giblets from 4 chickens
1 (10-ounce) package spinach
1 medium onion, chopped
4 garlic cloves, minced
2 bay leaves, crumbled
4 cups water
   Salt and pepper to taste
2 eggs
1 (2½-ounce) envelope matzo ball mix

Clean giblets; put in heavy soup pot with onion, garlic, bay leaves, and water, salt and pepper. Bring to a boil.

Reduce heat and simmer covered. May be cooked earlier in day or frozen for later.

Make matzo balls according to package directions.

Clean spinach and break leaves into smaller pieces. Add to pot. Cook for 5 minutes, or until giblets are tender.

Put matzo balls in pot and cook according to package directions.

Note: Precooked rice and additional water may be added to feed more.

HOME-STYLE STEW
Serves 4

1 pound white turkey meat, cut in cubes
1 (8-ounce) can peas with liquid
1 cup sliced carrots
1 chopped onion
½ cup chopped celery
1 can cream of chicken soup
   Salt and pepper to taste
1 raw potato, peeled and sliced
¼ teaspoon sage
1 (12-ounce) jar brown gravy

Place raw turkey meat in greased 2-quart casserole. Combine all other ingredients and pour over meat. Cover and bake for 5–6 hours at 275 degrees.

CHEF TOM'S PEANUT VEGETABLE SOUP
Serves 8–10

¼ cup butter
½ cup julienne carrots
½ cup julienne zucchini
½ cup julienne red *or* green pepper
½ cup shredded red cabbage
½ cup chopped onion
3 tablespoons flour
5 cups chicken broth
1 cup creamy peanut butter
1 cup light cream
   Salt and pepper to taste

In a large saucepan or Dutch oven melt butter. Add carrots, zucchini, red pepper, cabbage and onion; sauté 3 minutes. Add flour and stir until smooth. Gradually stir in chicken broth; bring to a boil. Stir in peanut butter; reduce heat and simmer 15 minutes.

Remove from heat. Stir in cream, salt and pepper. Garnish with chopped peanuts.

CARROT SOUP
Makes 11 cups

1/4 cup butter or margarine
1 large onion, chopped (about 1 cup)
4 large carrots, chopped (about 4 cups)
1 tablespoon sugar
4 cups liquid and braising vegetables from ham
2 cups water
Pepper to taste
Garnish; sprigs of fresh or dried thyme

In large pot melt butter; add onion; cook 5 minutes over medium heat until translucent. Add carrots; sprinkle with sugar; cook and stir 1 minute. Add braising vegetables, their liquid, and water. Bring to boil; reduce heat; cover, and simmer 40 minutes or until carrots are very tender. Skim off any surface fat. Purée soup in blender or force vegetables through food mill. Season with pepper. Sprinkle with thyme leaves for garnish.

CHEESY CHICKEN CHOWDER
Serves 8

- 8 tablespoons butter
- 2 cups carrots, shredded
- ½ cup onion, chopped
- ½ cup flour
- 3 cups chicken broth
- 4 cups milk
- 2 cups diced cooked chicken
- 1 cup corn, fresh *or* frozen
- 1 teaspoon Worcestershire sauce
- 8 ounces cheddar cheese, shredded
- 2 tablespoons white wine (optional)
- 1 teaspoon salt
- ½ teaspoon pepper

Melt butter in a skillet. Add carrots and onion; sauté until tender. Blend in flour. Add broth and milk. Cook and stir until thick and smooth. Add remaining ingredients and stir until cheese is melted.

MINESTRONE (THICK ITALIAN SOUP)

- 1 cup dried great northern beans
  Salt and pepper to taste
- 1 small head cabbage, coarsely cut
- 2 medium potatoes, diced (optional)
- 2 medium onions, finely cut
- 3 ribs celery, diced
- 2–3 (6-inch) zucchini, sliced
- 3 cups chicken broth *or* bouillon
- 4 carrots, peeled and sliced
- 6 cups tomatoes, fresh *or* canned
- 1 clove garlic
- 1 cup broken thin spaghetti *or* macaroni

Wash beans; parboil in water to cover; drain. Add chicken broth and 2 quarts water. Use a large 8-quart kettle; add salt and pepper. Cook slowly for 1 hour. In the meantime, prepare vegetables; add potatoes, carrots, garlic and onions. Cook for ½ hour. Then add zucchini, cabbage, celery and tomatoes; cook 20 minutes; add spaghetti; cook 15 minutes longer. Serve in bowl; top with grated cheese.

BROCCOLI CHOWDER

- 2 pounds fresh broccoli, coarsely chopped
- 2 (12½-ounce) cans chicken broth
- 3 cups milk
- 1 cup cooked, chopped ham
- 2 teaspoons salt (optional)
- ¼ teaspoon pepper

Cook broccoli in broth until tender. Add remaining ingredients and bring just to a boil.

Stir in:
- 1 cup light cream
- ½ pound grated *or* cubed Swiss cheese

Add to chowder and heat through, but *do not boil* as cheese will curdle. This broccoli chowder is a favorite at our house. It is easy to fix, and very filling. It's delicious with warm French bread and a fresh fruit salad.

FISH CHOWDER

- 1 pound fish fillets
- ½ cup chopped onion
- 2 tablespoons shortening, melted
- 2 cups cubed potatoes
- 1 cup boiling water
- ¾ teaspoon salt
  Pepper to taste
- 2 cups milk
- 1 (8¾-ounce) can creamed corn

Cut fish into 1-inch squares. Sauté onions in melted shortening until soft. Add potatoes, water, salt, pepper and fish. Cover and simmer for 15 minutes, or until potatoes are tender. Add milk and corn; serve immediately.

BEEF CHOWDER
Serves 8-10

- 1-1/2 pounds ground beef
- 1/2 cup chopped celery
- 1/2 cup chopped onions
- 1/3 cup chopped green pepper
- 2 (10-1/2 ounce) cans condensed cream of celery soup
- 2 (16-ounce) cans tomatoes, cut up
- 1 (17-ounce) can whole kernel corn
- 1/4 cup snipped parsley

Cook beef, celery, onions, and green pepper until meat is browned; drain. Add remaining ingredients and 1/2 teaspoon salt. Simmer, covered, for 20 minutes. Stir often. Add salt to taste.

CHILLY DAY BEEF HOT POT

- 1-1/2 pounds ground beef
- 3-1/2 tablespoons steak sauce
- 1 egg
- 1 (46-ounce) can vegetable-tomato juice
- 2 envelopes dry onion soup mix
- 1 (15-ounce) can red kidney beans, undrained
- 1 (14-ounce) can pinto beans, undrained
- 1 can mixed vegetables
- 1 cup fresh parsley, chopped

Mix ground beef with steak sauce and egg; shape into 1-inch meatballs. Heat vegetable-tomato juice to boiling. Stir in onion soup mix; cover; simmer 10 minutes. Place meatballs in simmering soup; cover; simmer 15 minutes. Stir in kidney beans, pinto beans, and mixed vegetables.

To garnish, sprinkle chopped parsley over individual servings of soup.

CHINESE HOT-AND-SOUR SOUP
Serves 5

½ pound boneless pork loin
½ teaspoon cornstarch
½ teaspoon soy sauce
4 cups chicken broth
3 tablespoons white vinegar
1 tablespoon soy sauce
1 can bamboo shoots
1 can sliced mushrooms *or* 1 cup fresh mushrooms
2 tablespoons cornstarch
2 tablespoons cold water
¼ teaspoon pepper
2 eggs, slightly beaten
2 whole green onions, chopped with tops
2 teaspoons red pepper sauce (to taste)
½ teaspoon sesame oil

Trim fat from pork and shred. Toss pork with ½ teaspoon cornstarch and ½ teaspoon soy sauce. Cover; refrigerate for 15 minutes.

Heat chicken broth, vinegar and soy sauce in 3-quart saucepan. Stir in bamboo shoots, mushrooms and pork. Heat to boiling; reduce heat. Cover and simmer 5 minutes. Mix 2 tablespoons cornstarch, water and pepper. Stir into soup. Add eggs, stirring with fork until egg forms shreds. Stir in green onions, pepper sauce and sesame oil.

QUICKIE CORN CHOWDER

1/4 cup butter
1 large onion, diced
1 large can cream-style corn
2 (7-ounce) cans tuna fish
3 cups milk
1 teaspoon seasoned salt
1/2 teaspoon salt
1/4 teaspoon pepper

Melt butter; sauté onions until lightly browned. Add remaining ingredients. Heat and serve.

Serve this with crusty rolls and a salad for a quick, nutritious meal.

WHITE BEAN SOUP
Serves 4

2 tablespoons margarine
⅓ cup diced celery
⅓ cup diced carrots
⅓ cup diced onion
Dash minced, dry garlic
1 (16-ounce) can white kidney beans
Dash dried thyme
⅛ teaspoon pepper
2 cups water
1 packet Pillsbury chicken gravy mix
1½ cups diced, smoked ham

Cook celery, onion, carrots and garlic seasoning in margarine in saucepan over medium-low heat for 5 minutes.

Add remaining ingredients; bring to a boil over medium-high heat. Reduce heat; cover and simmer for 20 minutes. Pour ½ cup of soup into blender and purée smooth. Return to pan and simmer 5 minutes longer.

SAVORY TOMATO-SPINACH SOUP
Serves 4

1 pound lean beef, cut into 1-inch cubes
4 cups beef bouillon
¼ teaspoon salt
4 potatoes, cubed
3 green onions, sliced
1½ pounds fresh spinach, washed and coarsely chopped
4 tomatoes, peeled and cut into wedges
¼ teaspoon nutmeg

Combine beef, bouillon, salt, potatoes and onions; cover; cook 20 minutes. Add spinach and tomatoes; cook 5 minutes. To serve: Sprinkle each serving lightly with nutmeg.

MICROWAVE COCK-A-LEEKIE SOUP
Serves 4

Tastes like it has simmered all day—but is ready in an hour.

4 cups chicken stock
2 leeks
2 carrots
4 chicken thigh/drumstick combinations, skinned
1 teaspoon white pepper

Trim the roots off the leeks and cut leeks into 2-inch pieces. Peel carrots and slice diagonally into thin slices. Put chicken stock, leeks, carrots, chicken and white pepper into a 3-quart microwave-proof casserole; cover (venting the cover if you have to use plastic wrap) and cook at MEDIUM (50 percent power) setting for 50 minutes to an hour (depending on the size of the thighs), stirring occasionally. Serve, accompanied with hot, crusty buttered bread.

GRANDMA'S BEEF RIVEL SOUP
Serves 4

1 pound rib boiling beef *or* chuck roast, cut in chunks
1 medium onion, finely chopped
2 quarts cold water
2 teaspoons salt
½ teaspoon pepper
1 large egg
¼ cup (or more) flour

Slowly boil beef with water, onion, salt and pepper until tender. Mix flour and egg with your fingers until in small chunks, called rivels. Add to broth and cook for 5 minutes. Serve in soup bowls with crackers or croutons. Beef could be cooked in Crockpot for convenience.

MEXICAN ABONDIGAS SOUP
Serves 8

5 cups water
1 onion, chopped
1 (7-ounce) can chili salsa
1 can stewed tomatoes
1 teaspoon coriander
1 pound lean ground beef
1/2 teaspoon garlic powder
1/4 teaspoon oregano
Salt and pepper to taste

Cook onion in salted water for 10 minutes. Add 2/3 can chili salsa. Add tomatoes and coriander; simmer for 30 minutes. Mix remaining ingredients into ground beef and form into small balls. Add meatballs to broth and bring to boil. Simmer 30 minutes.

When the Irish fled their country and its famines, we were glad they brought this taste to our shores.

SLOW-COOKER BEAN WITH BACON SOUP

1½ cups dry Northern beans
1 pound bacon
Salt and pepper to taste
Carrot shavings
Parsley
Water

Put beans in slow-cooker. Fill with water to about 2 inches from top. Add remaining ingredients and stir. Cook on high for about 9 hours (time will vary for different slow-cookers). Ingredients can be put in slow-cooker and kept in refrigerator overnight, so all you do in the morning is take it out and plug it in.

CAULIFLOWER SOUP
Serves 4–6

1 large cauliflower
2 onions, finely diced
1 clove garlic, finely minced
2 cups vegetable stock
3 tablespoons flour
2 cups milk
Chopped parsley

Cook cauliflower, onion and garlic in vegetable stock until very tender. Add flour dissolved in milk and stir soup until it comes to a boil. Simmer for 20 minutes. Sprinkle with parsley when served.

VEGETABLE BEEF SOUP
Serves 6

1 pound ground beef
1-1/2 cups cold water
1 medium onion, chopped
3 medium carrots, diced
3 medium potatoes, cubed
2 cups tomatoes or tomato juice
1/3 cup uncooked noodles
Salt and pepper to taste

Simmer beef and water 15 minutes. Add remaining ingredients. Simmer until vegetables are tender.

YANKEE CHOWDER
Serves 6

1 can condensed cream of mushroom soup
3 soup cans water
1 can condensed turkey noodle soup
1 can condensed vegetarian vegetable soup

Stir mushroom soup until smooth in a large saucepan; gradually stir in water. Add remaining soups. Heat thoroughly, stirring often. (115 calories per serving)

TORTILLA SOUP
Serves 4–6

1 (18-ounce) jar Ortega Mild Green Chile Salsa
1 (13¾-ounce) College Inn Chicken Broth
1 small zucchini, halved and sliced
1 cup cooked garbanzo beans
2 tablespoons Ortega Diced Jalapeños Tortilla Chips, coarsely broken
¾ cup shredded Monterey Jack cheese

In saucepan, combine first 5 ingredients; simmer 5–7 minutes. Arrange a shallow layer of chips in serving bowls. Ladle in soup; top with cheese. Serve immediately.

THREE-BEAN SOUP
Serves 10-12

1 cup dried red kidney beans
1 cup dried great northern beans
1 cup dried pinto beans
Water
2 tablespoons cooking oil
2 onions, chopped
1 cup chopped carrots
1 cup chopped celery
1 ham bone with ham
1 bay leaf
Salt and pepper

In large bowl, soak all the beans together in 6 cups water overnight. The next day, drain and rinse. In 5-quart Dutch oven, heat oil. Add onions, carrots, and celery; cook for a few minutes. Add 7 cups water; drain soaked beans; add with ham bone and bay leaf. Cover and bring to boil over high heat. Reduce heat to low, and simmer gently for 1-1/2 hours or until beans are tender. Remove ham bone to bowl; cool until easy to handle. Cut ham off bone; discard bone. Cut ham into bite-size pieces; return to soup. Heat through. Add salt and pepper to taste.

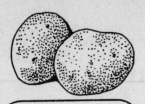

HAM-VEGETABLE CHOWDER
Serves 10–12

2 cups ham, cubed
2 medium onions, chopped
5 cups potatoes, cubed
1½ cups water
1 quart milk
2 tablespoons butter
2 tablespoons flour
¼ teaspoon baking soda
1 (6-ounce) can tomato paste
1 cup corn

Combine ham, onion, potatoes and water. Cook until soft, then add milk. In a separate pan melt butter and add flour, baking soda and tomato paste. Heat, stirring until smooth. Add ham mixture and corn; bring to a boil. Serve.

A LAWYER'S POTATO SOUP

1½ cups minced leeks, including some green
¼ cup minced onion
1 large clove garlic, minced
3 tablespoons minced carrots
4 tablespoons butter *or* rendered chicken fat
4 cups chicken stock
1½ cups diced potatoes
1½ cups heavy cream
Salt
White pepper
Beau monde seasoning

Sauté leeks, onion, garlic and carrots in butter or fat until leeks are soft. Do not brown. Add stock and potatoes. Cover and bring to a boil. Simmer until potatoes are tender. Pour into blender and purée. Add cream. Return to stove; reheat, but do not boil. Season to taste with

salt, pepper and beau monde. If soup is too thick, thin with more stock or half-and-half.

One tasty bowl equals a full meal. The secret of success is in the beau monde seasoning and in taking the time to purée.

FRESH TOMATO SOUP
Serves 6

12 fresh tomatoes, peeled (or 1 large can)
1 quart boiling water
1 onion
1 carrot
½ turnip
1 stalk celery
Salt and pepper to taste
1 tablespoon sugar
1 cup milk
1 tablespoon butter
2 tablespoons flour

Dice all vegetables very fine. Put into water and simmer for 1 hour. Season with salt, pepper and 1 tablespoon sugar. Add milk. Thicken with flour which has been mixed in ⅓ cup water. Add butter and season to taste. Simmer for 5 more minutes.

FISH CHOWDER
Serves 2

1 teaspoon butter
1/4 cup finely diced onion
1/2 pound lean white fish
1 teaspoon minced parsley
1 bouillon cube
3/4 cup milk
Salt and pepper

Place butter in small saucepan. Add onion and let cook about minute. Cut fish in 1-inch cubes and add to onion. Add 3/4 cup water, parsley, and bouillon cube. Bring to boil. Let simmer, covered, over low heat, until fish is done, about 5 minutes. Add milk and season to taste with salt and pepper. Heat thoroughly.

DIFFERENT TOMATO SOUP
Serves 6

1 pint canned tomatoes (crushed fine with potato masher, or strained tomatoes may be used)
1 medium-sized potato, peeled and grated
2 tablespoons butter
1/2 cup water
1 medium-sized onion, grated
1/8 teaspoon soda
3-4 cups milk
Salt and pepper to taste

Mix together the tomatoes, grated potato, butter, and water. Cook and stir over medium heat about 5 minutes, until butter melts, and potato begins to thicken the tomatoes. Add salt and pepper to taste. Stir in the soda, which prevents curdling; add the milk. Add the grated onion. Stir over low heat and cook to desired temperature. Preparation time: 45 minutes.

HEARTY ALPHABET SOUP

½ to 1 pound stew meat *or* round steak
1 (1-pound) can stewed tomatoes
1 (8-ounce) can tomato sauce
1 cup water
1 package onion soup mix
1 (16-ounce) package frozen mixed vegetables
1 cup uncooked alphabet macaroni

Cut beef into cubes. Combine meat, stewed tomatoes, sauce, water and soup mix. Cover and cook in Crockpot on low for 6–8 hours. Turn to high; add vegetables and macaroni. Cover; cook on HIGH 30 minutes, or until vegetables are done.

GOLDEN PUMPKIN SOUP

Serves 4-6

1 cup onion, chopped
1/2 cup celery, chopped
2 tablespoons butter or margarine
2 cups chicken broth
1-1/2 cups mushrooms, sliced
1/2 cup rice, uncooked
1/4 teaspoon salt
1/4 teaspoon curry powder
1/4 teaspoon tarragon
1 (16 ounce) can pumpkin
2 tablespoons margarine
Salt and pepper to taste

Sauté celery and onion in margarine, while potatoes are cooking. Mash potatoes and add all ingredients. Add more milk, if a thinner soup is desired. Bring to a boil and remove from heat. This is a delicious and rich-tasting soup made with evaporated milk. Try it, you'll like it!!

CREAM OF BROCCOLI SOUP

Makes 2 quarts

2 teaspoons chopped onion
3 teaspoons butter or margarine
3 teaspoons flour
1-1/2 teaspoons salt
3 cups milk
3 cups chicken broth
3 chicken bouillon cubes dissolved in 3 cups boiling water
1 (10 ounce) package frozen chopped broccoli, slightly thawed
2 cups carrots, sliced
Pepper

In large saucepan, sauté onion and butter until tender. With a whisk, stir in flour and salt. Gradually add milk, chicken broth, and bouillon cubes, stirring constantly; bring to a boil. Add broccoli and carrots. Cook over low heat (do not boil), stirring occasionally, about 25 minutes until carrots are tender. Add pepper to taste. Serve hot.

EASY CREAM OF BROCCOLI SOUP

Makes 8 cups

2 (10 ounce) packages frozen chopped broccoli
2 cans cream of mushroom soup
2-2/3 cups milk
3 tablespoons butter
1/2 teaspoon tarragon
Dash pepper

Cook broccoli; drain well. Add remaining ingredients and simmer over low heat until thoroughly heated.

CREAMY CARROT SOUP

2 tablespoons butter
1/4 cup chopped onion
1 rib celery, chopped
2 cups carrots, pared and sliced
2 cups chicken broth
1 cup milk or half-&-half
1 teaspoon salt
1/4 teaspoon nutmeg
1/8 teaspoon pepper

Melt butter; add onion and celery; cook until tender. Add carrots; cook 5 minutes. Add broth and bring to boil. Cover; cook over medium heat for 20 minutes until carrots are tender. Puree in blender. Add milk, salt, nutmeg, and pepper. Simmer 5-10 minutes, but do not boil.

CREAM OF MUSHROOM SOUP

Serves 4-6

1 cup (1/4 pound) mushrooms
2 tablespoons chopped onion (1 medium)
2 tablespoons butter
2 tablespoons all-purpose flour
2 cups chicken stock or beef broth
1/2 cup light cream
1/4 teaspoon salt
1/4 teaspoon ground nutmeg
1/8 teaspoon white pepper

Slice mushrooms through cap and stem; cook with 2 tablespoons onion in butter for 5 minutes. Blend in flour; add broth. Cook; stir until slightly thickened. Cool slightly; add cream and seasonings. Heat through; serve at once.

ITALIAN RICE AND PEA SOUP

1/3 cup olive oil
1 slice bacon, chopped
1 slice ham, chopped
1 small onion, chopped
1 tablespoon parsley, minced
1 package frozen peas
1 quart soup stock or water
1/2 cup uncooked rice
Salt and pepper
3 tablespoons grated Parmesan cheese

Sauté onion, bacon, ham and parsley in oil until light brown. Add peas; cook 5 minutes, stirring frequently. Add liquid and bring to a boil. Add washed rice, seasonings, and cheese; cook over medium heat until rice crushes easily between fingers. Serve very hot.

NOODLE EGG DROP SOUP

Serves 4

2 cans (10-3/4 ounce each) chicken broth
4 cups water
1-1/2 cups fine egg noodles, uncooked
2 eggs, beaten
2 tablespoons chopped parsley
2 tablespoons butter

Bring chicken broth and water to boil; gradually add noodles, stirring occasionally; cook 8 minutes. Reduce heat to low, stir in eggs. Simmer 3 minutes longer. Remove from heat; stir in parsley and butter.

CORNED BEEF CHOWDER
Serves 5

3 cups milk
1 can cream of potato soup
1 (10 ounce) package frozen
    Brussels sprouts, thawed
1 can corned beef, broken up

In a large saucepan, blend 1-1/3 cups milk and soup. Cut up Brussels sprouts and add to soup. Bring to boil. Reduce heat; simmer 15 minutes. Add remaining milk and beef. Heat through.

POTATO HAM CHOWDER
Serves 6

4 potatoes
2 tablespoons margarine
1/2 cup diced onions
2 cups water
1 teaspoon salt
1/8 teaspoon pepper
4 tablespoons flour
1/3 cup water
2 cups milk
1 (12 ounce) can whole kernel corn
2 cups diced cooked ham

Peel and dice potatoes. In large saucepan, melt margarine. Add onion, and cook until tender. Add potatoes, 2 cups water, and seasonings. Cover; simmer until potatoes are done. Make a paste of flour and 1/3 cup water; add to potato mixture. Add milk and cook until slightly thickened. Stir in corn and ham. Heat thoroughly, but do not boil.

MAINE CORN CHOWDER
Makes 9 cups

5 slices bacon
2 medium onions, sliced
3 cups diced, pared potatoes
2 cups water
1 teaspoon salt
1/2 teaspoon pepper
1 (1-pound, 1-ounce) can cream-
    style corn
2 cups milk

Cook bacon in Dutch oven until crisp. Drain on paper towels. Set aside. Sauté onion in bacon drippings until soft. Add potatoes, water, salt, and pepper. Bring to a boil. Reduce heat; cover and simmer about 15 minutes until potatoes are tender. Add corn and milk. Heat thoroughly. When serving, garnish with crumbled bacon.

CHILI

1 pound chunk beef
1-1/2 pounds ground beef
1 pound pork, cut into 1/4-inch
    cubes
1 large onion
1 can beer
Chili powder to taste
1 teaspoon salt
Sugar to sweeten
1 tablespoon oregano
1 (16 ounce) can kidney beans
1 (16 ounce) can butter beans
1 (16 ounce) can garbanzo beans
1 (No. 2-1/2) can tomatoes
1 (15 ounce) can tomato sauce
1 (6 ounce) can tomato paste
1 (16 ounce) can mushrooms
    (optional)
1 (16 ounce) can northern beans
1 cup beef broth made from bouillon
Garlic powder to taste
Add more tomato juice, as needed

Brown beef, pork, and onion; place in large kettle. Add all the rest of ingredients. If very thick, add water and tomato juice; simmer several hours until flavors are blended and meat is tender.

LUMBERJACK CHILI

2 pounds ground beef
1 large onion, diced
1/2 green pepper, diced
4 stalks celery, diced
1 large can tomato juice
1 can whole tomatoes
2 cans red kidney beans
2 tablespoons chili powder
1 teaspoon garlic powder
1 teaspoon celery salt
1 teaspoon Italian seasoning
1/2 teaspoon pepper

Brown beef and drain well. Sauté onion, green pepper, and celery. Combine all in large saucepot with remaining ingredients. Simmer for about 1 hour. Freezes well, and is very good reheated.

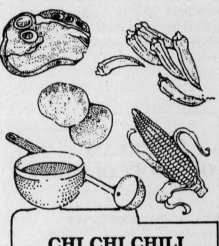

CHI CHI CHILI

1-1/2 pounds chopped meat or
    ground chuck
1-1/2 cups onion, cut up
1-1/2 celery, chopped
2 cloves garlic
2 teaspoons salt
1 teaspoon sage
2 tablespoons chili powder
1 tablespoon paprika
1 teaspoon thyme
1 bay leaf
2 cans kidney beans or chili beans (if
    you like it hotter)
1 large can tomatos
1 small can tomato paste

Brown meat, onion, garlic and celery. Add remaining ingredients and simmer 1 to 2 hours.

TOMATO SOUP ALA HERBS
Serves 8

An attractive, hearty soup using herbs to make it appear more elegant.

1 medium onion, chopped
1 clove garlic, minced
2 tablespoons butter or margarine
4 cups water
2 pounds ripe tomatoes, peeled and chopped
2 carrots, thinly sliced
4 red potatoes, unpeeled, and cubed
2 stalks celery, chopped
1 chicken bouillon cube
1/2 teaspoon fresh or 1/4 teaspoon dried of the following herbs: thyme, basil, and rosemary
Salt and pepper to taste

In large kettle or Dutch oven, sauté onion and garlic in margarine or butter. Stir in water, tomatoes, carrots, potatoes, celery, bouillon cube and spices. Bring to boil; reduce heat and simmer, covered, about 45 minutes or until vegetables are well-done.

CREAMY RUTABAGA SOUP
Serves 6

3 cups cubed rutabaga
2 chicken bouillon cubes dissolved in 1-1/2 cups boiling water
1 small onion, chopped
2 tablespoons margarine
1/4 teaspoon celery salt
1/2 teaspoon salt
Dash of pepper
1 teaspoon sugar
1-1/2 cups milk
1 cup light cream
Nutmeg

Sauté onion in margarine; add rutabaga, bouillon cubes, and water. Cook until very soft. Press through sieve (or use blender). Add remaining ingredients, except cream and nutmeg. Add cream; heat through but do not boil. Serve hot, sprinkled with nutmeg, bacon bits, or toasted croutons.

CREAM OF PEANUT SOUP
Serves 6

1/2 cup butter or margarine, melted
1 cup celery, thinly sliced
1 medium onion, minced
2 tablespoons flour
2 quarts chicken broth
1 cup creamy peanut butter
1 cup light cream or evaporated milk
1/4 cup fresh snipped parsley
1/4 cup coarsely chopped peanuts

In 3- or 4-quart saucepan, melt butter. Add celery and onion. Cook until lightly browned, stirring constantly. Stir in flour. Blend well. Gradually stir in chicken broth. Bring to a boil. Stir in peanut butter. Simmer 15 minutes. Just before serving, reheat over very low heat. Stir in cream. Garnish with snipped parsley and chopped peanuts.

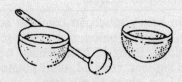

BOUNTIFUL BEAN SOUP
Serves 6

1 pound dry navy beans
2 quarts cold water
1 meaty ham bone
1 bay leaf
1/2 teaspoon salt
6 whole black peppercorns
Vinegar to taste

Rinse 1 pound beans. Add 2 quarts cold water. Bring to a boil and simmer 2 minutes. Remove from heat. Cover; let stand 1 hour. Do not drain. Add remaining ingredients. Cover; simmer 3 hours. Remove ham bone. Mash beans slightly, using potato masher. Cut ham off bone. Add ham to soup. Cook 30 minutes more. Season to taste. This is a wonderful nutritious soup; prepare in a slow cooker or slow pot.

CREAMY PIMIENTO SOUP
Serves 7

2 tablespoons butter or margarine
3 tablespoons flour
1/4 teaspoon salt
1/8 teaspoon pepper
1 teaspoon onion, grated
3 cups milk
4 cups chicken broth
3/4 cup pimientos
Chopped parsley, for garnish

In a saucepan melt butter; add flour, seasonings, and onion. Place milk, broth, and pimientos into food processor; pulse 5 times; add to flour/butter mixture. Cook, stirring constantly, until thickened. Sprinkle chopped parsley on individual servings.

SOME LIKE IT HOT VICHYSSOISE

1/4 cup butter
1 large onion, sliced (1 cup)
8 small Idaho® potatoes, pared, halved
3 medium carrots, sliced
1 quart water
1 tsp ground ginger
3/4 tsp salt
1/8 tsp pepper
2 cups milk
1 tbsp soy sauce
2 tbsps chopped scallion

In large saucepot or heavy kettle melt butter; saute onion until tender. Add potatoes, carrots, water, ginger, salt and pepper. Bring to a boil. Reduce heat. Simmer 30 minutes or until vegetables are tender. Remove 4 potato halves; dice and set aside. Puree remaining vegetables and cooking liquid in blender or food processor. Return to saucepot. Stir in milk, soy sauce and cubed potatoes; heat. Sprinkle soup with scallions before serving.

SPONGE SOUP

Serves 16-20

12 eggs
1-1/2 pounds ground beef
14 tablespoons flour (heaping)
14 tablespoons grated Parmesan cheese (heaping)
1 tablespoon salt
1 tablespoon baking powder

Beat eggs until frothy. Then mix in the ground beef, flour, grated Parmesan cheese, salt, and baking powder. Knead ingredients together. Spread in a 9x12-inch cake pan, and bake 25-30 minutes at 350 degrees. Remove from oven, let cool, and cut into 1/2-inch cubes. Place the cubes in a beef broth and reheat. The mixture also can be made ahead and frozen until the day before serving.

END-OF-THE-GARDEN SOUP

1-1/2 pounds beef soup meat
3 quarts water
1-1/2 cups green beans
1-1/2 cups potatoes
2 cups carrots
1 cup turnips
1 cup sweet corn
1 onion
1 clove garlic
Salt and pepper to taste

Wash all vegetables and chop. Combine vegetables, meat, and water; boil slowly for about 4 hours. Serve with crackers.

Very good for those cool fall evenings.

SHERRIED WILD RICE SOUP

Serves 4

2 (10-ounce) packages frozen white and wild rice combination
2 tablespoons butter or margarine
1 tablespoon onion, minced
1 tablespoon celery, minced
1 tablespoon carrot, minced
1/4 cup flour
4 cups chicken broth
1 cup light cream
3 tablespoons dry sherry
2 tablespoons chives, minced

Prepare rice according to package directions. In a saucepan, melt butter; sauté vegetables until tender. Blend in flour; cook 2 minutes; blend well. Stir in the prepared rice; simmer 5 minutes. Blend in cream, broth, and sherry. To serve, garnish each individual serving with minced chives.

SHRIMP BISQUE

Serves 4

1 cup celery, finely chopped
1 cup diced potatoes
1/2 cup onion, diced
1 cup water
Salt and pepper to taste
2 cups half-and-half
2 tablespoons all-purpose flour
1/2 pound fresh, boiled shrimp (or 8-ounce package frozen)
2 tablespoons butter

In heavy saucepan combine celery, potatoes, onion, water, and seasonings. Bring to boil; reduce heat and simmer, covered, until potatoes are done, about 15 minutes.

Blend half-and-half and flour together; stir into potato mixture. Add shrimp and butter. Cook, stirring constantly, until thickened.

Chowders are well known in the northeast part of our country because of the origination. This inviting dish takes its name from the French word, chaudière, a large kettle used by French settlers to cook soups and stews. These settlers often contributed part of their daily catch to a community kettle, adding potatoes and corn.

BASQUE BREAD SOUP

Serves 4

2 large cloves garlic, lightly crushed
1/4 cup olive oil
4 cups water
2/3 cup fine stale bread crumbs, toasted
1 teaspoon salt
2 eggs, slightly beaten
Salt and pepper to taste

In a small heavy skillet, sauté garlic in oil over moderately high heat until golden brown. Remove and discard the garlic; keep oil warm. In a saucepan, bring water to a boil and stir in the toasted bread crumbs, oil, and salt. Remove the pan from the heat; whisk in the eggs. Season with salt and pepper. Ladle into heated bowls.

ROCKY MOUNTAIN SOUP

Serves 8

3 cups water
1-1/4 cups dried pinto beans
3 slices bacon, chopped
2 cloves garlic, minced
1/2 cup chopped onion
1 (1-pound) can tomatoes, cut up
2/3 cup uncooked brown rice
1 teaspoon salt
1/2 teaspoon paprika
1/4 teaspoon pepper

Rinse beans. In a large kettle or Dutch oven, combine beans and 3 cups water. Bring to boiling. Reduce heat; simmer 2 minutes. Let stand one hour. Drain. Add 5-1/2 cups fresh water to beans. Simmer, covered, 1 hour. While beans are simmering, cook bacon until almost crisp. Add onion and garlic. Cook until vegetables are tender, but not brown, stirring occasionally. Stir bacon mixture, tomatoes, rice, salt, pepper, and paprika into bean mixture. Bring to boiling. Cover and simmer for 45 minutes to 1 hour or until rice and beans are tender. Stir occasionally.

GOLDEN ONION SOUP
Makes 5-1/2 cups

2 cups finely chopped onion
1/4 cup butter
2 cups water
1-1/2 cups (10-3/4 ounce can)
  cream of chicken soup
2 slightly beaten eggs
1 teaspoon salt
1/4 teaspoon nutmeg
1-2/3 cups undiluted Carnation
  evaporated milk

Sauté onion in butter until tender. Add water. Bring to boil; reduce heat and boil gently for 20 minutes, stirring occasionally. Combine chicken soup, eggs, salt, and nutmeg in small bowl. Add to onion mixture. Cook over medium heat, stirring continually, until mixture comes to a boil and thickens. Stir in milk. Heat to serving temperature.

HEARTY LENTIL SOUP

1 cup lentils
Small chopped onion
1/2 can tomato sauce
Salt and pepper to taste
1 cup cooked elbow macaroni
1 package frozen cauliflower
2 tablespoons olive oil
3 cups water
1 teaspoon sugar
Grated cheese

Brown onion in oil. Add remaining ingredients, except macaroni; cook until cauliflower is tender. Add cooked macaroni. Before serving, sprinkle with grated cheese.

MEATY SPLIT PEA SOUP
Serves 8

1 pound lean ground pork
1-pound package dry split peas
2 medium potatoes, peeled, chopped

3/4 cup onion, chopped
1/2 cup chopped celery
2 teaspoons seasoned salt
1/2 teaspoon garlic powder
1/4 teaspoon pepper
6 cups water

Brown ground pork in skillet, stirring until crumbly; drain. Combine with remaining ingredients in Crockpot. Cook, covered, on low for 10 to 12 hours; stir before serving.

GREAT GRANDMA'S OLD-FASHIONED SOUP

Veal shank, broken in two
Beef marrow bone
5 diced carrots
2 diced onions
5 diced potatoes
1 diced green pepper
2 or more stalks cut up celery
1 medium can tomatoes
1/8 teaspoon summer savory
1/8 teaspoon salt
Pepper to taste

Cover veal and marrow bone with cold water; cook for several hours until meat is nearly done. Add vegetables and seasonings. Cook until meat and vegetables are tender. If a more hearty soup is wanted, macaroni, noodles or a tablespoon of barley may be added.

POTATO SOUP

6 cups potatoes
1 onion, chopped
1 small can evaporated milk
2 cups milk or half and half
2 stalks chopped celery
2 cups cream
Toasted bread cubes, for garnish

Sauté onion and celery in butter; add broth, mushrooms, rice, and seasonings. Cover; simmer 25 minutes or until rice is cooked. Stir in pumpkin; cook 5 minutes more. Stir in cream; heat thoroughly. Garnish with toasted bread cubes.

POTATO SOUP WITH RIVELS

2 pounds white potatoes, peeled and
  cubed
1-1/2 quarts water or chicken broth
2 stalks celery, diced
Parsley to taste
1/8 teaspoon pepper
2 eggs
1/2 cup flour

Boil potatoes in chicken broth with celery, parsley; salt and pepper to taste.

Rivels:
Beat the eggs and flour together with a fork. Drizzle the mixture from a spoon into the cooked potato soup. Boil for about 10 minutes.

When my mother, who is now 84 years old, was a young girl of about 9 years, she used to visit her father's sister. Her father was a Pennsylvania Dutch descendent and lived in the back hills of central Pennsylvania. Her favorite dish made by this aunt was potato soup with what she called rivels.

POTATO BROCCOLI CHEESE SOUP

4 or 5 baking potatoes with skins, cut
  into bite-sized pieces
1 large or 2 small onions, cut into
  small pieces
2 bunches broccoli flowerets,
  chopped into bite-size pieces
3 carrots, cut into small pieces
1-1/4 sticks butter
3 tablespoons arrowroot
1 pint milk, plus some
Grated cheese

Cook all vegetables together in water and a little milk. Add arrowroot to 1/4 stick melted butter; stir with fork. Add 1 stick butter; melt. Add milk and grated cheese; stir and heat thoroughly.

CAULIFLOWER-HAM CHOWDER

2 cups diced potatoes
3/4 cup diced celery
1 (13-3/4-ounce) can chicken broth
1/4 cup water
2 tablespoons butter
1/8 teaspoon white pepper
2 cups sliced cauliflower
1/2 cup diced onions
1 cup cream
1-1/2 cups milk
3 tablespoons cornstarch
2 cups diced cooked ham

In large saucepan cook cauliflower, potatoes, onions, and celery covered in chicken broth until almost tender (about 10 minutes). *Do not drain.* Add butter to melt. In mixing bowl, gradually stir in milk and cream. Blend water, cornstarch, and pepper; stir into milk mixture. Pour over vegetables. Cook and stir until thickened and bubbly. Stir in ham. Simmer over low heat for 10 minutes. Season to taste. Garnish with parsley.

CLAM CHOWDER
Serves 6-8

1 cup potatoes, diced
1 small onion, diced
1 tablespoon butter
2 tablespoons flour
3 cups whole milk
Pinch of pepper
1/2 teaspoon salt, or to taste
1 (8-ounce) can minced clams

Simmer potatoes and onion together in small amount of water until tender. Melt butter in small pan, then blend in flour making a smooth paste. Drain juice from clams and blend into butter and flour mixture. Add to cooked potatoes and onions; stir in milk and clams. Heat to serving temperature, *but do not boil.* Season to taste and serve.

CHEESE VEGETABLE CHOWDER
Serves 8-10

2 cups chopped cabbage
1 cup celery slices
1 cup thin carrot slices
1 (16-ounce) can cream-style corn
1 teaspoon salt
1/4 teaspoon thyme
2-1/2 cups (10 ounces) shredded American process cheese
1 cup onion slices
1 cup peas
1/2 cup (1 stick) butter
3 cups milk, reconstituted
1/8 teaspoon pepper

Sauté cabbage, onion, celery, peas, and carrots in butter in saucepan 8-10 minutes, stirring frequently. Add corn, milk, and seasonings; heat over low heat for 15 minutes, stirring occasionally. Add cheese; stir until melted. Makes approximately 2 quarts.

ITALIAN BEAN SOUP
Serves 8

1 cup dry navy beans
1 teaspoon salt
1 (8-ounce) can tomato sauce
1 cup chopped onion
1 cup chopped carrots
1/2 cup chopped green pepper
2 cloves garlic, minced
2 beef bouillon cubes
1-1/2 teaspoon each crushed dried basil and oregano, or 3 teaspoons Italian seasoning mix
1/2 cup macaroni

Rinse beans; add 8 cups water. Soak overnight. Do not drain. Stir in 1 teaspoon salt and remaining ingredients, except macaroni. Cover and simmer 1-1/2 hours. Stir in macaroni and cook, uncovered, until macaroni is done, about 15 minutes.

Our neighbors to the south certainly knew how to cure any ills with this savory broth.

FRENCH MARKET BEAN SOUP

1-1/2 cups mixed beans
2 or 3 smoked ham hocks
1 pound smoked sausage, thinly sliced
1 large onion, chopped
Juice of 1 lemon
1 (16-ounce) can tomatoes
2 cloves garlic, chopped
1 (4-ounce) can green chilies, chopped
1 (8-ounce) can tomato sauce
Salt and pepper to taste

Rinse and drain beans; cover with water; soak overnight. Cook in same water with ham hocks and onion until tender, about 3 hours. Remove meat from bones and return meat to mixture. Add remaining ingredients. Simmer 30-60 minutes. Soup should be thick, but add small amount of water, if desired.

CABBAGE AND TOMATO SOUP
Serves 8-10

1 small head of cabbage
2 cans tomato soup
1 (16-ounce) can tomatoes, cut into quarters
1 large onion, sliced thin
2 tablespoons freshly-squeezed lemon juice
1/2 cup firmly-packed brown sugar
1/2 pound chuck steak, cubed
1/2 cup ground gingersnaps

Place cabbage in stock pot. Cover with hot water. Simmer over medium-low heat for 30 minutes; stirring occasionally. Add remaining ingredients. Simmer uncovered 1-1/2 hours, stirring occasionally.

FAMILY FARE CHICKEN VEGETABLE SOUP

1 cup potatoes, cut into small squares (diced)
4 cups chicken stock or broth
1 teaspoon salt
1/8 teaspoon pepper
1 cup onions, thinly sliced
1 cup carrots, diced
1 cup celery, chopped
1 cup fresh green beans, cut in 2-inch pieces
2 cups cooked chicken, diced
1 cup zucchini, sliced

In saucepan over medium heat, bring potatoes to boiling point in enough salted water to cover. Cook potatoes 5 minutes; drain and set aside. In large saucepan, heat stock to boiling. Season with salt and pepper. Add onion, carrots, and celery; simmer 5 minutes. Stir in green beans and chicken; heat soup to boiling. Add zucchini and potatoes; simmer 1 minute longer.

CREAMY ASPARAGUS SOUP
Serves 4

1 (10-ounce) package frozen asparagus
1/2 cup chicken broth
2 egg yolks
1/4 cup whole milk
1/2 teaspoon salt
1/4 teaspoon pepper
2 drops Worcestershire sauce
Parsley for garnish
Paprika for garnish

In large pan, combine asparagus and chicken broth; heat to simmer and cook, covered, for 8 minutes. Cool. Put in blender or food processor, and blend until smooth. Add egg yolks and blend well. Return asparagus mixture to pan; stir in milk, salt, and pepper; add Worcestershire sauce. Heat well, but do not boil. Top with parsley and paprika.

TACO SOUP
(teenage favorite)
Makes 3-1/2 quarts

1 pound lean ground beef
2-1/2 quarts chicken stock
1 (2-1/2-ounce) package taco seasoning mix
1/2 teaspoon cumin
1/2 teaspoon salt
1/4 teaspoon pepper
2 cups green onions, thinly sliced
2 cups tomatoes, chopped
1 (18-ounce) can pitted black olives, drained and sliced
1 (14-ounce) package corn chips
4 cups iceberg lettuce, shredded
2 cups cheddar cheese, shredded

In medium-size skillet, brown ground beef. Drain well and set aside. In large skillet, combine the chicken stock, taco seasoning mix, cumin, salt, pepper, and ground beef. Bring to a boil. Reduce heat and simmer covered for 10 minutes. Add green onions, tomatoes, and black olives. Simmer another 10 minutes. Ladle into bowls; top with chips, lettuce, and cheese.

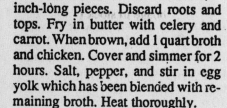

COCK-A-LEEKIE SOUP
Serves 4
(dates back to the 14th century)

1 dozen leeks
1 ounce butter
2 stalks celery, chopped
1 carrot, chopped
1-1/2 quarts chicken broth
1 cup cooked chicken, diced
Salt and pepper to taste
1 egg yolk

Wash and trim leeks. Cut into 1/2-inch-long pieces. Discard roots and tops. Fry in butter with celery and carrot. When brown, add 1 quart broth and chicken. Cover and simmer for 2 hours. Salt, pepper, and stir in egg yolk which has been blended with remaining broth. Heat thoroughly.

CREAMY TOMATO SOUP
Serves 4

1 diced potato
2 diced carrots
2 diced celery stalks
1 medium onion, chopped
2 bay leaves
1-1/2 teaspoons dried basil
3/4 teaspoon oregano
1/4 teaspoon chili powder
1/4 teaspoon pepper
1-1/2 cups stock

Place all ingredients in saucepan. Bring to a boil; reduce heat; and simmer, covered, for 10 minutes or until tender.
Then stir in:
1 (16-ounce) can undrained tomatoes
2 tablespoons tomato paste
1/3 cup tiny pasta, cooked

Simmer 5 minutes more; remove from heat and stir in 1 cup low-fat yogurt. Serve immediately.

VEGETABLE BEEF SOUP
Serves 8

1 pound ground beef
1 large can tomatoes, whole
1 can tomato soup
1 small onion, chopped
2 cups water
1 can lima beans, drained
1 can whole-kernel corn, undrained
1 cup sliced carrots
1 cup potatoes, cut up
1 cup diced celery
1/4 teaspoon salt
1/4 teaspoon pepper

Combine beef, tomatoes, soup, and onion in cooker. Add water, beans, and vegetables. Add salt, pepper, and other spices of preference. Stir well. Cook at lowest setting, 4 to 6 hours.

CHICKEN SOUP

1 large chicken, cut up
2 eggs
Juice of 2 lemons
2 teaspoons salt
8 cups water

Boil chicken* and salt in water about 2 hours. Remove chicken from broth; skin and debone; dice.

Beat eggs until light. Slowly add lemon juice; add 1 cup warm broth very slowly. Add to remaining broth with diced chicken and continue to heat through.

*For a different taste add finely chopped carrots, celery, and onion to the chicken when originally cooking.

A wonderfully-flavored and hearty soup such as this one needs only warm bread with butter, a tossed salad, and a dessert to make a filling meal.

Soups date back to prehistoric man when he combined bones, meat, water, and hot rocks in animal skin bags to produce a tasty brew. In ancient Roman cookbooks, the first known printed cookbooks contained recipes for soup. Both Queen Elizabeth I and Queen Victoria drank a cup of mutton broth to begin each day. The first soup "restorative" (later to be known as restaurant, and serve other foods) was established in Paris in 1750.

George Washington deserves credit for increasing the popularity of soup in our country. He requested that his personal cook, with few provisions, create a warm meal for his troops at Valley Forge. But it was our European ancestors who brought with them their favorite soups, and over the years, these soups have been adapted and blended to use local ingredients to suit a variety of tastes.

---

1 (16-ounce) can stewed tomatoes
1 (10-1/2 ounce) can condensed beef broth
1 soup-can water
1 teaspoon chili powder
1/2 teaspoon salt
1/2 teaspoon Worcestershire sauce
1 cup cooked peas

Brown meat in large, heavy Dutch oven or kettle. Drain off fat. Add onion and celery; cook until vegetables are done. Stir in tomatoes, beef broth, water, chili powder, salt, and Worcestershire sauce. Cover and cook until all is tender, about 15 minutes. Stir in peas; heat through.

HOT DEER CHILI
Serves 4-6

2 pounds coarsely ground venison
3 tablespoons chili powder
1 teaspoon black pepper
1 medium onion, chopped
1 bell pepper, chopped
1/2 teaspoon chopped jalapeño pepper
1 small can tomatoes (already seasoned with peppers, or regular tomatoes if others are unavailable)
1 (20-ounce) can tomato juice
1/2 teaspoon garlic salt
1/4 teaspoon salt
1 tablespoon oil
1/2 cup water

Sauté onion, bell pepper, and jalapeño pepper in oil in large skillet or pan until onion is clear; add meat and cook until meat loses its redness; add chili powder and black pepper. Mix well and cook 2 minutes, then allow it to set for 3 minutes. Add tomatoes, tomato juice, and salts. Heat to boiling, then simmer for 1 to 1-1/2 hours. Add water, as needed.

Note: You may use beef instead of venison.

---

2 tablespoons cooking oil
2 cups chopped onions
2 cloves garlic, minced
1 (1-pound) can tomatoes, cut up
1 beef bouillon cube
2 tablespoons chili powder
1-1/2 teaspoons salt
1 teaspoon dried oregano leaves
1 teaspoon ground cumin
2 (15-ounce) cans pinto or kidney beans

Brown meat in hot oil in Dutch oven. Add onion, garlic, tomatoes, bouillon cube, chili powder, salt, oregano, and cumin. Cover and simmer 1-3/4 hours. Add undrained beans; simmer 15 minutes.

QUICK & EASY CHILI CON CARNE
Serves 5

1 pound ground beef
1 cup onion, chopped
1 (1-pound) can kidney beans
1 (8-ounce) can tomato sauce
1 teaspoon salt
2 teaspoons chili powder
1 bay leaf

Stir and sauté ground beef and onions together until beef is well done. Add kidney beans, tomato sauce, salt, chili powder, and bay leaf. Cover and cook slowly for 1 hour.

BEEF STEW WITH DUMPLINGS
Serves 6

2 (24-ounce) cans beef stew
1 cup water
2 cups Basic Campers' Mix
1 cup milk

Combine canned stew and water. Bring to a boil. Combine Basic Campers' Mix and milk. Spoon onto hot stew. Cook, uncovered, over low coals for 10 minutes; cover and cook 10 minutes longer.

CHILI-BEEF SOUP
Serves 6

1/2 pound ground beef
1/2 cup chopped onion
1/2 cup chopped celery

AMERICAN CHILI
Serves 8

2 pounds stewing beef, cut in 1/2-inch cubes

HEARTY POLISH STEW

1/4 cup butter or margarine, divided
1 pound stewing beef, cut in 1-inch cubes
1 large onion, chopped (1 cup)
1 medium apple, cored, unpeeled, chopped (1 cup)
1 clove garlic, minced
1 pound sauerkraut, drained, rinsed well
1 can (14 1/2 oz) tomatoes, drained, chopped
1 1/2 cups beef broth
7 small Idaho® potatoes, unpared, cut in chunks
1/2 pound Polish sausage (Kielbasa), cut in 3/4 inch slices
3/4 tsp caraway seeds
1/4 tsp pepper

In a Dutch oven or large, heavy kettle melt 2 tbsps butter; brown meat quickly over high heat. Reduce heat to medium. Add remaining 2 tbsps butter; cook onion, apple and garlic until tender. Stir in sauerkraut and tomatoes. Gradually stir in broth, scraping up bits from bottom of pan. Add potatoes, sausage, caraway seeds and pepper. Cover. Simmer 1 hour 10 minutes or until meat is tender.

OYSTER STEW
Serves 4

1 quart milk
1/4 cup butter
1 teaspoon Worcestershire sauce
1 teaspoon salt
2 tablespoons flour mixed with 2 tablespoons water
1 pint oysters (with liquid)
Cayenne pepper

Put all ingredients, except oysters and cayenne pepper in a kettle. Cover; cook and stir well. Add oysters. Cook on low, until oysters curl. Sprinkle with cayenne pepper; serve hot with crackers.

COUNTRY FISH STEW
Serves 3

1 pound frozen fillets of perch, haddock, or other choice
2 teaspoons cooking oil
2 teaspoons cornstarch
1/4 cup cold water
1-1/2 teaspoons instant minced onion or 2 tablespoons fresh grated
1/2 teaspoon salt
1/4 teaspoon black pepper
1/4 teaspoon ground nutmeg
1 cup half-and-half
1 (8-1/2 ounce) can whole kernel corn, undrained
Chopped parsley for garnish

Thaw fish if frozen; cut into 1-inch pieces. In 3-quart saucepan, heat oil. Dissolve cornstarch in cold water; add seasonings. Stir into heated oil. Gradually add half-and-half, stirring constantly. Add fish and corn. Cook over medium heat, stirring often, for 8-10 minutes, or until fish flakes easily when tested with a fork. Garnish with chopped parsley.

FISH CHOWDER

1-1/2 pounds cod or haddock
2 cups diced potatoes
1 cup diced carrots
1 quart water
1/2 pound salt pork, diced
1 onion, chopped
2 tablespoons flour
1 pint milk
Salt and pepper

Cut fish into small pieces; remove bones and skin. Cook fish, potatoes, and carrots in water for 15 minutes. Fry the salt pork until crisp; remove from drippings; cook onion in drippings for a few minutes. Add flour and stir until well blended. Add milk.

Stir this mixture into fish and vegetables with the seasonings, and simmer 10 minutes longer, stirring frequently.

CORN CHOWDER
Serves 5

1/2 pound bacon
1 medium onion, chopped
2 medium potatoes, peeled and chopped
2 cups half-and-half
1 (17-ounce) can cream style corn
1/2 teaspoon salt
Pepper
1/2 cup milk

Fry bacon in a heavy Dutch oven until crisp; remove, reserving 2 tablespoons drippings in Dutch oven. Crumble bacon; set aside.

In reserved drippings, sauté onion until tender; add potatoes and water. Cover and simmer 15-20 minutes or until potatoes are tender. Stir in half-and-half and milk, corn and seasonings. Cook over medium heat, stirring frequently, until thoroughly heated.

Sprinkle each bowl with bacon.

CORN CHOWDER
Serves 4-6

1 tablespoon butter
3 slices bacon
1 large onion, chopped
4 large potatoes, peeled and diced
3 cups milk
1 cup creamed corn, fresh or canned
2 cups corn kernels
1 teaspoon salt
1 teaspoon finely chopped parsley

Heat butter in a large heavy pan. Add bacon and onion; cook until tender. Add potatoes and cook over medium heat for 5 minutes. Stir in 2 cups milk. Bring just to a boil. Cover and simmer until potatoes are tender. Gently stir in the creamed corn, whole kernels, and remaining milk. Heat through; season and sprinkle with parsley. Serve with croutons and sliced cooked sausage.

CABBAGE BEEF SOUP

1-1/2 pounds stewing beef, chopped
1 teaspoon salt
1/2 teaspoon pepper
2 bay leaves
1 cup chopped celery
1/2 cup chopped onion
4-5 medium carrots, sliced
1 cup chopped cabbage
Pinch of oregano
1 (#2 can) Italian style tomatoes
1 tablespoon Worcestershire sauce
1 beef bouillon cube

Place meat in 3 quart kettle; cover with cold water. Add salt, pepper, and bay leaves. Bring to boil; then turn heat to low. Add celery, onion, carrots, and cabbage. Simmer 2-1/2 hours or until meat is tender. Remove bay leaves. Cut meat into small pieces; return to kettle. Add oregano, tomatoes, Worcestershire sauce, and bouillon cube. Simmer 30 minutes. Serve.

MEATBALL SOUP ITALIANO

Serves 6

6 cups tomato juice
1.5 ounce package spaghetti-sauce mix, Italian style
1 small onion, diced
1 cup uncooked small-shell or elbow macaroni cooked according to package instructions
3/4 cup diced green pepper
3/4 cup diced celery
4-ounce can mushrooms, diced
Meatballs, browned (recipe below)
1 tablespoon vegetable oil
Grated Parmesan or Romano cheese

In large, kettle, mix tomato juice and spaghetti-sauce mix; place over medium heat. While juice is heating, brown meatballs in vegetable oil in heavy frying pan over medium heat. Add to juice mixture. Using same frying pan, sauté vegetables until onion is transparent, about 15 minutes. Add to juice mixture; simmer 30 minutes stirring occasionally. Add cooked macaroni; bring to simmer. Serve in bowls with a teaspoon of grated cheese sprinkle on top.

Variation: Replace macaroni with 15-ounce can ravioli or its equivalent of fresh of frozen ravioli or tortellini cooked according to package instructions.

A green salad with an Italian dressing, garlic toast or hard-crust Italian bread and a dessert will make a good meal for a hungry group.

Meatballs:
Makes 16

1/2 pound lean hamburger
2 teaspoons dried minced onion
2 tablespoons seasoned bread crumbs
1 tablespoon grated Parmesan or Romano cheese
1/2 teaspoon Italian herb seasoning
1 egg, slightly beaten
Salt and pepper to taste

Mix together well and form into 3/4 to 1-inch meatballs. (Note: Recipe can be doubled.) After browning, meatballs can be simmered about 30 minutes in your favorite spaghetti sauce and served over spaghetti or other pasta.

DUMPLINGS WITH DILL GRAVY

75 to 100 years old

Dumplings:
1 cup flour
2 teaspoons baking powder
1/4 cup milk
2 eggs
4 slices toast, buttered, cut into fine squares
1 large canning kettle
Water

Mix in order given. Mold into 2 large dumplings. Let stand few minutes before boiling. Make sure kettle full of water is boiling before adding dumplings. Boil 30 - 35 minutes, covered (don't take cover off until done). Remove with slotted spoon onto platter. With heavy thread, cut into slices.

Dill Gravy:
2 tablespoons butter
2 tablespoons flour
1/4 teaspoon salt
Dash pepper
1/2 to 3/4 cup beef broth or 1 beef bouillon cube
1 tablespoon fresh dill, finely chopped   (or more to taste)
1/2 cup sour cream

Melt butter in skillet over low heat. Add flour, salt and pepper; mix until flour is lightly browned. Remove skillet from heat, gradually add beef broth or bouillon cube and dill. Return to stove; bring to boil, stirring constantly. Cook 1 - 2 minutes longer. Remove from heat. Add sour cream stirring constantly.

CABBAGE PATCH STEW

1 medium head cabbage, sliced and cooked until tender
1-1/2 pounds ground beef
2 tablespoons oil
2 medium onions, sliced thin
1/2 cup diced celery
16-ounce can red kidney beans, drained
2 cups tomatoes
6 ounce can tomato paste
Salt, pepper and chili powder to taste
2 cups grated cheese

Brown beef in hot oil; add onion and celery; cook until transparent. Add beans, tomatoes and rest of ingredients; simmer for 15 minutes. In a greased larger casserole, place layer of cabbage, layer of meat mixture; repeat. Top with 2 cups grated cheese. Bake at 350 degrees for 45 minutes.

QUICK POTATO SOUP

1 medium potato, peeled and cubed
1 medium onion, peeled and chopped
2 cups milk
1 teaspoon chicken flavor bouillon granules, or one cube
1 tablespoon sugar
1 cup dried potato flakes
Pinch white pepper
2 slices bacon, diced
1/4 cup smoked ham or diced, boiled ham
2 quarts of water (more or less)

In saucepan, fry bacon until partially cooked, *not* crisp. Drain off most fat; add chopped onions. Cook until transparent. Add water, ham, chicken flavor bouillon, to hot bacon. Simmer until all is tender, about 15 minutes. Add sugar, pepper, and half of dried potato flakes, stirring well until all is mixed. Simmer an additional 10 minutes. Add rest of potato flakes, stirring well, then all milk. Simmer another short time until soup is well thickened. Add diced potato; cook until soft.

Note: If a thinner soup is wanted, add additional milk. Skim milk powder, or canned milk works well, as long as it is added slowly and never boiled, only simmered.

If a brighter soup is wanted, add cubed red pepper, or a few canned or frozen sweet peas at the same time as the potato flakes. When checking for taste, a bit of salt can be added, but as the ham, bacon, and chicken bouillon are cooked, salt may not be needed.

POTATO SOUP
Serves 4-6

2 (10-1/2 ounce) cans of chicken consommé
1 soup can water
2 cups diced potatoes
2 scallions, chopped
1 soup can milk
1 teaspoon Worcestershire sauce
1/2 cup sour cream

Combine consommé, water, potatoes, and scallions in a large saucepan; bring to a boil. Reduce heat; simmer until potatoes are tender, about 12 minutes. Blend smooth in a blender; return to saucepan. Stir in milk and Worcestershire sauce; heat. Stir in sour cream. Can be eaten hot or well chilled.

IRISH CREAM OF POTATO SOUP
Serves 6

4 stalks celery and leaves
2 medium onions
1 medium carrot
1-1/2 cups water
2 chicken bouillon cubes
1-1/2 cups cooked, mashed potatoes
1 tablespoon butter
2 cups half-and-half

Chop celery, onions and carrot; add water and simmer 30 minutes. Strain through sieve (large tea strainer will work). Stir bouillon cubes into strained vegetable-water. While hot, pour over potatoes, stirring until dissolved. Rub through strainer to make sure no lumps remain. Add butter and half-and-half; heat. Sprinkle paprika and parsley flakes on top.

If you have never tried bisques, you do not know what you have missed. The definition of a bisque is a thick, rich creamy soup with shellfish as its base. Bisques always have been popular in the southern states, most of which border a waterway, But today, all regions enjoy their own variety of this thick soup. We will wager that the official definition does not match the taste of this hearty soup which is served both as a first course at dinner or as lunch, all by itself.

EASY POTATO-CHEESE SOUP
Serves 6

1 package au gratin potatoes
1 (#303) can chicken broth
3 cups water
1/4 cup carrots, finely diced
1/4 cup celery, finely diced
1 small can Pet milk
Chopped parsley

Combine contents of potato package, including cheese sauce mix, broth, water, carrots, and celery in a 3-1/2 quart saucepan. Bring to a boil, stirring occasionally. Reduce heat and simmer, covered, for 15 minutes or until potatoes are tender. Remove from heat; add milk. Garnish with parsley.

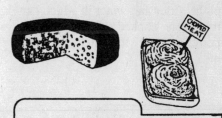

HAMBURGER SOUP

1 pound hamburger
1 cup chopped onion
1 cup celery
1 cup diced potatoes
1 quart tomatoes
2 large carrots, grated medium
1 tablespoon salt
1 bay leaf
1/4 teaspoon basil
1/4 teaspoon thyme
1/4 teaspoon fresh ground pepper
2 tablespoons beef bouillon
6 cups water
2 small cans whole kernel corn
1 small can yellow wax beans
1 cup frozen peas

Fry hamburger with onion until done. Add everything else except corn, beans, and peas. Simmer 30 minutes. Add last 3 ingredients and simmer another 5 minutes. A really great "hurry up" meal, tastes like it took hours to prepare.

CREAM OF CARROT SOUP

Serves 4 to 6

1 bunch of carrots
1 small onion
Sprig of parsley
1/4 cup of rice
2 tablespoons butter or drippings
1-1/2 teaspoons. salt
Few grains of cayenne
2 cups water
2 cups scalded milk
2 tablespoons flour

Chop enough carrots to make 2 cups; cook in water until tender. Press through sieve, saving cooking water. Cook rice in milk in double boiler. Cook onion in butter or fat; add flour and seasonings. Mix carrots with rice and milk, add butter or drippings, flour and water in which carrots were cooked.Bring to boiling point; serve. If too thick, thin with milk.

CREAMED ZUCCHINI SOUP

Serves 6-8

Here is a great way to use wonderful zucchini. We are always looking for new serving ideas.

2 cups grated zucchini
2 cups water
1 tablespoon dried minced onion
2 chicken bouillon cubes
Grated pepper
1 teaspoon garlic powder
1 teaspoon dillweed
1/2 teaspoon nutmeg
1(13-ounce) evaporated milk
1/2 cup water
2 tablespoons cornstarch

In a 2-quart casserole combine zucchini, water, onion, bouillon cubes, pepper, garlic powder, dillweed, and nutmeg. Microwave for 8 minutes on HIGH. Puree in blender. Pour back into bowl.

In a small dish combine the cornstarch with the 1/2 cup water; mix well. Pour into the puree, add the can of milk, and microwave the entire mixture until thick, for 5-8 minutes on HIGH. Refrigerate to cool. Serve as a cold soup with garnish of paprika and parsley.

CREAM OF WILD RICE SOUP

Serves 4

1/2 cup wild rice
10-3/4 ounce can condensed chicken broth
1 cup water
1/4 cup chopped onion
1 small bay leaf
1/2 teaspoon dried basil, crushed
4-ounce can sliced mushrooms, drained
1/4 cup fresh parsley, snipped or 1/8 cup dried
2 cups of light cream or milk
1 tablespoon flour
1/4 cup shredded carrot

Rinse rice. In 3-quart saucepan, combine rice, water, broth, onion, carrot, bay leaf and basil; cover, simmer 45 minutes. Remove bay leaf. Add mushrooms and parsley. Stir cream (or milk) into flour; add to soup. Cook and stir until mixture thickens. Cook and stir 1 minute more. Season to taste with pepper.

CREAM OF SPINACH SOUP

Serves 8

2 tablespoons butter
1 leek, chopped, or 6 to 8 green onions, cut in 1-inch pieces
1 clove garlic, cut in half
1 can (13-3/4 ounce) chicken broth
2 packages (10-ozs. each) fresh spinach, cleaned
1 medium potato, shredded
3 cups milk
1 teaspoon salt
1/8 teaspoon nutmeg
Pepper
Dairy sour cream (optional)

In a 5-quart dutch oven, melt butter over medium heat; sauté leek and garlic until tender, but not browned. Add 1/2 cup of chicken broth, spinach and potato. Simmer, covered, over medium heat, stirring occasionally, about 15 minutes. In bowl of food processor, place chopping blade; add spinach mixture. Process just until blended. Carefully return spinach mixture to Dutch oven. Add remaining chicken broth, milk, salt and nutmeg; stir until blended. Cook, covered, over medium heat for 15 minutes or until hot. Season with salt and pepper as desired. Garnish with dollop of sour cream.

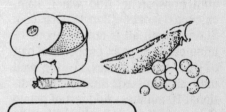

ORIENTAL CHICKEN NOODLE SOUP

Serves 6

6 chicken thighs, (about 1-1/2 pounds)
6 cups water
1 cup frozen green peas
2 medium eggs
2 (3 ounce) packages dried ramen or Oriental noodles for soup
Soy sauce or salt

In 5-quart Dutch oven, heat chicken thighs and water to boiling. Cover; simmer chicken over low heat until fork-tender, about 20 minutes. Transfer chicken to bowl; cool until easy to handle. Skim off and discard all fat from surface of broth. Remove and discard skin and bones from chicken. Tear chicken into pieces. Add peas to broth; cook for 1 minute. In cup, beat eggs lightly, just to break yolks. Drizzle eggs into soup. Add noodles and seasoning packets. Cook just until noodles soften. Stir in chicken. Add soy sauce or salt to taste.

BEEF STEW

2 pounds beef chuck roast
2 medium onions, peeled and quartered
1 pound carrots
16-ounce can tomatoes
2 cups water
1 tablespoon basil
1 teaspoon pepper
5 potatoes, peeled and quartered

Cube beef; sauté in small amount of fat; slice onions and sauté in fat. Place beef, onions, carrots, tomatoes, basil, pepper and water into large covered pot. Bring to boil; simmer 2 hours. Add potatoes the last 45 minutes.

GREEN PEPPER STEW

Economy dish, serves 4

1 onion, chopped
4 tablespoons shortening
2 cups water
2 green peppers, chopped
2 tomatoes, chopped
1 teaspoon salt
1/2 teaspoon black pepper
4 medium sized potatoes, diced
2 tablespoons flour

Brown onion in shortening. Add water, peppers, tomatoes, salt and pepper. Cook for 20 minutes. Add potatoes and cook until potatoes are soft but not mushy. Mix flour with small amount of water. Add just enough to vegetables to thicken.

GERMAN BROWN STEW AND NOODLES

50 years old

1-1/2 pounds stew beef, cubed
2 tablespoons Crisco
1 large apple, pared and shredded

1/2 cup carrots, shredded
1/2 cut water
1/2 onion, sliced
1 clove garlic, minced
2 beef bouillon cubes
4 tablespoons cornstarch
1/4 cup cold water
1/4 teaspoon Kitchen Bouquet

Brown meat in Crisco; drain. Add apple, carrots, onion, 1/2 cup water, salt, pepper, garlic and bouillon cube. Place in saucepan; bring to boil; simmer about 2 hours. Combine cornstarch with 1/4 cup cold water and Kitchen Bouquet; add to meat mixture. Stir until thick and serve over hot noodles.

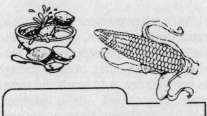

SEAFARER'S TOMATO CLAM CHOWDER

Makes 10 cups

3 slices bacon, chopped
1 onion, chopped
2 ribs celery, chopped
1 clove garlic, minced
2 cups tomato juice
2-1/2 cups potatoes, diced
1 (28 ounce) can whole tomatoes, undrained and cut
1/4 teaspoon salt
1/2 teaspoon dried whole thyme
1 (8 ounce) bottle clam juice
2 (6-1/2 ounce) cans minced clams, undrained
4 tablespoons cornstarch

In a Dutch oven, cook bacon until lightly browned. Add onion, celery, and garlic; sauté until tender. Add tomato juice and next 5 ingredients. Cover; cook 25 minutes or until potatoes are tender. Drain clams; reserve liquid. Mix cornstarch and clam liquid; stir until smooth. Carefully stir clams and cornstarch mixture into vegetables. Gently boil about 2 minutes, stirring constantly, until slightly thickened.

CHASE THE CHILLS WINTER CHOWDER

1 pound dried lima beans
1 large onion, chopped
2 large ribs celery, chopped
1/4 cup butter
1/4 cup flour
1 teaspoon salt
Pepper to taste
3 cups heavy cream
16-ounce can Italian plum tomatoes
16-ounce can corn
1/4 pound sharp Cheddar cheese, grated

Rinse dried lima beans and soak in 6 cups water for 6 hours or overnight. Drain and cook beans for about 1 hour in large pot with 6 cups fresh water. In large saucepan, sauté onion and celery in butter until slightly tender. Thoroughly blend in flour, salt and pepper. Add cream and bring to a gentle boil. Add beans and their liquid; add remaining ingredients. Bring again to a boil; adjust seasonings before serving.

SMOKY CORN CHOWDER

Serves 6

1/2 cup chopped onion
1/4 cup margarine or butter
1/4 cup all-purpose flour
1 teaspoon salt
1/8 teaspoon pepper
4 cups milk
1 (17 ounce) can whole kernel corn, drained
1 (12 ounce) package fully-cooked smoked sausage links, sliced
1 (8-1/2 ounce) can Lima beans, drained

In saucepan cook onion in margarine or butter until tender, but not brown. Blend in flour, salt, and pepper. Add the milk all at once; cook and stir until thickened and bubbly. Stir in corn, sausage, and Lima beans. Simmer 10 minutes.

Tasty TRIMMERS

DIETER VEGETABLE SOUP

1 head cabbage
5 carrots
4 stalks celery
1 large onion
5 tomatoes *or* 15-ounce can tomatoes
6 beef bouillon cubes
6 cups water

Chop all vegetables coarsely. Add water and bouillon cubes; bring to a boil, then simmer about 45 minutes, or until vegetables are tender. (145 calories per serving)

JIFFY MINESTRONE
Serves 8

4 cups coarsely chopped cabbage (½ medium-size head)
1 medium onion, coarsely chopped
¼ cup parsley, chopped
1 clove garlic, chopped
1 teaspoon salt
1 teaspoon oregano
¼ teaspoon pepper
3 tablespoons oil
5 cups beef broth
1 (16-ounce) can tomatoes *or* 2 cups chopped fresh
¼ pound spaghetti, broken up

1 medium zucchini, sliced
1 (16-ounce) can red kidney beans

In Dutch oven, over medium heat, sauté cabbage, onion, parsley, garlic ,salt, oregano and pepper in oil, stirring often, 5 minutes, or until cabbage is crisp-tender. Add broth and tomatoes; bring to boil. Stir in spaghetti, zucchini and beans. Cook, stirring occasionally, for 10 minutes, or until spaghetti is of desired doneness. (200 calories per serving)

TOMATO-CHEESE TOPPER
Makes 1 cup

¾ cup vegetable cocktail juice
¼ cup chopped green pepper
1 tablespoon all-purpose flour
1 teaspoon Worcestershire sauce
Dash hot pepper sauce
4 ounces pasteurized process cheese spread, cubed
Hot potato skins *or* baked potatoes

In 1-quart saucepan, stir together vegetable juice, green pepper, flour, Worcestershire and hot pepper sauce. Over medium-high heat, heat to boiling, stirring often. Reduce heat to low. Stir in cheese until melted. Spoon over potato skins or baked potatoes. (26 calories per tablespoon)

CHICKEN BREASTS WITH MUSTARD SAUCE AND RICE
Serves 6

1 cup regular long-grain rice
3 whole chicken breasts, skinned, boned and cut in half
1 cup water
1 teaspoon salt
½ teaspoon thyme leaves
2 tablespoons butter *or* margarine
1 green onion, thinly sliced
2 tablespoons flour
1 tablespoon prepared mustard
¼ cup chopped parsley

Prepare rice as label directs. Meanwhile, in a 10-inch skillet over high heat, heat chicken, water, salt and thyme leaves to boiling. Reduce heat to low; cover and simmer 10 minutes, or until chicken is fork-tender, turning breasts once. With slotted spoon, remove chicken to warm platter; reserve liquid. In a 1-quart saucepan over medium heat, melt butter; add green onion and cook until tender, stirring occasionally. Stir in flour and mustard until blended. Gradually stir in the reserved liquid; cook, stirring constantly, until sauce is thickened and smooth. Pour sauce over chicken. Toss rice with parsley and serve with chicken. (300 calories per serving)

CASSEROLE PORK STEW
Serves 6

1 pound lean pork pieces, 1 inch square (fat trimmed off)
3 medium potatoes (about 1 pound), cut in 1½-inch pieces
1 (16-ounce) bag carrots, cut into ½-inch pieces
1 medium green pepper, cut into thin strips
1 medium onion, sliced
1 medium tomato, cut in thin wedges
2 beef bouillon cubes
1 cup water
1 tablespoon flour

Place all ingredients, except flour, in 2½-quart or larger casserole. Evenly sprinkle flour over top of pork mixture. Cover casserole and bake in a 350-degree oven for 1¾ hours, or until pork and vegetables are tender. Stir occasionally. (235 calories per serving)

STIR-FRIED BROCCOLI
Serves 4

1 (10-ounce) package frozen broccoli spears, partially thawed
1 tablespoon vegetable oil
1 small onion, sliced
1 (4-ounce) can sliced mushrooms, drained
3 tablespoons soy sauce

Cut broccoli spears into 1 to 2-inch lengths. Heat oil in non-stick skillet. Add remaining ingredients. Cook, stirring constantly over high heat 2–3 minutes until broccoli is just tender. (67 calories per serving)

TOMATO SKILLET CABBAGE
Serves 4

1 (16-ounce) can tomato wedges in tomato juice, drained (reserve liquid)
1 teaspoon instant beef bouillon
3 cups shredded cabbage

In medium skillet, heat reserved tomato juice and bouillon until bouillon is dissolved. Stir in cabbage. Cover tightly; cook for 3 minutes, stirring occasionally. Stir in tomatoes; cover and cook until cabbage is crisp tender and tomatoes are heated through, 3–5 minutes. (45 calories per serving)

DIETWISE STUFFED POTATOES
Serves 4

2 large baking potatoes
½ cup cottage cheese
1 bouillon cube, dissolved in ¼ cup boiling water
1 tablespoon chopped onion or scallion
2 tablespoons parsley
1 teaspoon lemon juice
¼ teaspoon salt
Dash pepper
1 tomato, cut in wedges
1 lemon, cut in wedges

Scrub potatoes. Dry and prick with a fork. Bake at 425 degrees for 50 minutes, or until soft. Cut in half lengthwise. Scoop out potato from each half without breaking skin. Place potato in large mixing bowl. Add cottage cheese, dissolved bouillon, scallions, parsley, lemon juice, salt and pepper; beat until smooth. Spoon into potato skins. Place on baking sheet and bake at 350 degrees for 10–15 minutes, until potato is lightly browned. Serve with wedges of tomato and lemon. (90 calories per serving)

SAGE AND ONION STUFFING

4 medium onions, peeled and cut in thick slices
1/2 cup water
4 whole cloves
6 whole peppercorns
1 teaspoon powdered sage or 6 fresh sage leaves, chopped
2 cups bread crumbs
6 tablespoons melted butter
Salt and pepper to taste

Put onion slices, water, cloves, and peppercorns into a saucepan. Cover and simmer until onions are tender. Discard cloves and peppercorns. Reserve the cooking liquid. Roughly chop onions and add them to the bread crumbs; add sage. Stir in melted butter, then taste and add salt, pepper, and additional sage to suit your taste. If the stuffing is too dry for your taste, add some of the reserved cooking liquid.

Enough for an 8-pound goose. Double the recipe for a 12-14-pound turkey.

SKILLET SALAD
Serves 4

2 ribs celery, cut into ¼-inch slices
1/2 green bell pepper, sliced into small pieces
1 small onion, chopped
1/3 cup water
1½ teaspoons flour
2 tablespoons vinegar
1 teaspoon prepared mustard
2 teaspoons sugar
Dash pepper
Lettuce to taste, torn into small pieces

In a skillet place celery, pepper, onion and water. Bring to boil over medium-high heat. Mix flour, vinegar, mustard, sugar and pepper together. Add to mixture in skillet; cook and stir constantly until thickened and bubbly. Remove from heat and stir in lettuce. Toss well. (45 calories per serving)

LAZY BEEF CASSEROLE
Serves 4

- 1 pound lean beef chuck, cut into 1½-inch cubes
- ½ cup red wine
- 1 (10-ounce) can beef consommé, undiluted
- ¼ teaspoon rosemary
  Freshly ground black pepper to taste
- 1 medium onion, chopped
- ¼ cup fine, dry bread crumbs
- ¼ cup all-purpose flour

Put meat in a casserole with wine, consommé, pepper, rosemary and onion. Mix flour and bread crumbs; stir into liquid.

Cover and bake at 300 degrees for about 3 hours. (A lower temperature and longer cooking time may be used if it is more convenient.)

Serve with rice or noodles. (350 calories per serving or 450 calories with ½ cup of rice or pasta)

BURGERS WITH MUSHROOM SAUCE

- 1 pound extra-lean ground beef
- 1 small onion, chopped
- 1 tablespoon dry vegetable flakes
- 1 teaspoon Worcestershire sauce
- ½ teaspoon salt (optional)
- ¼ teaspoon pepper
- 1 teaspoon prepared horseradish
- 8 ounces sliced, fresh mushrooms
- 1 teaspoon soy sauce
- ¼ teaspoon dry mustard
- ¼ cup white wine
- 1 tablespoon cornstarch
- ¼ cup water

In medium mixing bowl combine ground beef, onion, vegetable flakes, Worcestershire sauce, salt, pepper and horseradish. Form into 4 patties. Place in 12 x 8-inch baking dish. Microwave on HIGH, 5–9 minutes, or until meat is no longer pink. After half the cooking time, remove patties and set aside, reserving meat juices. Add remaining ingredients. Microwave on HIGH for 6–9 minutes, or until sauce is thickened and mushrooms are tender, stirring 2 or 3 times. Return patties to dish. (198 calories per serving)

FISH CREOLE
Serves 4

- ½ cup sliced celery
- ½ cup chopped green pepper
- 1 onion, thinly sliced
- 1 (8-ounce) can tomato sauce
- ½ teaspoon salt
- ½ teaspoon chili powder
- ¼ teaspoon garlic powder
- ¼ teaspoon dried oregano leaves
- ¼ teaspoon dried thyme leaves
- 1 pound fish fillets

Combine celery, green pepper and onion in an 8-inch square microwave dish. Cover with plastic wrap. Microwave on HIGH for 2½–3 minutes, or until just about tender. Add remaining ingredients, *except* fish. Cover.

Microwave on HIGH for 2–3 minutes, or until mixture boils. Push vegetables to side of dish; arrange fillets in dish. Spoon vegetables and sauce over fish. Cover. Microwave on HIGH 4–4½ minutes, or until fish flakes apart easily, rotating dish once. (125 calories per serving)

ONION SOUP
Serves 4

- 2 teaspoons margarine
- 2 cups sliced onions
- 1 clove garlic, minced
- 4 cups water
- ¼ cup dry sherry
- 4 packets (4.5 grams each) low-calorie instant beef-flavor broth mix
- 1 teaspoon chopped fresh parsley
- ⅛ teaspoon dried thyme leaves
- ⅛ teaspoon white pepper

In 2-quart saucepan, sauté onions and garlic in margarine until onions are softened, about 2 minutes. Add water and remaining ingredients; stir well to dissolve broth mix. Simmer 15–20 minutes. (25 calories per serving)

BEEF TERIYAKI
Serves 6

- 1½ pounds sirloin steak
- ½ cup soy sauce
- ½ cup dry white wine
- 1 clove garlic, minced
- 1 teaspoon ginger
- 1 tablespoon cornstarch
- 3 packets artificial sweetener

Slice beef into ½-inch strips. Arrange in shallow casserole. Combine soy sauce, wine, garlic and ginger. Pour over meat; cover and refrigerate. Marinate 2 hours. Broil beef 1½ minutes on each side. Pour marinade into saucepan. Add cornstarch and cook over medium heat until sauce thickens. Remove from heat; stir in sweetener. Serve sauce over meat. (203 calories per serving)

SPICY BEEF DIP
Serves 4

- 1 cup plain low-fat yogurt
- 3 tablespoons dairy sour cream
- 2 packets (4.5 grams each) low-calorie beef-flavor broth mix
- 1 tablespoon drained prepared horseradish
- 1 teaspoon Worcestershire sauce

In small bowl, combine ingredients. Cover with plastic wrap and refrigerate at least 30 minutes to blend flavors. Stir dip and serve with vegetables. (65 calories per serving)

STEWED VEGETABLE MEDLEY
Serves 4

- 1 teaspoon vegetable margarine
- 3 cups cabbage, finely shredded
- 6 ribs celery, thinly sliced
- ½ green pepper, thinly sliced
- 1 large onion, thinly sliced
- 4 tomatoes, peeled and diced
- 1 teaspoon seasoned salt
- ½ teaspoon paprika
  Black pepper to taste

Heat margarine in bottom of saucepan; add all other ingredients. Stir with a fork; cover and bring just to a boil. Lower heat, simmer 8–10 minutes, or until vegetables are tender. (74 calories per serving)

SWEET POTATO AND APPLE CASSEROLE
Serves 8

- 4 small sweet potatoes (1½ pounds), peeled and sliced
- 2 apples (1 pound), cored and sliced
  Cooking spray
- 3 tablespoons sugar
- ½ teaspoon cinnamon
  Dash white pepper
- 2 teaspoons low-calorie margarine, melted

Layer half each of potatoes and apples in an 8-inch square dish coated with cooking spray. Combine sugar, cinnamon and pepper; sprinkle half of mixture over potatoes and apples. Drizzle with half of melted margarine. Repeat with remaining potatoes, apples and other ingredients. Cover and bake in a 350-degree oven for 1 hour. (120 calories per ½-cup serving.)

DELUXE CHICKEN BREASTS

- 4 cups hot cooked light spaghetti; set aside
- 2 cups grated zucchini
- 1 cup chopped green pepper
- 1 cup chopped mushrooms
- ½ cup chopped onion
- 2 cloves chopped garlic
- ½ teaspoon oregano
- ½ teaspoon dried basil
- ½ teaspoon salt
- 1 cup low-fat cottage cheese
- 4 chicken breast halves, skin removed and split in half
- 1 (1-pound, 12-ounce) can whole tomatoes

Combine zucchini, green pepper, mushrooms, onion, garlic, salt, basil and oregano in a blender; blend only.

Divide mixture in half. Stir cottage cheese into half the mixture, reserving other half for the sauce. Blend vegetable-cottage cheese stuffing mixture until smooth. Spoon 1½ tablespoons of stuffing into center of each piece of chicken. Press together and secure with toothpicks or string. Set aside.

Place tomatoes and reserved vegetable mixture in a large skillet; heat thoroughly over medium heat. Place stuffed breasts in the tomato mixture; cover and simmer for 20–25 minutes over medium heat. Serve over hot spaghetti. (273 calories per serving)

FINNISH CARROT CASSEROLE
Serves 6

- 2 cups cooked brown rice
- 1 cup skim milk
- 2½ cups shredded carrots
- 2 eggs
- 2 teaspoons brown sugar

- ¼ teaspoon ground nutmeg
  Salt to taste
- 2 tablespoons crushed high-vitamin cereal flakes

Add cooked rice to milk in saucepan. Simmer, uncovered, until most of the liquid reduces and mixture is creamy, about 10 minutes. Mix with remaining ingredients, except cereal crumbs, in 2-quart casserole. Sprinkle with crumbs. Bake, uncovered, in preheated 325-degree oven for approximately 50 minutes until set. (146 calories per serving)

SAUCY CHICKEN WINGS
Makes 10

- 2 pounds chicken wings (10 wings
- 1½ cups seasoned vegetable juice cocktail
- 1 tablespoon soy sauce
- 2 large cloves garlic, minced
- 1 teaspoon ground ginger or
- 2 teaspoons grated fresh ginger
- ⅛ teaspoon sesame oil
- 1 tablespoon cornstarch
- 2 tablespoons water

Spray 10-inch nonstick skillet with vegetable cooking spray. Over medium heat, cook chicken wings, half at a time, until browned on all sides. Spoon off fat. Return wings to skillet. Add vegetable juice, soy sauce, garlic, ginger and sesame oil. Reduce heat to low. Cover; simmer 20 minutes. Uncover; simmer 10 minutes more, or until wings are fork-tender.

Remove chicken to serving platter; keep warm. In cup, stir together cornstarch and water until smooth; gradually stir into vegetable juice mixture. Cook until mixture boils and thickens, stirring often. Serve sauce over wings. (113 calories per serving)

TURNIPS GLAZED WITH HONEY AND LEMON
Serves 4

2 large turnips (1 pound) peeled and cut into ½-inch cubes
2 tablespoons honey
1 tablespoon Weight Watchers margarine
½ teaspoon lemon rind
⅛ teaspoon black pepper
1¼ cups water

In medium saucepan over moderate heat bring 1¼ cups unsalted water to boil. Add turnips; cook, covered, for 15–20 minutes, or until fork-tender. Drain and add honey, margarine, lemon rind and pepper to turnips. Warm, uncovered, over low heat, shaking pan gently for 2–3 minutes, or until margarine has melted and turnips are lightly glazed. (83 calories per serving)

DIETER'S DELIGHT

1 pint dry-curd cottage cheese
1 (3-ounce) package orange gelatin
1 (11-ounce) can mandarin oranges, drained
1 small can crushed pineapple in own juice, drained
1 (4-ounce) carton Cool Whip

Place cottage cheese in large bowl with lid. Pour gelatin over it and mix gently. Add pineapple and oranges; mix gently, then fold in Cool Whip and seal. For dessert, use 1 scoop and put cherry on top. For salad, place on lettuce leaf topped with chopped nuts. Before each serving, gently whip. Will keep 1 week.

ASPARAGUS WITH CHEESE
Serves 4

1 pound fresh asparagus spears *or* 1 (10-ounce) package frozen asparagus spears
2 ounces (½ cup) processed Swiss cheese, shredded
2 tablespoons chopped canned pimiento
2 teaspoons sesame seed, toasted

In a 10-inch skillet, cook asparagus spears in boiling salted water until tender. Drain. Toss together cheese, pimiento and sesame seed. Sprinkle over spears. Heat in a 350-degree oven just until the cheese melts. (78 calories per serving)

LIGHT 'N' LUSCIOUS CHILLED TORTE
Serves 5

½ cup fructose
2 tablespoons cornstarch
1⅓ cups skim milk
⅓ cup water
1 egg, well-beaten
1 teaspoon vanilla
1½ squares unsweetened chocolate, melted
1 (10-ounce) angel food loaf cake
1 tablespoon finely chopped nuts

In a saucepan combine fructose and cornstarch; mix to blend. Stir in skim milk and water. Cook, stirring constantly, until mixture begins to thicken. Stir small amount of hot mixture into egg; return egg mixture to pan. Continue cooking until mixture just comes to a boil and thickens. Stir in vanilla and chocolate. Cover surface with waxed paper; chill. Slice cake horizontally, making 3 layers. Fill and frost cake layers. Sprinkle nuts over top of cake. Chill several hours before serving. (150 calories per slice)

BAKED VEGETABLES AND CHEESE

Marvelous hot or cold.

1 carrot (¾ cup); thinly sliced
½ tomato, diced
½ medium zucchini (¾ cup), thinly sliced
1½ teaspoons minced parsley
⅛ teaspoon Italian seasoning
⅛ teaspoon salt
1 slice low-fat pasteurized process cheese

Preheat oven to 350 degrees. In an 8-inch pie plate, layer carrot, zucchini and tomato. Sprinkle with parsley, Italian seasoning and salt. Cover with foil. Bake 30 minutes, or until vegetables are crisp-tender. Meanwhile, cut cheese into ½-inch strips. When vegetables are tender, remove foil. Arrange cheese strips to form a crisscross design on top of vegetables. Return to oven and bake until cheese is slightly melted, about 2 minutes. (165 calories per serving)

ITALIAN-STYLE POPCORN
Serves 6

3 tablespoons butter *or* margarine
3 tablespoons grated Parmesan cheese
½ teaspoon dried oregano leaves, crushed
6 cups popped popcorn

In small saucepan over low heat, melt butter with cheese and oregano; cook 2 minutes. In large bowl, pour butter mixture over popcorn; toss until well-coated. Store at room temperature in covered container. (86 calories per serving)

AMANA GIBLET DRESSING

1-1/4 to 1-1/2 pounds boneless beef chuck, cut in 3/4 inch cubes
3 sets of chicken giblets (heart, gizzards, and livers)
1 medium potato, peeled and cubed
1 medium onion, coarsely chopped
2 celery stalks, chopped
4 slices bread
1 teaspoon poultry seasoning or 3/4 teaspoon dried sage
1/4 teaspoon dried thyme
1/8 teaspoon freshly ground black pepper
1-1/2 teaspoons salt
1/2 cup chicken broth

Place beef cubes in a pan. Cover with water and simmer until tender (about 50 minutes). Cool in broth. Meanwhile, put giblets into another pan; cover with water and simmer for 20 minutes. Remove broth and let cool. Put beef, hearts, livers, and fragments of flesh from the gizzards into the bowl of a food processor and process briefly. Add potato, onion, celery, bread, poultry seasoning, thyme, pepper, and salt. Process again. Pour in sufficient chicken broth to make the mixture cohere. This stuffing is good in chicken or turkey. It can also be used to stuff vegetables such as squash or cabbage leaves. Enough for a 12-pound turkey. To serve it as a side dish, bake covered in a greased pan at 350 degrees for 30 minutes.

CORN BREAD DRESSING

2 (8-1/2-ounce) packages corn muffin mix, mixed and baked as directed on package
5 cups croutons
8 slices bacon, cooked and crumbled (reserve 3 tablespoons drippings)

1/3 cup butter or margarine
2 cups chopped celery
1 cup chopped onion
2 (10-3/4-ounce) cans condensed chicken broth
1/2 cup water
1 egg, slightly beaten
2 tablespoons snipped fresh parsley
2 teaspoons poultry seasoning

Cut muffins in 1/2-inch cubes. In large shallow casserole, combine corn muffin cubes and croutons. Stir gently. Set aside. Preheat oven to 325 degrees. In large skillet, heat reserved bacon drippings and the butter. Add celery and onion. Sauté over medium heat until vegetables are tender, about 5 minutes. Remove from heat. Stir in bacon, chicken broth, water, egg, parsley, and poultry seasoning. Add to corn muffin mixture. Toss gently to coat. Cover. Bake until hot, about 1 hour.

SHERRY AND WALNUT STUFFING

1 medium onion, chopped
4 tablespoons butter
1 tablespoon oil
1/4 pound chicken livers (optional)
2 cups bread crumbs
1 large apple, peeled and cored
1 cup walnuts, chopped
1 teaspoon dried tarragon
3/4 cup medium sherry
Salt and pepper to taste

Gently cook chopped onion in a mixture of 2 tablespoons butter and 1 tablespoon oil until it is tender. Remove from pan. If you are using chicken livers, cut each of them into four pieces and sauté for 1-2 minutes or until the outside is browned while the inside remains tender. Put the bread crumbs into a large bowl and add onions and livers. Grate the apple into the mixture. Add walnuts and

tarragon and stir to blend. Stir in the sherry. Melt the remaining butter and add to mixture. Taste for seasoning. Add pepper and salt as desired. This makes enough for a 6-pound roasting chicken. Double the recipe for a 12-pound turkey.

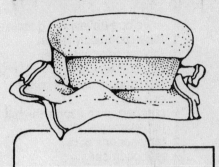

WILD RICE STUFFING WITH FRUIT AND HAZELNUTS

1 cup wild rice
4 cups water
16 dried apricots, each cut into 3 pieces and soaked in water for 1 hour
3 tablespoons raisins
1/4 pound red or green grapes, halved and seeded
1/4 cup chopped hazelnuts
1 teaspoon cumin seeds
1/4 teaspoon cinnamon
Pinch powdered cloves
Rind of 1 lemon, grated
Black pepper, freshly grated
Pinch salt
2 tablespoons butter, melted but not hot

Rinse wild rice under cold running water. Put into a saucepan with the water. Cover and simmer for 40 minutes. At this stage the water will have been absorbed and the rice will be tender, though not without a bite to it. Tip the rice into a large bowl. Drain apricot pieces, and add these to wild rice along with raisins, grapes, and hazelnuts. Briefly pound the cumin seeds in a mortar and stir them into the wild rice mixture. Stir in the grated lemon rind, cinnamon, and cloves. Season to taste with black pepper and salt. Stir in the melted butter.

Enough to stuff a 4-5 pound duck or 8 Cornish game hens. This recipe is also a good pilaf to serve with roast lamb.

BLENDER CHOCOLATE MOUSSE
Serves 4

- 1 egg
- 1 envelope unflavored gelatin
- 1 tablespoon cornstarch
- 1 tablespoon cold water
- 1 cup boiling water
- 2 tablespoons instant coffee granules
- ½ cup part-skim ricotta cheese
- ½ cup skim milk, cold
- 2 tablespoons cocoa
- ⅛ teaspoon salt
- 9 packets dry artificial sweetener

Combine egg, gelatin, cornstarch and cold water in blender or food processor. Blend to moisten gelatin and cornstarch. Add boiling water; blend until gelatin dissolves. Add remaining ingredients and blend until smooth. Chill until set.

To serve: Blend mixture until smooth and pour into dessert dishes. Serve immediately. (104 calories per serving)

DIABETIC THANKSGIVING CHEESECAKE
Makes 36 squares

- 1 (3-ounce) box any flavor sugar-free gelatin
- 8 ounces light cream cheese
- 1 package D-Zerta topping, whipped according to directions
- 2 cups graham cracker crumbs
- 22 packages Sweet 'N' Low
- 7 tablespoons stick margarine

Dissolve gelatin in 1 cup warm water. Set aside to cool. Stir together 6 packages Sweet 'N' Low with graham cracker crumbs. Add melted margarine. Press 2 cups of crumb mixture firmly into a 9 x 13-inch pan. Reserve rest of crumbs for top.

Cream 16 packages Sweet 'N' Low with cream cheese. Stir in whipped topping. Pour mixture over crust and sprinkle with remaining cracker crumbs. Chill 3–4 hours. Also freezes well. (37 calories per square)

YUMMY APPLES
Serves 4

- 1 pound apples, peeled, cored and cut into ½-inch cubes
- ¼ cup raisins
- ¼ cup water
- 1 ounce pecans, roasted and chopped
- 1¼ teaspoons vanilla extract, divided
- ¾ teaspoon cinnamon, divided
  Sugar substitute to equal 1 teaspoon sugar
- ½ cup plain non-fat yogurt

Combine apples, raisins, water, pecans and 1 teaspoon vanilla in 1-quart casserole. Cover dish with vented plastic wrap; microwave at HIGH, 3 minutes. Let stand 5 minutes. Stir in ½ teaspoon cinnamon and sugar substitute; cool. Meanwhile, prepare topping. In small bowl, combine yogurt, the remaining ¼ teaspoon *each* cinnamon and vanilla. To serve, divide apple mixture among 4 dessert dishes; top each serving with 2 tablespoons topping. (138 calories per serving)

LIME-COTTAGE CHEESE SALAD
Serves 4

- 2 envelopes lime D-Zerta gelatin
- 2 cups hot water
- 2 teaspoons vinegar
- ⅛ teaspoon salt
- ½ cup cottage cheese
- 2 teaspoons pimiento grated
- 1 teaspoon grated onion

Dissolve gelatin in hot water. Stir in vinegar and salt; pour 1 cup mixture in a 3-cup mold. Chill until partially set. Chill remaining gelatin mixture until slightly thickened. Fold in cheese, pimiento and onion. Pour over layer in mold. Chill until firm. Unmold on greens. (40 calories per serving)

DELECTABLE PIE
Serves 6

- ¼ cup milk
- 2 envelopes (4-serving size) diet vanilla pudding and pie filling
- 3¼ cups milk
- 10 ladyfingers, split

In a medium-size bowl, stir together thoroughly the ¼ cup of milk and 2 packages vanilla pie filling. Add 3¼ cups milk and bring to a boil, stirring constantly. Cool 15 minutes; stir occasionally. Lightly grease pie pan and line bottom with split ladyfingers. Pour cooled vanilla mixture over ladyfingers. Chill until set. Top with 1 tablespoon of low-calorie whipped topping per pie wedge when ready to serve. (115 calories per serving)

WHIPPED TOPPING
Serves 8

- ¾ cup evaporated skim milk
- ¼ cup apple juice *or* cider
- 1 teaspoon vanilla extract
- 8 packets Equal
- ½ teaspoon dried lemon peel
  Pinch of nutmeg

In deep narrow bowl combine all ingredients. Freeze until partially frozen, about 1½ hours. Beat at highest speed until stiff, about 5 minutes. Serve immediately. Spoon on fresh fruit, cakes, pies or ice cream. (28 calories per serving)

GINGER SPICE COOKIES
Makes 3 dozen

- ¼ cup vegetable oil
- 3 tablespoons diet margarine
- 1 tablespoon skim milk
- 1 egg
- ½ teaspoon vanilla extract
- ½ teaspoon salt
- 1 teaspoon baking powder
- ½ teaspoon cinnamon
- ½ teaspoon ginger
- ¼ teaspoon ground cloves
- 1½ cups all-purpose flour

Topping:
- 12 packets Equal
- ½ teaspoon cinnamon

Glaze:
- 12 packets Equal
- ½ teaspoon cinnamon
- 2 tablespoons boiling water

Cookies: Beat together oil and margarine. Add milk, egg and vanilla; beat well. Combine dry ingredients; blend into liquid mixture. Roll out to ⅛-inch thickness and cut into 2-inch rounds. Place cookies on baking sheet sprayed with non-stick coating. Bake at 375 degrees for 7 minutes. Add either topping or glaze while warm.

Topping: Combine Equal and cinnamon in plastic bag. Place warm cookies in bag and shake to coat.

Glaze: Combine Equal and cinnamon in boiling water. Brush over cookies while warm. (122 calories per serving of 3 cookies)

SPICED PEARS IN WINE
Serves 6

- 6 medium pears
- ½ cup rosé wine
- ½ cup water

- 4 (3-inch) long cinnamon sticks
- 2 teaspoons grated lemon peel
- 1 teaspoon whole cloves
- ⅛ teaspoon ground allspice

Peel pears with apple corer; remove cores from bottoms of pears; leave stems on. In 10-inch skillet over medium-high heat, heat pears and remaining ingredients to boiling. Reduce heat to low; cover and simmer 30 minutes, or until pears are tender, turning pears occasionally. Cover and refrigerate. To serve, discard the cinnamon sticks and cloves. Arrange pears with wine sauce in a deep serving dish or serve in individual bowls. (100 calories per serving)

DUTCH APPLE PANCAKE
Serves 4

Batter:
- 4 eggs
- ½ cup all-purpose flour
- ½ teaspoon baking powder
- ⅛ teaspoon salt
- ½ cup skim milk
- 2 tablespoons diet margarine, melted
- ⅛ teaspoon cinnamon

Filling:
- 2 tablespoons diet margarine
- 1 large tart apple, pared and sliced ¼-inch thick
- ½ teaspoon cinnamon

Glaze:
- 8 packets Equal
- ½ teaspoon cinnamon
- 3 tablespoons boiling water

Combine batter ingredients in blender or food processor; mix until smooth. Let rest 30 minutes. For filling, melt margarine in a 10-inch ovenproof skillet. Add apple slices; sprinkle with cinnamon and toss over low heat for 3 minutes. Pour batter over apples and place in preheated 425-degree oven for 15 minutes. Reduce heat to 350 degrees for 15 minutes. Remove from oven. Blend glaze ingredients and drizzle over top of pancake.

BREAKFAST BISCUITS
Makes 12 biscuits

- 2 cups sifted flour
- 3 teaspoons baking powder
- 1 teaspoon salt
- 2 tablespoons diet margarine
- ¾ cup skim milk

Stir the flour, baking powder and salt together, then cut in the diet margarine with a fork or pastry blender. Add milk and stir just until mixture forms a ball. Turn batter out onto a floured board and knead lightly. With floured hands pat out to ½-inch thickness. Cut into 2-inch biscuits with a biscuit cutter or an empty juice can. Spray a non-stick cookie tin with cooking spray. Arrange the biscuits at least an inch apart. Bake in a preheated 450-degree oven for 10–14 minutes. Cool on a rack. These biscuits may be frozen in plastic bags and reheated in a toaster oven or microwave. (90 calories per serving)

FLUFFY CHIFFON DESSERT
Serves 4

- 1 cup hot water
- 1 cup cold water
- 1 (3-ounce) package fruit-flavored gelatin
- ½ cup non-fat dry milk

Prepare gelatin according to package directions. Chill until partially set. Using blender or mixer, whip non-fat dry milk in gelatin until fluffy. Serve immediately, or allow it to reset in refrigerator. (112 calories per serving)

CORN BREAD STUFFING

For the corn bread:
1-1/2 cups cornmeal
2 cups all-purpose flour
2 tablespoons sugar
1 teaspoon salt
4 teaspoons baking powder
2 eggs, lightly beaten
2 cups milk
4 tablespoons melted butter

Grease 2 (8-inch) pans. Preheat oven to 450 degrees. In a large bowl, mix cornmeal, flour, sugar, salt, and baking powder. Stir in eggs, milk, and melted butter until well-mixed. Pour into the prepared pans and bake at 450 degrees for 30 minutes. Cool and then crumble.

For the stuffing:
1 large bag Pepperidge Farm or other bread crumbs
2 large onions, peeled and chopped
6 outside sticks of celery, chopped
1 stick butter, melted
2 apples, unpeeled, cubed
2 teaspoons poultry seasoning or to taste
2-3 cups giblet or chicken broth, warm
Salt and pepper, to taste

Combine corn bread and bread crumbs in a large bowl. Cook onions and celery in butter until until they are softened (about 8 minutes). Add these to the crumbs along with apples and poultry seasoning. Stir in the broth, adding sufficient to make a cohesive mixture. Taste for seasoning. Add salt and pepper if necessary.

This is enough stuffing for an 18-pound turkey.

SAUSAGE AND CELERY STUFFING

1 pound ground pork
1 pound hot or sweet Italian sausage
2 cups dried bread crumbs

2 cups celery, chopped into 1/4-inch pieces
1-2 eggs, slightly beaten

Combine pork and sausage. (The easiest way is to mix them with your hands.) Add the bread crumbs and celery. Add one slightly beaten egg to bind the mixture. If it seems too stiff, add the other egg.

Enough for a 14-pound turkey. Make in half quantities for a 6-pound roasting chicken.

ESCALLOPED OYSTERS
Serves 6-8

1 cup crushed saltine crackers
1 pint shucked oysters (about 24), drained
1/2 teaspoon salt
1/4 teaspoon cayenne pepper
1/2 cup heavy cream
1/2 cup fresh bread crumbs, lightly toasted
4 tablespoons unsalted butter, cut into small pieces

Preheat oven to 400 degrees. Sprinkle 3/4 cup of the crushed saltines into a large shallow baking dish. Add the oysters in a single layer. Season the cream with the salt and cayenne; drizzle the cream evenly over the oysters.

Toss the remaining 1/4 cup crushed saltines with the toasted bread crumbs and sprinkle them over the entire dish. Dot with the butter. Bake in the middle of the oven until the oysters are plumped and the crumb topping is light golden brown, about 20 minutes.

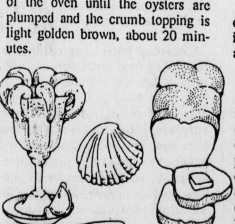

PICKLED CORN ON COB

Shuck and clean ears of corn. Boil about 10 minutes while still on the cob. Whole ears of corn may then be packed into a clean crock, or kernels cut from cob. Add a solution of salted water, (1/2 cup plain salt *not iodized* to 1 gallon water). In 2 weeks, corn may be eaten from cob, or cut off and fried in butter or other fat.

Unless you want to can corn, you may use it right from crock.

TOMATOES SHRIMPLY DELICIOUS
Serves 4

4 large tomatoes
1 tablespoon margarine
1/3 cup finely chopped onion
1/3 cup chopped celery
2 tablespoons chopped green pepper
1/2 pound (Bay) small cooked shrimp
1/4 cup soft bread crumbs
1 teaspoon Worcestershire sauce
1/4 teaspoon salt
1/4 teaspoon ground pepper
1/4 teaspoon dill weed
2 tablespoons grated cheddar cheese

Remove pulp from tomatoes, being careful not to break shells. Put shells in a 1-quart shallow baking dish; set aside.

Melt margarine in 8-inch skillet. Add onion, celery, and green pepper; sauté over low heat, 5 minutes. Cut up shrimp. Mix tomato pulp, shrimp, and chopped vegetables. Add bread crumbs, Worcestershire sauce, salt, pepper, and dill weed. Mix well. Fill each shell with 1/4 of the mixture. Sprinkle each with 1/4 of the cheese (1/2 tablespoon). Bake in preheated 375-degree oven for 20 minutes. (140 calories per serving.)

LIME MOUSSE

1 (3-ounce) package sugar-free gelatin
⅔ cup boiling water
1 tablespoon fresh lime juice
2 cups vanilla non-fat yogurt
½ teaspoon rum extract
¼ teaspoon coconut extract
1 cup crushed pineapple, drained (no sugar added)
2 egg whites
2 kiwifruit, peeled and sliced

Dissolve gelatin in boiling water; pour into blender container. Add lime juice, yogurt and extracts. Process at low speed until smooth, about 45 seconds. Add pineapple; process at medium speed until pineapple is almost puréed, about 1 minute. Transfer to large bowl. Place egg whites in medium bowl; beat with electric mixer until stiff peaks form. Fold egg whites into gelatin mixture; pour into decorative 1½-quart mold. Chill overnight, or until set. Garnish with kiwifruit. (51 calories per serving)

FRUIT MELANGE
Serves 12

1 (16-ounce) can pitted dark sweet cherries (water pack), drained and halved
1 pint fresh strawberries, sliced (2½ cups)
1 medium cantaloupe, cut into balls (about 2½ cups)
1 (15¼-ounce) can pineapple chunks (juice pack), drained
½ cup low-calorie orange marmalade
¼ cup hot water
1 teaspoon finely chopped candied ginger
1 medium-large banana, sliced (1 cup)
Fresh mint

Chill fruits; layer cherries, strawberries, melon and pineapple in compote or large glass bowl. Combine orange marmalade, hot water and candied ginger. Drizzle over fruit and chill. Arrange banana on top of fruit mixture. (To keep banana from darkening, dip in ascorbic acid color keeper or lemon juice mixed with a little water.) Garnish with mint. (87 calories per serving)

APPLE-RICE PUDDING
Serves 6

6 plain, unsalted rice cakes
2 medium (1 pound) Red or Delicious apples, cored and quartered
1 cup apple juice
⅓ cup non-fat dry milk
1 large egg
1 teaspoon ground cinnamon
1 teaspoon vanilla extract
Non-dairy topping (optional)

Preheat oven to 350 degrees. In a 1-quart ovenproof casserole break up rice cakes. In blender combine coarsely chopped apples, apple juice, dry milk, egg, cinnamon and vanilla. Pour mixture over rice cakes. Cover dish with foil. Bake 20 minutes at 350 degrees. Serve warm with non-dairy topping and apple slices, if desired. (100 calories per serving)

MOCK CHOCOLATE RUM TRUFFLES
Makes 3½ dozen *or* 14 servings

3 eggs
¼ cup water
2 tablespoons light rum
1 tablespoon frozen orange juice concentrate, thawed
26 packets Equal
⅓ cup cocoa
1⅓ cups fine, dry bread crumbs

Beat eggs with water, rum and orange juice concentrate until thick and lemon-colored, 5–7 minutes. Gradually add Equal. Fold in cocoa and bread crumbs. (Mixture will become very dense.) Shape rounded teaspoons of the mixture into balls. Let stand at room temperature until outsides are dry. Store in airtight container in refrigerator. (3 truffles per serving equals 73 calories)

LOW-CALORIE PEANUT BUTTER COOKIES
Makes 3½ dozen

1 cup *plus* 2 tablespoons all-purpose flour
½ cup artificial sweetener
1½ teaspoons baking powder
⅔ cup low-calorie peanut butter
¼ cup light cooking oil
1 egg
2 tablespoons water
1 teaspoon vanilla

Preheat oven to 375 degrees. Place flour, sweetener and baking powder in mixing bowl. Add peanut butter, cooking oil, egg, water and vanilla. Mix well. Shape into 1-inch balls and place onto ungreased cookie sheets. Flatten with fork and bake 10–12 minutes, or until lightly browned. (51 calories per cookie)

LOW-CALORIE PEACH SURPRISE

6 medium halves canned peaches
1 tablespoon brown sugar
Lemon rind, grated to taste
1 egg white, beaten
2 tablespoons sugar

Drain canned peaches. Put 6 halves on an ovenproof platter, hollow side up. Sprinkle halves with the brown sugar and lemon rind. Make a meringue of the egg white and 2 tablespoons sugar. Spoon meringue on peach halves in peaks. Broil or bake until peaches are heated through and meringue is delicately browned. (30 calories per serving)

STRAWBERRY BREAKFAST SPREAD
Makes 1 cup

1 teaspoon unflavored gelatin
¼ cup orange juice
1 cup mashed *or* puréed fresh strawberries *or* frozen unsweetened
6 packets Equal
1 tablespoon orange peel slivers
¼ teaspoon coriander

In small saucepan, sprinkle gelatin over orange juice. Let stand 1 minute. Heat over low heat until gelatin is dissolved and mixture comes to a boil. Remove from heat and stir into strawberries. Add remaining ingredients and stir to blend. Refrigerate until firm, 3–4 hours. Best when used within 1 week. (7 calories per serving)

SHERRIED CHICKEN AND RICE
Serves 6

2 whole chicken breasts, skinned, halved and boned
1 tablespoon oil
8 ounces fresh mushrooms, sliced
2 cups sliced carrots
1½ cups sliced onions
2 teaspoons parsley flakes
½ teaspoon savory *or* thyme leaves
½ teaspoon salt, if desired
⅛ teaspoon pepper
1 cup dry sherry
1 bay leaf
½ cup uncooked Minute Rice

Cut chicken into 3-inch strips. In large skillet, cook chicken in oil until lightly browned. Add remaining ingredients, except rice. Cover; simmer 20–30 minutes, or until vegetables are tender. Stir in rice. Cover; simmer an additional 5–10 minutes, or until rice is fluffy. (150 calories per serving)

NO-GUILT OATMEAL COOKIES
Makes 3 dozen

1 cup sifted flour
¼ teaspoon salt
⅔ cup sugar
½ teaspoon baking powder
¼ teaspoon baking soda
½ teaspoon cinnamon
1½ cups quick-cooking oatmeal
½ cup seedless raisins
½ cup cooking oil
1 egg
¼ cup skim milk

Sift together flour, salt, sugar, baking powder, baking soda and cinnamon. Mix in oatmeal and raisins. Beat in the oil, egg and milk until well-mixed. Drop by teaspoonfuls onto a cookie sheet, spacing them 1½ inches apart. Bake in a preheated 400-degree oven for 10 minutes, or until delicately browned. Cool on rack. (75 calories per cookie)

CHUNKY APPLE-SAUCE
Serves 8

9 fresh tart apples, pared, cored and chopped (about 3 pounds)
2 tablespoons lemon juice
2 teaspoons brandy extract
6 packets Equal sweetener
⅛ teaspoon cinnamon
⅛ teaspoon nutmeg
⅛ teaspoon allspice
⅛ teaspoon ginger

Combine apples, lemon juice and brandy extract in saucepan. Bring mixture to a boil. Reduce heat; cover. Simmer until soft, about 45 minutes. In food processor or blender, with on-off motion, purée mixture to desired consistency. Add sweetener and spices. Cool to room temperature. Refrigerate. (96 calories per serving)

CURRIED MUSHROOM SOUP
Makes 3¾ cups

1 (10¾-ounce) can condensed cream of mushroom soup
1¾ cups skim milk
1 (2½-ounce) jar sliced mushrooms
2 tablespoons minced green onion
¼ to ½ teaspoon curry powder
Parsley, if desired

Combine all ingredients, except parsley, in medium-size saucepan. Heat to boiling, stirring frequently. Serve immediately; garnish with parsley. (120 calories per serving)

MOLDED SHRIMP DELIGHT
Serves 4-6

1 pound small cooked, cleaned shrimp
2 (3-ounce) packages lemon gelatin
2 scant cups hot tomato juice
1 cup chopped celery
1 cup low-calorie sweet pickle relish, well drained
Pinch salt
1/2 teaspoon Worcestershire sauce
2 drops Tabasco

Dissolve gelatin in hot tomato juice. Stir in all remaining ingredients, except shrimp. Chill to egg white consistency and pour into mold. Add shrimp and place in desired design. Refrigerate until firm. Unmold on crisp greens and garnish as desired. (135 calories per serving)

Vegetable
DELIGHTS

MARSHMALLOW YAM CASSEROLE
Serves 6

- 3 cups whole yams (canned), drained and mashed
- ¼ cup brown sugar
- ½ teaspoon salt
- 1 teaspoon cinnamon
- 1 teaspoon nutmeg
- 1 tablespoon melted butter
- ¼ cup cream
- 1½ cups miniature marshmallows

Blend yams with sugar, salt, spice, butter and cream. Mix half the marshmallows with yams. Turn into greased baking dish. Top with remaining marshmallows. Bake in a moderate oven of 350 degrees for 20 minutes, or until mixture is puffy and marshmallows delicately browned.

TATER STICKS
Serves 4

- 4 baking potatoes, cut into wedges
- ½ cup margarine, melted
- 1 (2⅜-ounce) package taco seasoning mix

Dip potato wedges into melted margarine; shake with seasoning mix in plastic bag, coating well. Place skin side down on ungreased baking sheet. Bake at 350 degrees for 40 minutes, or until tender.

GREEN VEGGIE BAKE
Serves 6-8

- 2 tablespoons butter or margarine
- 1/2 cup chopped onion
- 1 teaspoon salt
- 1/4 teaspoon pepper
- 4 ounces sour cream
- 1 to 1-1/2 tablespoons cornstarch
- 1 cup broccoli
- 1 cup green beans
- 1 cup peas
- 1 cup American or cheddar cheese, grated
- 2 tablespoons butter or margarine, melted
- 1 cup Ritz (salad) crackers

Cook onion in 2 tablespoons butter until tender. Add cornstarch, salt, pepper, and sour cream; mix well. Stir in green vegetables. Put in casserole dish, top with grated cheese. Combine remaining 2 tablespoons butter and cracker crumbs; place on top of cheese. Bake at 350 degrees for 30 minutes. This recipe was created for those "timid" green–vegetable eaters. Also great for leftovers.

CREAMY ONIONS AND POTATOES

- 5 potatoes, peeled and quartered
- 8 small onions (or 2 large, quartered)
- 2 tablespoon margarine
- 1 tablespoon flour
- 1/4 cup heavy cream
- 3/4 water
- 1-1/2 teaspoons salt
- Pepper and paprika to taste

Grease 3-quart casserole. Place in potatoes and onion. In small saucepan, melt margarine; stir in flour. Combine cream and water; add to flour mixture; cook until mixture thickens. Add salt and pepper; pour over potatoes and onions. Sprinkle with paprika. Bake until tender in 350 degree oven.

EGGPLANT LAMB PIE
Serves 6

- 1 medium eggplant
- 4 tablespoons butter or olive oil
- 1½ pounds ground lamb
- 1 egg, beaten
- 1 medium onion, diced
- ½ teaspoon each salt and pepper
- ½ teaspoon curry powder (optional)
  Pinch of thyme and basil
- 1 tablespoon minced parsley
- 1 cup tomato sauce
- ⅓ cup buttered bread or cracker crumbs

Peel eggplant; cut into 1-inch cubes. Sauté in butter or oil until tender. Combine lamb, egg, onion, salt, pepper, curry powder, thyme, basil and parsley. Mix well with tomato sauce. Place half of the lamb mixture in greased baking dish or casserole; cover with half of eggplant. Repeat. Top with buttered crumbs. Bake at 350 degrees for 45 minutes.

TENDER ASPARAGUS BAKE

1 cup soft bread crumbs
1 pound asparagus, cut in 1-inch pieces and cooked
4 hard-cooked eggs, sliced
3 pimientos, cut in strips
2 tablespoons butter *or* margarine
2 tablespoons flour
¼ teaspoon salt
1 cup milk
1½ cups cheddar cheese, diced

Place half the crumbs in a greased, ovenproof dish. Alternate layers of asparagus, eggs and pimiento. Make a white sauce of the butter, flour, salt and milk. Pour over asparagus; dot with diced cheddar cheese and the remaining bread crumbs. Bake at 350 degrees for 30 minutes, until cheese is golden, melted and bubbly.

SINFULLY RICH SWEET POTATOES

3 cups cooked, mashed sweet potatoes
1 teaspoon vanilla
¼ cup butter
2 eggs, beaten
¾ cup sugar

Topping:
1 cup coconut
1 cup brown sugar
1 cup pecans, chopped
⅓ cup butter

Mix sweet potatoes, vanilla, butter, eggs and sugar; put into greased casserole. Mix topping ingredients and spread over mixture. Bake at 375 degrees until browned.

REFRIGERATOR POTATOES
Serves 10

5 pounds *or* 9 large potatoes
2 (3-ounce) packages cream cheese
1 cup sour cream
2 teaspoons onion salt (optional)
1 teaspoon salt
½ teaspoon pepper
2 tablespoons butter

Cook potatoes; drain and mash until smooth. Add remaining ingredients. Stir until fluffy. Cool. Place in refrigerator. When ready to serve, place in a 350-degree oven for 30 minutes, or heat on top of stove until hot. Keeps in refrigerator up to 2 weeks. These are great to have prepared ahead.

ZUCCHINI FANS
Serves 4

⅓ cup butter *or* margarine, softened
2 tablespoons minced fresh parsley
½ teaspoon dried, whole tarragon
⅛ teaspoon salt
⅛ teaspoon pepper
4 small zucchini
¼ cup water
2 tablespoons freshly grated Parmesan cheese
1 tablespoon soft bread crumbs

Combine first 5 ingredients; set aside. Cut each zucchini into lengthwise slices, leaving slices attached on stem end. Fan slices out and spread evenly with butter mixture. Place in a 15 x 10 x 1-inch jelly roll pan; add water. Bake at 400 degrees for 20 minutes, or until crisp-tender.

Combine cheese and bread crumbs; sprinkle on zucchini and broil 4 inches from heat for 2 minutes, or until cheese melts.

POTATOES AND TURNIPS COMBO
Serves 6

3 large potatoes, pared and quartered
3 large turnips, pared and quartered
2 cups water
1 teaspoon salt
¼ cup butter *or* margarine
¼ teaspoon pepper
⅛ teaspoon paprika
⅛ teaspoon dry mustard
3 tablespoon flour

Cook potatoes and turnips in saucepan with 2 cups water, and ½ teaspoon salt; drain; mash; reserve ½ cup of vegetable liquid. Heat butter in skillet; blend in remaining salt, pepper, paprika, dry mustard and flour.

Slowly add reserved vegetable liquid; cook, stirring constantly, until smooth and thickened. Add potato/turnip mixture; beat until light and fluffy.

TWICE-BAKED POTATOES
Serves 8

4 large baking potatoes, baked
¼ cup (½ stick) margarine
¾ cup milk
1 teaspoon grated onion
1 teaspoon salt
⅛ teaspoon pepper
¾ cup grated sharp cheddar cheese
Paprika

While hot, cut baked potatoes in half lengthwise. Scoop out insides; whip potatoes; add margarine. Gradually beat in milk. Stir in onion, salt and pepper. Spoon back into shells. Sprinkle with grated cheese. Bake in moderate 375-degree oven for 15–25 minutes, or until cheese melts. Sprinkle with paprika and serve.

HASH BROWN DELIGHT

2 (10-ounce) packages frozen hash brown potatoes
2 cups sour cream
1 can cream of chicken soup
1 stick or 1/2 cup melted butter
1 tablespoon salt
1 tablespoon onion
2 cups crushed cornflakes
1/4 cup melted butter
2 cups grated cheese

Thaw hash browns. Combine sour cream, soup, and 1/2 cup butter. Add salt, onion, and cheese; mix well. Add potatoes. Place mixture in a 9x13-inch baking dish. Combine 1/4 cup melted butter and cornflakes; sprinkle on top of mixture. Bake at 350 degrees for 50 minutes or until golden brown.

CROCK-STYLE BARBECUE BEANS
Serves 10-12

8 cups water
3 cans pork and beans
1/4 teaspoon salt
1/4 teaspoon pepper
1/4 teaspoon minced onion
1 small onion, chopped
1/2 cup brown sugar
2/3 cup syrup
3 tablespoons white sugar

Combine water, pork and beans. Add remaining ingredients and stir well. Cook on *low* for six hours, *high* for less than six hours. Stir before serving.

SPICY CARROT DISH

9 tablespoons butter
12 whole small carrots, scraped and sliced
½ teaspoon salt
2 tablespoons honey
   Pinch of marjoram

Melt 5 tablespoons butter in pan and add carrots, salt and good pinch of marjoram. Cover and cook very gently over low heat until carrots are tender. Add remaining 4 tablespoons melted butter and honey; let mixture boil up to 3 minutes, shaking the pan so carrots are covered and glazed with sauce. This is an interesting way to prepare carrots.

THREE-CORN CASSEROLE
Serves 6–8

½ cup butter, softened
1 cup sour cream
1 egg
1 (16-ounce) can whole-kernel corn, drained
1 (16-ounce) can cream-style corn
1 (9-ounce) package corn muffin mix

Preheat oven to 375 degrees. Mix butter, sour cream and egg. Stir in both corns. Blend in dry muffin mix and spoon into a well-greased casserole. Bake for 1 hour until puffed up, golden brown and crispy on top.

COUNTRY-STYLE FRIED CABBAGE
Serves 4

2 tablespoons bacon fat
1 medium head green cabbage (about 1-1/2 pounds), shredded
Salt and pepper

Heat bacon fat in 10-inch skillet. Add cabbage. Cook over low heat, stirring frequently, until light brown. Cover and cook, stirring occasionally, until crisp-tender, about 5 minutes. Sprinkle with salt and pepper. If desired, 2 tablespoons of cream and 1-1/2 teaspoons vinegar may be added before removing from heat. Also red cabbage may be fixed the same way; just substitute vegetable oil for bacon fat.

SWISS VEGETABLE MEDLEY
Serves 6

1 (16-ounce) bag broccoli, carrots, cauliflower combination, thawed and drained, *or* combine your own
1 (10¾-ounce) can condensed cream of mushroom soup
1 cup (4 ounces) shredded Swiss cheese
⅓ cup sour cream
¼ teaspoon pepper
1 (4-ounce) jar chopped pimiento (optional)
1 (2.8-ounce) can French-fried onions
½ soup can water *or* milk

Combine vegetables, soup, ½ cup cheese, sour cream, pepper, pimiento, ½ soup can water or milk and ½ can onion rings. Pour into 1-quart casserole. Bake, covered, at 350 degrees for 30 minutes. Top with remaining cheese and onions; bake, uncovered, for 5 minutes longer.

CREAMED CORN
Serves 6–8

1 (20-ounce) package frozen whole-kernel corn
1 pint whipping cream
1 teaspoon salt
2 tablespoons granulated sugar
2 tablespoons butter, melted and cooled
2 tablespoons all-purpose flour

In medium saucepan, bring corn, cream, salt and sugar to a boil. Reduce heat and simmer for 5 minutes. In a small bowl, whisk together melted butter and flour until smooth. Stir into corn mixture and cook until thickened. Serve at once.

ALMANDINE ASPARAGUS
Serves 2

8 asparagus spears, shaved, cooked halfway and well drained
2-1/2 tablespoons mayonnaise
2-1/4 tablespoons sweet relish
2 pieces of fillet of sole (about 1/2 - 3/4 pounds of sole) wipe dry
1/2 tablespoon chili sauce
1/2 teaspoon margarine
2 tablespoons slivered almonds, toasted

Preheat oven to 350 degrees. In a lightly buttered baking dish lay the asparagus down gently. Mix the mayonnaise and relish; spoon over the asparagus. Place the fish fillets on top over the asparagus. Spoon the 1/2 tablespoon chili sauce over all and top with almonds. Dot with margarine. Bake for 35 minutes or until the fish flakes easily with a fork.

GLORIFIED CABBAGE

1 small head cabbage, shredded
1 large onion, finely chopped
1 green pepper, finely chopped
1/4 cup green onion, chopped
2 ribs celery, sliced 1/8 inch think
2 tablespoons margarine
2 tablespoons vegetable oil
2 cloves garlic, minced
1/2 cup whipping cream
1 cup fresh bread crumbs (optional)
1-1/2 cups Cheddar cheese, shredded
2 tablespoons parsley, minced
1 teaspoon salt
1/2 teaspoon black pepper

Heat butter and oil in large saucepan; add onions, green pepper and celery; saute 5 minutes over low heat. Add cabbage and garlic; cook covered over low heat for 10 minutes or until cabbage is tender; stir in cream. Mix crumbs with 1/2 the cheese and the parsley; set aside. Add remaining cheese to cabbage mixture; stir in salt

and pepper. Turn into 1-1/2 quart buttered, shallow casserole. Top with crumbs-cheese mixture. Bake at 350 degrees for 20 minutes or until crumbs are golden and crisp.

CREAMED CABBAGE VEGETABLE DISH FROM 1891
Serves 4

1 medium head cabbage
1 gill (1/2 cup) cream
1 ounce butter (walnut size)
Salt and pepper to taste
1 cup water

Slice cabbage as for slaw. Cook in 1 cup water until tender; drain. Return to saucepan. Add cream and salt and pepper. Simmer two to three minutes.
NOTE: Milk may be used by adding a little more butter.

BAKED CREAM CABBAGE
Serves 6

1 medium head cabbage
1/2 cup boiling salted water
3 tablespoons flour
1/2 teaspoon salt
1-1/2 cups milk
1/4 cup bread crumbs
2 tablespoons butter

Shred cabbage very fine and cook 9 minutes in boiling, salted water. Remove cabbage; drain well. Place in buttered 1-1/2-quart casserole. Melt butter in saucepan; stir in flour and salt until smooth. Add milk gradually, continuing to stir until mixture thickens. Pour this sauce over cabbage and sprinkle breadcrumbs over top. Bake at 325 degrees for about 15 minutes or until crumbs are browned.

ZUCCHINI FRITTERS
Makes 2 dozen

2 large zucchini squash
3 eggs
1/2 teaspoon salt
1/4 teaspoon pepper
1/2 teaspoon sugar
1 teaspoon dried dillweed or 1 tablespoon fresh dill
2 cloves garlic (finely diced)
5 tablespoons flour
1 onion (diced)
Salad oil and margarine

Wash zucchini, do not peel. Dice coarsely; cover with water. Add 1 teaspoon salt and bring to boil for eight minutes. Drain in colander (about 15 minutes). While draining zucchini, heat salad oil and saute onion until soft. Beat eggs; add next 7 ingredients. Stir in drained, mashed zucchini. Mix until well blended, adding sauteed onions.

Drop batter by tablespoon into skillet in which you have 2 tablespoons salad oil and 1 tablespoon margarine. Fry zucchini fritters, a few at a time, until light brown on both sides, turning once.

Place on platter with paper towel to absorb, adding more oil and margarine to skillet as needed and add more batter.

Serve plain or topped with dollop of sour cream or plain yogurt.

ZUCCHINI SURPRISE
Serves 4
60 calories per serving

1 pound zucchini, sliced
8-ounce can mandarin oranges, drained
1/4 teaspoon nutmeg
Sprinkle cinnamon
1/4 cup pecans, chopped

Steam zucchini slices until tender. Add orange slices, nutmeg and cinnamon. Sprinkle with pecans; serve.

MUSHROOM SUPREME

1 (12 ounce) can whole mushrooms
2 beef bouillon cubes
1/2 cup hot water
4 tablespoons butter
2 tablespoons flour
1/2 cup light cream
Pinch of salt and pepper
1/2 cup bread crumbs
1/2 to 1 cup Parmesan cheese.

Saute mushrooms in butter gently for two minutes. Dissolve beef cubes in hot water. Melt butter and blend with flour in another saucepan. Add cream, salt, pepper, beef broth, and mushrooms to butter and flour mixture. Pour into buttered casserole. Top with cheese and bread crumbs, mixed together. Bake for 30 minutes at 350 degrees.

Great for mushroom lovers.

ASPARAGUS-TOMATO STIR FRY
Serves 4

1 pound fresh asparagus
1 tablespoon cold water
1 teaspoon cornstarch
2 teaspoons soy sauce
1/4 teaspoon salt
1 tablespoon cooking oil
4 green onions, bias sliced
 in 1-inch lengths
1-1/2 cup sliced fresh mushrooms
2 small tomatoes, cut in thin wedges
Hot cooked rice

Snap off and discard woody base of asparagus. Bias slice the asparagus crosswise into 1-1/2 inch lengths and set aside. If asparagus spears are not slender and young, cut up pieces, cook uncovered in small amount of boiling salted water about 5 minutes; drain well. (Celery, green beans, broccoli, etc., may be used in place of asparagus.) In small bowl, blend water into cornstarch. Stir in soy sauce and salt; set aside. Stir-fry asparagus and green onions in hot oil 4 minutes. Use a long-handled spoon to turn and lift the food with a folding motion. Add mushrooms; stir-fry 1 minute more. Stir the soy mixture again. Push vegetables up the sides of the wok; add soy mixture to center of wok. Let mixture bubble slightly, then stir into vegetables. Cook and stir till mixture is thickened and bubbly. Add tomatoes and heat through. Serve at once with cooked rice.

COMPANY ASPARAGUS
Serves 4-6

14-1/2 - ounce can green asparagus
10-1/2 - ounce can Cheddar cheese
 soup
2 hard-boiled eggs, chopped
1/2 cup toasted slivered almonds
1 cup buttered bread crumbs, divided

Combine asparagus, soup, eggs, almonds and 1/2 cup bread crumbs in buttered 1-quart casserole dish. Spread 1/2 cup bread crumbs over mixture. Bake uncovered at 375 degrees for 20 minutes.

ASPARAGUS WITH YOGURT DRESSING
Serves 4

1 pound fresh asparagus
1/2 cup plain yogurt
1 small clove garlic, crushed
1 tablespoon chopped parsley
1/4 teaspoon salt
1 small head Boston or Bibb lettuce
1 hard-cooked egg yolk; sieved

Snap off tough ends of asparagus. Remove scales with knife or peeler. Cook asparagus in boiling water about 10 minutes or until crisp-tender. Drain. Cool and place in refrigerator to chill. Combine yogurt with garlic, parsley, and salt; stir well. Chill. Place asparagus on bed of lettuce; top with yogurt dressing and sprinkle with egg yolk.

ASPARAGUS VINAIGRETTE
Serves 4

1 pound fresh asparagus (or 1 pound
 fresh whole green beans)
1 head fresh cauliflower (or 1 package
 frozen cauliflower)
1 can (7 ounce) artichoke hearts
Vinaigrette Dressing (below)

Cook asparagus or beans and cauliflower. Drain artichokes. Pour 1/4 cup Vinaigrette Dressing over each vegetable. Chill at least 1 hour. Arrange the three vegetables artistically on individual serving plates or on one large platter. Garnish with cherry tomatoes or parsley.

ASPARAGUS LOAF

1 carton half & half
1 sleeve package soda crackers
 crumbled
3 eggs, beaten
2 tablespoons butter
2 cans green asparagus spears, cut
Pinch of salt

Mix all ingredients together. Pour into buttered casserole. Bake at 350 degrees for 1 hour.

ASPARAGUS WITH HERBS
Serves 3 - 45 calories per serving

1-1/4 cups asparagus
1 tablespoon diet margarine
1/2 teaspoon salt
1/4 cup water
2 tablespoons chives, chopped
1/8 teaspoon seasoned salt
1/16 teaspoon pepper

Separate asparagus. Place margarine, salt, water, and chives in skillet; cover tightly. Bring to boil, add asparagus and cover again. Gently boil until asparagus is tender. Sprinkle with seasoned salt and pepper.

ZUCCHINI QUICHE

1 cup corn muffin mix
3 cups sliced small zucchini squash
1 medium onion, chopped
1/2 cup Parmesan cheese, grated
1/3 cup cooking oil
4 eggs, well beaten
Salt and pepper to taste
1 cup rich cream or half-and-half

Mix all ingredients together. Pour into a buttered 10" pie plate or quiche dish. Bake 45 minutes at 350 degrees. Can be frozen and baked when needed. If preferred, slice tomato or green pepper rings to place on top.

Nice served with relish plate of fresh vegetables and melon or other raw fruit for a luncheon.

ZUCCHINI ROUNDS

1/3 cup commercial biscuit mix
1/4 cup grated Parmesan cheese
Salt and pepper to taste
2 eggs, slightly beaten
2 cups shredded, unpared zucchini
2 tablespoons butter or margarine, softened

In a bowl combine biscuit mix, cheese, salt, and pepper. Stir in eggs just until mixture is moistened; fold in zucchini. For each round, drop 2 tablespoons mixture in soft butter or margarine. Fry 2-3 minutes on each side until brown.

This is an excellent summer luncheon dish or for a brunch.

ZUCCHINI APPLESAUCE

Makes 2 cups

2 medium zucchini, peeled and diced
2 apples, peeled, cored, and diced
1/4 cup sugar
2 whole cloves
1/8 teaspoon nutmeg
1/2 teaspoon salt
1 tablespoon lemon juice

1/4 teaspoon cinnamon
1/2 teaspoon vanilla extract
Water

In a large saucepan, bring to a boil the zucchini, apples, sugar, cloves, nutmeg, salt, and 1/2 cup water. Reduce heat, cover, and simmer for 20 minutes; stir occasionally. Remove cover; continue cooking until all liquid has evaporated. Discard the cloves, then mash until smooth. Stir in the lemon juice and cinnamon. Cover and refrigerate until ready to use.

SQUASH PILLOWS

1 yeast cake
1/2 cup lukewarm water
2/3 cup shortening
1 teaspoon salt
1/2 cup sugar
1 cup mashed cooked squash
1 teaspoon grated lemon rind
1/8 teaspoon mace
1 cup scalded milk
2 eggs
6 to 8 cups sifted flour

Mash squash. Add sugar, shortening, salt, lemon rind, mace and eggs. Blend well. Dissolve yeast in water. Add yeast mixture to milk and add to the first mixture. Add sifted flour to make a stiff dough. Mix well. Cover and let rise in a warm place until doubled in bulk. Shape into rolls; place in greased pans. Let rise in warm place until double in bulk. Bake at 325 degrees for 25 minutes.

STUFFED ACORN SQUASH

Serves 8-12

Water
4-6 acorn squash, halved crosswise and seeded
1 or 2 (6 ounce) boxes chicken-flavor stuffing mix, prepared according to package directions
Parsley sprigs (garnish)

Preheat oven to 350 degrees. Pour water into 1 large or 2 smaller baking pans to measure 1 inch deep. Arrange acorn squash in water with cut sides up, cutting a thin slice off ends so halves will stand upright. Bake, covered, for 45 minutes or until flesh is tender when pierced with fork. Fill each squash cavity with about 1/3 cup hot stuffing and garnish with parsley.

HOLIDAY STUFFED WINTER SQUASH

Serves 6

3 small acorn or butternut squash
3 green onions, chopped
1 tablespoon oil
1 cup finely-diced celery
1 bunch fresh spinach, coarsely chopped
3/4 cup whole wheat bread crumbs
1/4 teaspoon salt
1/4 cup almonds, finely ground
1 tablespoon butter

Halve and clean the squash. Bake in a 350 degree oven, for 35-40 minutes, or until tender. Sauté onions in oil until soft. Add diced celery. Cover and simmer on medium heat until just tender. Add spinach; stir to wilt. Combine bread crumbs with salt and ground almonds. Stuff the squashes with spinach; sprinkle crumb mixture on top. Dot with butter and return to oven for 10-15 minutes.

DEBBIE'S YUMMY BAKED BEANS

4 cans pork and beans, drained
1/2 cup minced onion
1/2 pound diced bacon
3/4 cup grape jelly
3/4 cup enchilada sauce

Fry onion and bacon; drain. Add jelly and enchilada sauce; mix well. Add beans; pour into casserole dish and bake, uncovered at 350 degrees for 1 hour. Serve hot.

SCALLOPED CARROTS

5 cups raw carrots, sliced or diced
1 onion, sliced
1/2 cup butter
1/2 pound Velveeta cheese
12 Ritz crackers

Cook carrots until done; drain. Sauté onion in butter. In baking dish, layer carrots and cheese. Pour onions and butter over top. Break up Ritz crackers and sprinkle over top. Bake at 350 degrees for 30-40 minutes.

GREEN BEAN AND CARROT COMBO
Serves 6-8

1 pound can green beans, drained
1 pound can sliced carrots, drained
1/2 teaspoon sugar
1/4 teaspoon salt
1/4 teaspoon onion powder
1 can cream of celery soup
1/4 cup milk

Combine all ingredients; mix well. Place in greased casserole and bake for 25-30 minutes at 350 degrees.

GLAZED CARROTS WITH BACON 'N ONION
Serves 4

1 pound carrots, scraped and sliced
   diagonally
3 slices bacon
1 small onion, chopped
3 tablespoons brown sugar
1/8 teaspoon pepper

Cook carrots, covered, in small amount of boiling water for 15 minutes or until crisp tender; drain. Cook bacon in skillet until crisp; crumble. Reserve 1 tablespoon drippings in skillet. Sauté onion in drippings. Add brown sugar, pepper, and carrots. Cook until heated; sprinkle with crumbled bacon.

COLORFUL CARROT RING
Serves 4

1/2 cup soft bread crumbs
3 eggs
1 small onion
1/4 cup parsley
1 tablespoon butter or margarine,
   melted
1/4 teaspoon cinnamon
1/4 teaspoon salt
1/8 teaspoon pepper
2-1/2 cups carrots, cooked
1 tablespoon brown sugar or
   maple syrup

Place all ingredients in food processor; process 1 minute or until carrots are cut very fine. Turn into an 8-inch ring mold; set in a shallow pan of water; bake at 375 degrees for 30 minutes or until set and firm. Unmold on serving plate; fill center with tiny peas.

POTATOES AND MUSHROOMS

8-10 small, new potatoes
1/4 cup butter, melted
2 tablespoons green onions or
   chives, chopped
1/2 pound mushrooms, chopped
1 cup meat stock
2 egg yolks
1 teaspoon lemon juice
Salt and pepper

Cook potatoes in jackets until tender. Drain and dry. Place in a casserole, adding butter and chopped onion. Beat egg yolks and add lemon juice, mushrooms, and meat stock. Season with salt and pepper. Pour over potatoes in casserole. Bake uncovered in preheated 350 degree oven for 30-40 minutes.

SWISS POTATOES

1-1/2 cups large baking potatoes,
   thinly sliced
1 teaspoon salt
1 teaspoon minced dried onion
2 eggs, beaten
1-1/2 cups milk, scalded
1/4 pound Swiss cheese, grated

Mix together all above ingredients, saving some grated cheese to sprinkle on top. Place into medium-sized, lightly-buttered casserole. Sprinkle top with reserved cheese. Place in preheated 350 degree oven and bake for 1 hour.

Recipe can be doubled easily.

POTATO CELERY SUPREME
Serves 4

4-6 medium potatoes, cut into small
   pieces
Salt and pepper to taste
1/3 stick margarine
1 can cream of celery soup
1/2 cup water

Put cut potatoes into greased casserole; add salt and pepper, margarine, soup, and water. Stir lightly. Bake covered in a 350 degree oven for 1-1/2 hours.

COUNTRY-FRIED POTATOES

2 tablespoons butter or margarine
2 tablespoons bacon drippings (or
   shortening)
6 cooked, pared, thickly sliced
   potatoes
1 medium onion, chopped
Salt and pepper to taste

Melt butter and drippings or shortening in heavy skillet. Add sliced potatoes and chopped onions to hot skillet. Season with salt and pepper. Cook over low fire until bottom crust is brown; turn, and brown other side.

10-MINUTE PECAN SQUASH

Serves 4-6

2 (12-ounce) packages frozen
  cooked squash
2 tablespoons butter
4 teaspoons instant breakfast drink
  (Tang)
1 teaspoon salt, if desired
Dash of pepper
6 tablespoons chopped pecans

Combine squash, butter, instant breakfast drink, salt, and pepper; cook as directed on package. Stir in pecans.

STUFFED PATTY-PAN SQUASH

4 patty-pan squash
4 slices bacon, cooked crisp
1/2 cup onion, chopped
3/4 cup bread crumbs
1/2 cup milk

Cook squash in boiling salted water for 15 minutes. Drain and cool. From the stem end cut a small slice; scoop out center, leaving 1/2-inch rim. Chop the squash which has been removed very finely. Sprinkle the squash cups lightly with salt. Sauté onion in bacon drippings; add crumbs, milk, and reserved squash. Fill cups; sprinkle crisp bacon on top. Place in flat casserole; bake at 350 degrees for 35 minutes.

SCALLOPED EGGPLANT

Serves 6

2 cups cooked eggplant
1/2 cup coarse cracker crumbs
4 tablespoons onion, minced
3 ounces cheese, grated
1 egg, beaten
1/2 cup milk
2 tablespoons margarine or butter

Peel eggplant and cut in 1-inch cubes. Cook in boiling salted water until tender, 8 minutes. Drain. Put eggplant, half of cracker crumbs, onion, and cheese in layers in buttered casserole. Combine egg and milk; pour over other ingredients. Dot with margarine and sprinkle with remaining cracker crumbs. Bake at 350 degrees for 30 minutes.

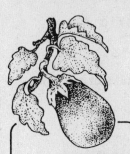

FRENCH FRIED EGGPLANT

1 medium eggplant, peeled and sliced
  into 1/2 x 2-inch strips
1 cup pancake flour
1 egg
1/4 cup water
1/2 cup Parmesan cheese, grated
Salt
Vegetable oil

Beat egg and water together. Dip eggplant strips into egg mixture; then roll in pancake flour. Drop into hot oil and cook until golden brown, about 2 - 3 minutes. Drain on paper toweling and sprinkle lightly with salt and Parmesan cheese. Serve hot!!

SAUCY ASPARAGUS

2 cans drained asparagus
1 cup cream of mushroom soup
1 can broken pieces mushrooms
1/4 pound squared American
  cheese
1-1/4 cups bread crumbs
1/2 stick butter

Grease a long flat casserole dish with butter. Place drained asparagus over bottom. Add cream of mushroom soup. Then add mushroom pieces and juice. Cover with Ameri-can cheese squares. Put bread crumbs over cheese and thinly sliced butter over top. Bake 25 minutes in 350 degree oven or until it bubbles up through and crumbs are browned. Can use 2 chopped hard cooked eggs, if desired, for garnish.

SAVORY SUCCOTASH

Serves 6-8

1 (1-pound) can (2 cups) French
  style green beans, drained
1 (1-pound) can (2 cups) whole
  kernel corn, drained
1/2 cup mayonnaise or salad
  dressing
1/2 cup shredded sharp cheese
1/2 cup chopped green pepper
1/2 cup chopped celery
2 tablespoons chopped onions
1 cup soft bread crumbs
2 tablespoons butter or margarine,
  melted

Combine first 7 ingredients; place in 9x9 inch casserole or 10x6x1-1/2 inch baking dish. Combine crumbs and butter; sprinkle over top. Bake in moderate oven 350 degrees for 30 minutes or until crumbs are toasted.

VEGETABLE BAKE

1 can Veg-All, drained
1/2 cup chopped celery
1/2 cup chopped onion
1/2 cup sliced water chestnuts
1 cup mayonnaise
1 cup celery soup
1 cup shredded cheese
1/2 stick margarine
20 Ritz crackers

Mix together all ingredients except margarine and crackers in a 2-quart casserole. Bake for 45 minutes at 300 degrees. Melt margarine. Mix with crushed Ritz crackers. Sprinkle over the top. Bake 15 additional minutes.

This is truly a super vegetable casserole, a crowd pleaser for church potluck suppers and one which carries and travels well.

Accent On Cooking

INDEX

INDEX

126

INDEX